Produced by Third Millennium Publishing,
a subsidiary of Third Millennium Information Limited

Designed by Matthew Wilson
Edited by Janet Sacks
Production by Bonnie Murray

Reprographics by Asia Graphic Printing Ltd
Printed by 1010 Printing International Limited on behalf of Compass Press Limited

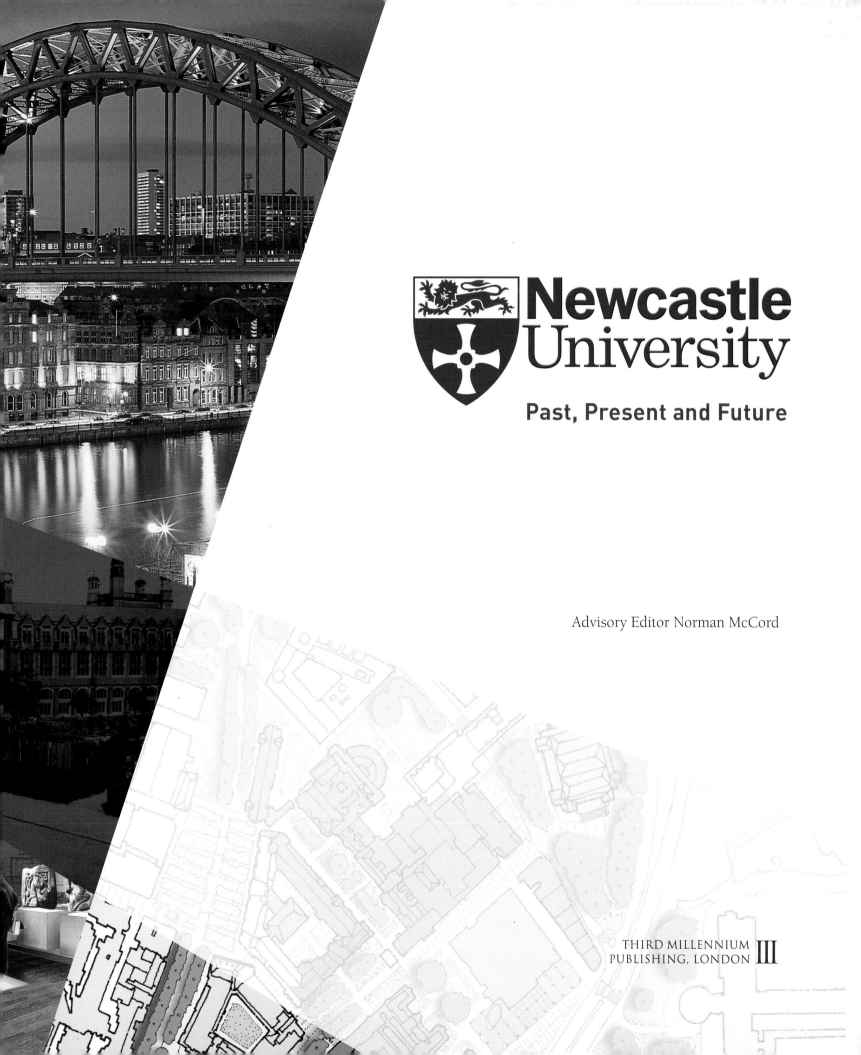

Newcastle University

Past, Present and Future

Advisory Editor Norman McCord

THIRD MILLENNIUM
PUBLISHING, LONDON III

Contents

08 THE CAMPUS TODAY

12 ORIGINS TO ARMSTRONG COLLEGE

30 A NEW CENTURY

57 FACULTY OF HUMANITIES AND SOCIAL SCIENCES

92
FACULTY OF
MEDICAL SCIENCES

114
FACULTY OF SCIENCE,
AGRICULTURE AND ENGINEERING

142
TRANSITION AND EVOLUTION

162
THE UNIVERSITY IN
THE 21ST CENTURY

Preface

At a moment when the commitment to a world-class future for university life in Newcastle is more than ever apparent, it is entirely appropriate that this volume should appear. Surprisingly, our University, despite excellent historical accounts by Professor Bettenson taking the story to 1972, has never possessed a true archive: the first-hand accounts and memories of many alumni of the Newcastle campus in its various incarnations, a number of which are to be found in this book, form a major contribution to this process.

Professor Norman McCord, Advisory Editor to the book, has pointed out that the evolution of our University has been a slightly unusual process, in that it not only celebrated a centenary in 1971, but can celebrate future anniversaries in 2008 (100 years), 2037 (100 years), 2034 (200 years), 2052 (200 years), and another centenary in 2063. Why this should be is only part of the story of this book, which for the first time offers a fully illustrated portrait of a unique institution which, triumphantly beginning the new century as the *The Sunday Times* 'University of the Year', has gone on to shape itself for a dynamic future. I'm delighted to welcome this publication and heartily commend it to you.

The Rt Hon Lord Patten of Barnes, CH

Chancellor
University of Newcastle upon Tyne

Visual Essay:
The Campus Today

The University of Newcastle upon Tyne has an unusual history which can be traced back to the founding of the School of Medicine and Surgery in 1834, located at that time in the Barber-Surgeons' Company's Hall in the Manors area of the city. By coincidence, 1834 was also the date of the establishment of the University of Durham which, by 1852, had an association with the School of Medicine in Newcastle. The first association between any English provincial medical school and a university, this was ironically a link that has been renewed over recent years through government initiatives to increase medical student numbers and hence doctors in the National Health Service, with the first two years' training of University of Newcastle medical students now being undertaken at a new medical school at the University of Durham.

Having become the University of Durham College of Medicine by 1870, the affiliation to the University of Durham strengthened with the development of the buildings around the present quadrangle [1] including, in 1888, the north-east wing of Armstrong College, the home at that time of the University of Durham College of Physical Science. From this time, Durham University's teaching through this second college in Newcastle expanded into science and, in due course, the arts. Armstrong College, now the Armstrong Building [2], was essentially the first of the buildings which – together with the Department of Agriculture (1914) now occupied by the School of Architecture, Planning and Landscape [3], and the (Old) Library (1926, extended in 1960) [4 & 5], all of which are now listed – form the heart of the present-day campus.

The two colleges were first linked through the development of a Students' Union Building [6] in 1925 for shared use by both colleges. It is a building whose

distinctive appearance, together with the adjoining arched entrance to the Armstrong Quadrangle [7] now visually characterizes the University of Newcastle. By 1937 Armstrong College and the College of Medicine had become King's College, Newcastle, and in the following year a new Medical School building was completed which, in 1939, was opened by King George VI. Known as the King George VI Building [8] and occupying a corner location between St Thomas's Street and Queen Victoria Road, this building forms the south-west corner of today's campus and is now occupied by the School of Biological Sciences in the Science, Agriculture and Engineering (SAgE) Faculty.

The greatest contribution to the establishment of the University's main campus came in 1946 when, through a compulsory purchase order, the College had the right, indeed the obligation, to develop the area bounded by Barras Bridge, St Thomas's Street, Queen Victoria Road and Claremont Road. From this time there has been continuous evolution into the University of today, and the present campus has grown through development and acquisition. The post-war construction of the Chemistry

(Bedson) Building (1949) [9], the Stephenson Building (1951) [10] – primarily for Mechanical Engineering – and the Cassie Building (1956) [11] for Civil Engineering all quickly followed.

In 1958 the Museum of Antiquities [12], built to house the Romano-British collection of the Society of Antiquaries of Newcastle, was completed alongside the arched entrance to the Quadrangle. In the same year, the College came to the rescue of the Natural History Society of Northumberland, Durham and Newcastle upon Tyne since it became responsible for the running of the Hancock Museum [13]. The Hancock Museum building is soon to be extended and refurbished, and will then be known as the Great North Museum. In addition to natural history exhibits, it will house the contents of the Shefton (Greek artefacts) Museum and the Museum of Antiquities, which is to be demolished to create a new quadrangle between the Armstrong Building and the Union Society building.

1962 saw the development of the Herschel Building [14] for the Department of Physics, designed by the eminent architect Sir Basil Spence, the architect of the

rebuilt Coventry Cathedral. The building gives access to the Curtis Auditorium, the first large lecture theatre on the campus.

On 1 August 1963, King's College, the University of Durham, was reconstituted as the University of Newcastle upon Tyne and has in due course taken its place as one of the Russell Group of universities. Even at this time it was recognized that the temporary car park on the west side of Barras Bridge was hardly appropriate for this prominent location facing the new, and now listed, Arne Jacobson-inspired Civic Centre. Since then the Playhouse Theatre was constructed and completed in 1970 on what was the site of a Presbyterian church, later known as Grey Hall. The theatre has undergone extension and improvement and was opened as the Northern Stage in 2006.

1964 saw the opening of the new Refectory Building incorporating a ballroom. As part of this development the Union Society building was extended to include a debating chamber dramatically located over Kings Road but, due to its poor condition and the increasing cost of maintenance, the chamber was demolished in 2004. 1964 also saw the completion of the Agriculture Building [15] further along Kings Road and adjoining the Old Brewery buildings and St Thomas' Street. Completing the group of new buildings on the campus area as defined by the 1946 compulsory purchase order is the Claremont complex [16]. Built in 1968 by the eminent architects Sheppard Robson, the 11-storey-high complex, part of which spans Claremont Road, at that time intended to become a quiet internal University road, was, until the development of the new Medical School, the largest building on the University campus.

In 1970, the administrative offices of the new university, previosuly spread across many buildings,

were brought together into two adjoining blocks of terraced houses (Kensington [17] and Park [18] Terraces). These were linked in 1994 by a new building designed to accommodate the expanding Personnel and Finance Offices.

The 1980s saw the further westerly extension of the campus beyond the Ridley Building complex of 1973 [19] with, in 1983, the development of the new Medical School, comprised of the Cookson and William Leech Buildings. This is the largest building complex within the University and has recently been increased in size to accommodate significantly increased medical student numbers. In 2002 the Cookson Building was extended by the construction of a new award-winning 400-seat (David Shaw) lecture theatre [20] dramatically located over the entrance to the Medical School and the Henry Wellcome Building for Neuroecology [21], which houses the Institute of Neuroscience together with researchers in biology and psychology relocated from unsuitable accommodation in the Ridley Building. The development of the Royal Victoria Infirmary has also resulted in Haematology accommodation being moved

into a new building in one of the courtyards at the Medical School.

Increasing student numbers and hence bookstock soon outgrew the Old Library and prompted the establishment of the Robinson Library [22], which was opened in 1982. It was designed by local architects FaulknerBrowns and is located to the east of the A167 over which it is accessed via a covered pedestrian bridge. The building was extended in 1995, since when it has provided open-access computer facilities in addition to its extensive stock of books, periodicals and papers. The Old Library has itself been redeveloped to provide open-access language learning [23] and computer facilities – and in its newer section – a research beehive providing facilities for the incubation of research ideas as well as the Courtyard, a popular, centrally located meeting place and restaurant.

Significant government investment in promoting higher quality research in British universities since 1998 has led to the development of a range of new multi-award-winning buildings including the Paul O'Gorman Building [24] housing the Northern Institute for Cancer Research (NICR) and the Devonshire Building [25], home to the University's new Institute for Research on Environment and Sustainability (IRES).

The new Henry Wellcome Building for Biogerontology [26] at the General Hospital is the first new building on a whole new campus for the University where facilities for research into the health of the elderly are being developed. This was joined in early 2006 by the new Newcastle Magnetic Resonance Centre [27]. Additional to its facilities on the main campus and at the General Hospital, in 2001 the Faculty of Medical Sciences also relocated and developed its Institute of Human Genetics at the International Centre for Life designed by Sir Terry Farrell. To cater for the University's world-leading research in the field of stem cells it has subsequently developed the Life Knowledge Park at the International Centre for Life in the Bioscience Building, now linked to its Genetics accommodation by an elevated bridge link.

John Lambert

22 23 24

25 26 27

11

01

Origins to Armstrong College

FROM COLLEGE OF PHYSICAL SCIENCE TO ARMSTRONG COLLEGE

Armstrong College was much more than its name implied. It was not just the result of one person's philanthropy, nor was it just a college. Rather, it was what the term 'university college' implies, a space where a wide range of disciplines was housed, professions trained, degrees awarded, academic staff employed and students progressed to graduation. But the College was not granted full university status until the mid-20th century, leaving Newcastle trailing behind similar institutions in Birmingham, Liverpool, Leeds and Manchester. There were two main reasons for this. The first was that the connection with Durham, so valuable in the early years of the Newcastle colleges, now stood in the way of independence. The other was that the colleges' champions failed for many years to co-ordinate a campaign for that objective.

Universities in the 19th and 20th centuries came into being via many routes, so Newcastle should not be seen as abnormal. Durham itself began as a child of the University of Cambridge, nurtured into existence by the cathedral and its clergy. If there was no clear pathway to university status, perhaps we might learn more by asking first what resources were needed, what preconditions there were for the birth of a university?

Our organizing principles here are space, curriculum and networks. Without donations, gifts and purchases of property, no part of the University could have been established, developed and maintained. The management of bequests and estates posed ever-changing problems for the universities, illustrated by the struggle to fund professorships, the impact of the agricultural depressions of 1850–70, and the intricacies of the Universities and Colleges Estates Acts of 1858 and 1860.

There are several factors determining the success of a network (in the sense of an interlocking community held together by a range of intellectual concerns). These include geographic proximity over time; maintenance of a group of sufficient size to provide a catalytic effect; relations over time between persons of great intellect; connection with leaders, friends and above all rivals of status; maintenance and improvement of the material base for the network. Armstrong College was not able to acquire enough of these features early enough to promote the catalytic effect for an early breakaway from Durham.

What shaped the College's history from 1871? The demand for surgeons and doctors in Newcastle, from an expanding industrializing region, was a major factor in the decision to found the College of Medicine in 1834, as was pressure, in other disciplines, for qualified engineers, architects, chemists and biologists from the shipbuilding, iron and steel industries, mining and agriculture for the College of Physical Science in 1871. Durham had become the victim of its clerical roots, and its governors baulked at the call to develop non-humanistic disciplines aimed at saving bodies and enhancing well-being rather than saving souls. But it fell to the irascible Dean of Durham and Governor of the University, Dean Lake, to turn pressure from the North of England Institution of Mining and Mechanical Engineers, the Literary and Philosophical Society, the Natural History Society of Northumberland, Durham

Right: Armstrong College, now known as the Armstrong Building, was opened in 1904. It was named for William, Lord Armstrong, 1810–1900 (below), a benefactor of the University

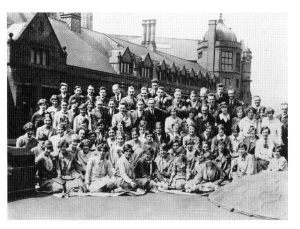

and Newcastle and the Society of Antiquaries into a policy. The Workers Education Association offered useful support and liaison from 1911 and an Extra-Mural Board of Studies was added. But Newcastle had no independent network or champions prior to 1871 prepared to place its interests above those of Durham.

Lake looked to a group of associates – champions from industry Isaac Lowthian Bell and William Armstrong, banker and historian, Thomas Hodgkin, along with R.S. Newall and Robert Spence Watson – for advice and support. After several false starts, on 11 March 1871, the Durham Senate agreed a grant of £1,000 so that a college could be established in Newcastle 'to provide advanced scientific education in the north region and especially to teach science as applied to English mining, agriculture and manufacture', on condition that a similar sum be raised by public subscription. With agreement secured, the

founders didn't wait for the desired sum to arrive from subscription and the College was opened on 1 October. The donations covered the appointment of tutors and some administrative costs, but accommodation had to be rented or borrowed from sympathetic bodies such as the Coal Trade Chambers Company, the Wood Memorial Hall Trustees, and the Literary and Philosophical Society. The paucity and poor quality of accommodation, especially in terms of a library, laboratories and lecture theatres, nurtured a sense of crisis and cramped ambition for three decades.

In Newcastle, it was the challenge to purchase land at Lax's Gardens (now the Quadrangle) in 1894 that was the single galvanizing act, bringing the diverse stakeholders in the city and region together on a mission, a policy and a practice that led to the expansion of the College. The College of Physical Science was renamed Armstrong College in 1904, and

Far left: Armstrong College: (clockwise from top left) the Stephenson engineering Laboratory, the main entrance, Professor Lebour, King's Hall, electrical laboratory, Sir Isambard Owen, the Council Chamber

Above: Armstrong College, 1950s

Bottom: Art students on the roof of the Hatton Gallery in the 1920s

Two founders of Armstrong College: solicitor Robert Spence Watson 1837–1911 (above) and treasurer Thomas Hodgkin 1831–1913 (right)

the financial skills of the Treasurer, Thomas Hodgkin, the rewards of knowledge and skills transfer to the city and region could not be realized.

How was knowledge constructed and organized in the new college? The College of Physical Science awarded a Bachelor's degree after three years' full-time or up to six years' part-time study, and a Master of Science after a further two years of study. A doctorate was awarded for 'original work' spread over seven years, so long as candidates were over 30 years of age. By 1893, students could study at a University Extension Department for University of Cambridge degrees as affiliates, but no hostel accommodation was yet available, a state of affairs unchanged even by 1912. Fees were kept low, remissions frequently granted, and scholarships slowly added to encourage access, but the original college was a private body and had to cover its costs. As with most institutions at the time, the degree structure moved from the founding specialisms in Mining, Physics and Mathematics to embrace the arts and humanities, including Philosophy, Latin, Greek and History, supplemented with studies in Arithmetic, Physical and Political Geography, Algebra and Languages. Degrees in Architecture, Naval Architecture, Fine Art and Law were added by 1932–3 and accommodation for 79 students was provided in 1932.

Subjects rapidly became more specialist, so that by 1893 degrees in Agriculture included instruction in chemistry, botany, veterinary anatomy and pathology, mechanics, surveying, entomology and book-keeping. Teaching was provided by a very small number of lecturers and professors. Examinations were regular and compulsory. For scientific studies, attendance at laboratories was compulsory, admission tickets had to be paid for and a certificate of attendance at not less than three classes over a fixed period was required. Students could be affiliated to Durham or Armstrong College, but all had to defer to the College regulations, with 'disorderly conduct on the part of any student, within the precincts of the College' resulting in special punishment. There were no religious tests for membership of the University and women were allowed entry.

Armstrong College's metamorphosis into the University of Newcastle upon Tyne came about variously from disillusion with the restraining power of the parent body, the clericalism and conservatism of Durham University, and envious eyes cast on the city universities emerging elsewhere. Recovery from the

the main buildings were opened officially by King Edward VII in 1906, followed by the opening of the School of Art in 1911 and the Agriculture Block in 1926. The Prince of Wales opened the new Mining Building in 1929. The Dove Marine Laboratory, founded in 1897, opened its new building at Cullercoats in 1908, and land was bought for forestry, dairy, marine and zoological research.

Once established, the College's future lay in the hands of a prickly yet enterprising network of individuals displaying divergent talents but with focused aims and missions. The founding fathers in this early period were the Principals, William Garnett (1884–94) and Henry Palin Gurney (1894–1904), both holders of the Chair in Mathematics; Dr John Theodore Merz, philosopher and industrialist; the zealous solicitor Robert Spence Watson; and two Governing Body members who sat on the University Council, William Cochrane and Robert Robey Redmayne. Other sponsors included city councillors, alumni and practitioners of various industries who looked to the College and its staff to provide a supply of qualified scholars, solutions to local problems and induction in the newest ideas from home and abroad. Without the land, the network and

deprivations of both world wars was slow, and so the final battle for sovereignty was left until the 1960s. King's College was in effect a parallel institution to Durham University rather than a constituent division. Its student body, specialization of disciplines, degree and quality of space and equipment had passed the critical mass that identified a university in that period. The birth of the new university from its old parent bodies of Armstrong College and the College of Medicine, by way of King's College, was eventually welcomed by Parliament, City and College in 1963. Restructuring of the College of Physical Science into Durham College of Science, Newcastle upon Tyne, in 1883, had only added to the identity crisis of the adolescent University of Newcastle, as did the penultimate transformation, the merging of Armstrong College and the College of Medicine into King's College, in 1937.

The champions who took the institution from college to university were the new professors and managers rather than the clergy, businessmen and councillors (though the patronage of Robinson and Cookson, whose benefactions took place after the University's independence, should not be forgotten). It is fitting that the names of the buildings on campus, used now to navigate the University and its disciplines, include Bedson, Daysh, Merz, Percy and Stephenson.

John Gibbins

NEWCASTLE IN THE 19TH CENTURY

When the 19th century opened, Newcastle was already an important centre with a long history. Romans and Anglo-Saxons had appreciated the value of this key crossroads site where major north–south and east–west routes met. Normans had christened the town when they built their new castle in 1080. During the Middle Ages, Newcastle was one of the nation's most important boroughs, a trading centre and a military base on the often fought-over Anglo-Scottish border. This military significance declined after the Union of the Crowns in 1603, apart from flurries of action during the Civil War and the Jacobite risings of 1715 and 1745.

The commercial significance of the town continued to increase, with the coal trade of the Tyne expanding at the heart of the process. Initially, the urban area was small by later standards. The first census credited Newcastle with a population of only 28,000 in 1801,

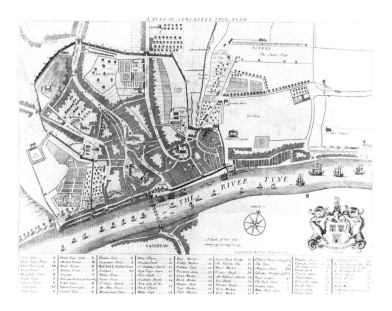

but the scene was set for accelerating growth. An early change came in 1835, when the borough was enlarged by the addition of Byker, Elswick, Heaton, Jesmond, Walker and Westgate. Local control was exercised by relatively small social groups who dominated the town's economy and also managed its political, social and philanthropic activities. Connected by a great variety of personal, social, commercial and recreational links, this oligarchy was already exhibiting a capacity for innovation and development in many different facets of the town's life. There were coal mines, metalworking enterprises and shipyards within the town's boundaries, and also a great variety of workshops and commercial enterprises. As the centre of an expanding region, Newcastle was already providing important services for its hinterland. The commercial side of the coal trade was concentrated here. Banking and insurance, including maritime insurance for the Tyne's growing shipping interests, were also based here. A growing professional

Map of Newcastle in 1736

An engraving of a 19th-century colliery by Thomas Hair (1810–75)

Above: The Lit and Phil Society, where public discussion of a College in Newcastle began in 1831 with a paper by Thomas Greenhow

Above right: HMS Victoria, a battleship built by the Armstrong company, passing the Swing Bridge on her way to sea

group was prominent in the town, including lawyers, doctors, teachers and ministers of religion.

The late 18th and earlier 19th centuries saw the proliferation of a variety of institutions for intellectual, cultural and philanthropic purposes. They included the Infirmary, the Dispensary, two maternity charities, asylums for the blind and the deaf and dumb, and even an institution for the rehabilitation of prostitutes. At the centre of cultural and scientific interests, the Literary and Philosophical Society (Lit and Phil), founded in 1793, spawned specialist societies for archaeology and natural history, and after more than two centuries still plays an active part in the city's life. Such societies brought together many individuals from the elite groups of Newcastle and its surrounding region, groups much concerned with the local economy. The scientific interests of the Lit and Phil were concentrated in early years on coal mining and other local industries, and this connection was central in institutions like the Mechanics' Institute of 1824, which had accumulated a library of 8,000 books by 1840, and the North of England Institution of Mining and Mechanical Engineers of 1852, which brought together coal owners and colliery managers in the study of technical matters affecting the coalfield.

Contacts such as these played important roles in some of the technical breakthroughs that marked these years, including developments in mining techniques, the coming of the railways and a dramatic shift in ship design. By 1850, Tyneside shipyards had developed the iron-built screw-propelled merchant ship that was to replace the old wooden sailing vessels. The first successful innovation here was the iron-built collier, which brought such major savings in the cost of

shipping coal that it consolidated the North East's hold on the key London market and facilitated dramatic future growth in coal sales at home and abroad. From this limited application, the new vessels proliferated into the various types of merchant shipping which carried the unprecedented growth in international trade that marked the period 1850–1914.

Similar developments occurred in a variety of other industries, including chemicals, pottery, glass, engineering, iron and steel, stimulated by the cheap energy available from the Great Northern Coalfield during the great age of coal, iron and steam. Much of this industry lay outside Newcastle, but the dramatic expansion of the region's industries enhanced the town's importance as the centre of the commercial and service facilities that these industries required. The enormous growth in coal shipments from the Great Northern Coalfield was of much more than local importance. Most of this coal was exported to an arc of European countries, ranging from the Baltic to the Mediterranean. It constituted a vital part of the energy supplies for the industrialization and urbanization of the whole of western Europe, at a time when Europe played such a dominant role on the world stage. It was from Newcastle that this traffic was administered.

By the mid 19th-century, Newcastle's population had grown to nearly 88,000, an unprecedented and unforeseeable growth which presented serious social problems in a society where central and local government played only a limited role and produced a standard of performance that did not always inspire confidence in a tax- and rate-paying electorate. By the 1850s, Newcastle had developed some of the worst slums in England. The once thriving quayside area had become rundown and overcrowded, as more prosperous inhabitants moved out to new suburbs. This decline was exacerbated by such events as the influx of poor Irish immigrants following the potato famine of the 1840s. There was also a catastrophic fire and explosion in riverside Gateshead in 1854, which devastated much of the tenemented housing on the Newcastle quayside, increasing the overcrowding in the remaining structures.

The second half of the 19th century saw gradual attempts at tackling the city's social problems. Economic development was among the causes of some of these problems, but it also provided the enhanced resources that could boost local government income and increase spending power among local workers. Rateable value of property in Newcastle rose from £449,000 in 1870 to £1,641,000 in 1907. In 1882, the city's Medical Officer of Health had a staff of nine, which by 1907 had grown to 37, not counting the staff employed in the city's own hospitals by that time. Improvements in local transport, better roads, suburban railways and urban tramway systems facilitated a spread of the expanding population into healthier suburbs with greatly improved housing provision. By 1900, Newcastle's death rate, a horrendous 36.7 per thousand in 1865, had fallen permanently to below 20 per thousand, despite a huge increase in the city's population to 215,000. By the end of the century, there had been parallel improvements in the provision of schools, sanitation and medical services.

In 1900, Newcastle was a great city, known worldwide and justly seen as the lynchpin of a region that had become a leading player in the creation of the modern world.

Norman McCord

Newcastle Central Station in the 19th century

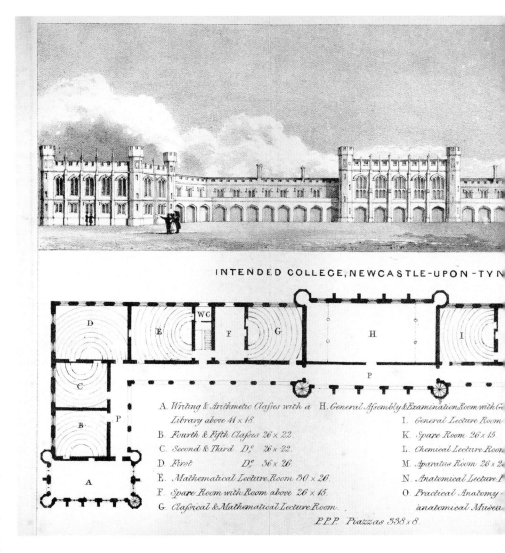

INTENDED COLLEGE, NEWCASTLE-UPON-TYN

A. *Writing & Arithmetic Classes with a Library above 44 x 48*
B. *Fourth & Fifth Classes 26 x 22.*
C. *Second & Third D.°   26 x 22.*
D. *First   D.° 36 x 26.*
E. *Mathematical Lecture Room 30 x 26.*
F. *Spare Room with Room above 26 x 15.*
G. *Classical & Mathematical Lecture Room.*
H. *General Assembly & Examination Room with G*
I. *General Lecture Room*
K. *Spare Room 26 x 15*
L. *Chemical Lecture Room*
M. *Apparatus Room 26 x 2*
N. *Anatomical Lecture R*
O. *Practical Anatomy anatomical Museu*
P.P.P. Piazzas 338 x 8.

ORIGINS OF THE COLLEGE OF MEDICINE

'The Expediency of Establishing in Newcastle an Academical Institution of the Nature of a College or University for the Promotion of Literature and Science, more especially amongst the Middle Classes of the Community, briefly considered.' Thus was entitled a paper read by Mr Thomas M. Greenhow to the Newcastle Literary and Philosophical Society on 5 April 1831. Dismissing Oxford and Cambridge as 'open only to the upper and more wealthy classes' and London as 'the last place where a prudent father would … entrust a youth', he asserted that 'in no country in Europe are the means of obtaining a liberal and systematic course of academic instruction so sparingly supplied … as in England'. He went on to challenge his audience: 'What expedient, then, remains to supply this lamentable deficiency … but to establish for ourselves a College or University.'

John Green's plan for a new university building

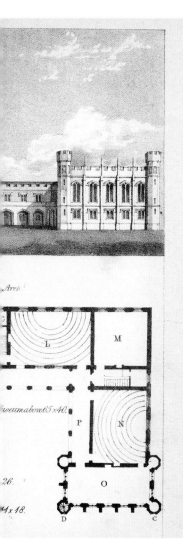

Greenhow, a surgeon, had a vision of the potential greatness of Newcastle that enshrined access to education in literature and science for its citizens. He emphasized the benefits of languages to merchants, of engineering to those in the shipbuilding and mining industries and of academic training to those entering the professions. 'As a situation favorable for a flourishing and beneficial school of medicine', he said, 'Newcastle possesses many eminent advantages'. He ended by proclaiming that the new institution 'would … shed a glory over a town which is already so rapidly increasing in extent, in beauty, and in commercial importance.'

The paper was well received. Two months later Greenhow read a further paper setting out his detailed proposals for the building, financing and governance of the new institution. He specified the courses of study and enumerated the subjects to be taught in the medical curriculum. At his suggestion, a committee was appointed to draw up a formal prospectus. This was approved by the Society 12 months later, as were the plans for a handsome building designed by John Green. At a public meeting held in the Guildhall on 28 January 1833, a resolution to carry forward the proposals was unanimously agreed.

The story of these beginnings is worth telling because it foreshadowed the unfolding of the history of our University: the successful development of a medical school, early pre-eminence in mining and marine engineering, the burgeoning of teaching and research across a wide range of disciplines, and ultimately the creation of an institution of distinction far beyond Thomas Greenhow's dreams.

Unfortunately, the joint-stock company set up to finance the venture did not attract the necessary support and the scheme failed. Perhaps press comment, so often corrosive of noble aspiration, played its part. The response of the *Tyne Mercury* was to 'regard the project as chimerical' and 'the baseless fabric of a vision'. Nor was there much support in other influential quarters.

One of the members of the committee set up to implement the Greenhow proposals was John Fife, destined later to be Mayor of Newcastle and to be knighted for his part in the suppression of the Chartist riot on Forth Banks. He too was a surgeon, with consulting rooms in Bell's Court, a close off Pilgrim Street. In October 1832, with the Greenhow initiative still in embryo, Fife with five colleagues embarked upon a course of lectures in Medicine in premises adjacent to

Sir John Fife, who established the Newcastle upon Tyne School of Medicine and Surgery in 1834

his rooms. The success of the course emboldened Fife and his colleagues to establish themselves as the Newcastle upon Tyne School of Medicine and Surgery, formally inaugurated and opened on 1 October 1834. They rented the vacant hall of the 'Worshipful Company of Barber-Surgeons and Wax and Tallow Chandlers' in the Manors, made some structural alterations, and henceforth referred to it as Surgeons' Hall.

We can but speculate on the circumstances in which John Fife, within a year of accepting his role in the Greenhow plan, was to become the dominant figure in the establishment of a new medical school from which Greenhow was excluded. Grey Turner, a charitable historian, simply balances Greenhow's lofty idealism against the humbler practicality of those wishing to get things started on a smaller scale. Embleton, pondering the question more critically, does not impugn Fife's honour but comments obliquely on some of his less attractive qualities and on his lack of support for Greenhow.

There is no record of animosity between Fife and Greenhow. Together they had founded a Hospital for Diseases of the Eye in 1822. In 1836, their names were linked in the curious business of the petitioning of Lord Glenelg, Secretary for the Colonies, on the selection by phrenology of convicts for deportation to New South Wales to which, apparently, his Lordship had expressed disinclination. Fife's submission was in character. He was a man of awesome energy and obsessional

Bell's Court, where John Fife had consulting rooms and where the first lectures in Medicine took place

From top: Gibb's certificate showing the Barber-Surgeons' Hall; the Disruption document, 1851; the programme for the Northumberland Road Foundation Stone ceremony, 1867

Right: The gardener's cottage which provided a temporary home for the Medical School in 1851–2

punctuality; regarded by some as 'a very presumptious young man', he had imperturbable self-confidence. His petition asserted that 'natural dispositions are indicated by the form and size of the brain, to such an extent as to render it quite possible … to distinguish men of desperate and dangerous tendencies from those of good dispositions'. Greenhow's petition, submitted with 16 other signatories, was more cautious. It commended phrenological selection provided its reliability could be demonstrated on the basis of a controlled experiment. Before the days of imaging, it was perhaps reasonable to conjecture that human characteristics, known or supposed to be associated with the degree of development of particular regions of the brain, might be reflected in the contours of the skull.

During the early years of the School, the numbers of students and staff gradually increased. The lists of both, faithfully recorded by Embleton, contain many names prominent in the folklore of Newcastle medicine. Amongst the students who attended the Bell's Court lectures was John Snow, famous for his work on the transmission of cholera and for administering chloroform to Queen Victoria at the birth of two of her children.

Charles Gibb, a student and later Lecturer in Anatomy, had a surgical practice renowned throughout Northumberland and Durham. His name is immortalized in 'The Blaydon Races', the Tyneside anthem:

> *Some went to the dispensary*
> *an' some to Doctor Gibb's,*
> *an' some to the Informary*
> *to mend thor broken ribs.*

Successful though the School was, relations among staff members were not always harmonious. To some extent they were in competition with one another, their livelihoods depending on the success of their practices. The prestige of involvement in the School could attract public awareness and the lecture room could provide an opportunity to impress on rising generations of doctors eligibility for their patronage. The lack of any financial

reward rankled. For a time, new appointees to lectureships were even required to contribute an entrance fee of £40 to the School.

It was against this background that a row flared up over the appointment of a surgeon to one of the districts of the Poor Law Union. Dr Embleton, a Poor Law Guardian of significant influence, failed to support a colleague in his own department and gave preference to an old friend and fellow student. So bitter was the ensuing row that reconciliation proved impossible and the extreme measure of dissolution became inevitable. What was to become known as the 'disruption' occurred on 25 June 1851. Two rival factions immediately emerged and set up competing teaching establishments. A group comprising the majority of former staff established the Newcastle upon Tyne College of Medicine, whilst the minority, under the leadership of John (now Sir John) Fife, named their enterprise the Newcastle upon Tyne College of Medicine and Practical Science.

On one occasion the unseemly split between leading members of the profession degenerated into the unlawful plundering by the minority faction of museum specimens held in store, pending agreement on their disposal. This outrage was the subject of an epic poem in the style of a border ballad that ran to 50 verses. It was quoted in extenso by both Embleton and Grey Turner, but readers of this account are to be spared.

The upheavals of 1851 were not just organizational. A plan to drive the North Shields and Berwick Railway through Newcastle meant the demolition of Surgeons' Hall and its replacement by a new building, designed by John Dobson, on Victoria Street. Completed in the year of the 'disruption', it was immediately occupied by the College of Medicine and Practical Science, owing to

Westmorland House adjoining the
Lit and Phil.
Engraving by T.M. Richardson

Fife's dominant influence with the Barber-Surgeons. Its now homeless rival sought refuge in the only surviving building on the Manors site, the house formerly occupied by the gardener. After an uncomfortable winter in overcrowded accommodation, Westmorland House, an old mansion adjoining the Lit and Phil building, was acquired. It failed to provide all the necessary accommodation and a new building, again designed by Dobson, was erected in its orchard. Thus did Orchard Street acquire its name.

In 1850, a year before the 'disruption', the idea was first mooted of establishing a link between the College of Medicine and the University of Durham. Negotiations initiated by Dr Embleton and the Venerable Charles Thorp, Warden of the University, eventually led to the rather clumsy renaming of the new college of the majority as the 'Newcastle upon Tyne College of Medicine in connection with the University of Durham'. The academic advantage of the link with Durham, coupled now with recognition by the Society of Apothecaries, the Royal College of Surgeons of England and the University of London, gave this college a clear lead over its rival. The ailing College of Medicine and Practical Science sought reconciliation. This was achieved in a most civilized manner, one of those most prominent in negotiating the settlement being none other than Thomas Greenhow, who had accepted an appointment as Lecturer in Medical Ethics in 1856. The union was completed in time for the 1857 session, which was opened with great cordiality, the Warden of the University of Durham presiding.

From these turbulent beginnings developed a medical school that prospered in ensuing years, readily adapting to advances in medical science and medical practice. It changed its name yet again in 1870, when strengthening links with Durham determined that it should become the University of Durham College of Medicine, Newcastle upon Tyne. By this time, it had grown to be the largest provincial medical school in England.

But the hunger of the railways was not yet assuaged. The North Eastern Railway Company proposed an extension of the Central Station into Orchard Street, requiring the demolition of the College. By 1887, it was so overcrowded that it readily acquiesced and, in November of that year, the foundation stone of a new building in Bath Road, later renamed Northumberland Road, was laid by Algernon George, 6th Duke of Northumberland. Remarkably, this fine building was completed in time for the opening of the 1888 session. An extra wing was added in 1906, the year in which the new Armstrong Building was opened by King Edward VII. On the same wet day in July, he opened the Royal Victoria Infirmary, replacing the old infirmary on Forth Banks. This brought the teaching hospital closer to the College of Medicine, to the benefit of students in the clinical years of their training.

After the turbulence of its early years, the College of Medicine thus enjoyed an era of uninterrupted academic development, physical expansion and growing reputation. Many of its teachers achieved professional distinction and many of its students made their mark at home and abroad. These largely untroubled years extending over half a century were to end abruptly in 1914 with the outbreak of war.

David Shaw

The Hancock Museum, which houses a natural history collection

CULTURAL FOUNDATIONS: THE UNIVERSITY MUSEUMS

The tale of the University's museums begins in 1743 with the ornithologist Marmaduke Tunstall. A man with wide interests, he arranged his mansion at Wycliffe on the Tees to house his 'invaluable collections of manuscripts, books, prints, coins, and gems, besides a spacious museum stored with rare birds, and many other curiosities relating to natural history'. In 1791, his collection was bought for £700 by the solicitor and noted antiquary, George Allan of Blackwell Grange, Darlington, but after Allan's death in 1800 the collection was allowed to decay until the Literary and Philosophical Society of Newcastle upon Tyne (known to all as the Lit and Phil) bought it in 1822 for £400.

Newcastle in the 19th century was a centre of intellectual activity, and anybody of any note was a

The opening of the Museum of Antiquities in 1960

member of one or more of the great societies that thrived in the city. Many of these societies started life as sub-groups of the Lit and Phil, which had been founded in 1793 with a very wide remit, covering most of the sciences as well as the arts. These interests led to the Society acquiring scientific collections, but their collecting really took off when they bought the Allan Museum. The decision had its opponents, but their objections were overruled and in 1827, George Townshend Fox, a prominent benefactor of the Society, published his *Synopsis of the Newcastle Museum*.

When Fox retired, the Lit and Phil found they had to appoint a Museum Committee to cope with the increasing number of artefacts that were being donated, as well as the resulting financial burden. In 1829, it was decided to form the Natural History Society of Northumberland, Durham and Newcastle upon Tyne, with its own membership and its own subscription income, to run the natural history part of the Lit and Phil. Matters did not run smoothly: later that year the Annual General Meeting of the Lit and Phil robustly rejected the idea that the Natural History Society should buy the collection. They did, however, agree that the Natural History Society take over 'the superintendence and arrangement' of the museum but declared that there be a 'mutual understanding … that the museums [ie the various collections] be not separated'.

By 1831, the Natural History Society had already decided to open a gallery on a site next to the Lit and Phil building on Westgate Road. A proposal of the Lit and Phil 'to combine its funds with those of the Antiquarian and Natural History Societies to secure the accommodation under one roof, of our various collections' was put forward. The museum was called the Newcastle Museum and it opened to the public in December 1834.

The Society of Antiquaries of Newcastle had been formed when, on 23 January 1813, 17 gentlemen met in the Long Room of Loftus's Inn 'for the purpose of adopting the best measures to promote enquiry into antiquities in general, but more especially those of the North of England and of the counties of Northumberland, Cumberland and Durham in particular'. Monthly meetings were held in the Keep of the New Castle and from the start artefacts were collected. Soon their rooms on the ground floor of the Lit and Phil were overflowing and, in 1849, the Society of Antiquaries removed their collection of archaeological artefacts to the newly renovated Keep.

the University, was employed in 1956 to catalogue the Antiquaries' collection and oversee the move.

The Joint Museum of Antiquities was opened in April 1960. Better known internationally than locally, it holds a surprisingly large and impressive collection of archaeological artefacts, ranging in date from the Palaeolithic period to 1600 AD. Although its present collecting policy restricts its acquisitions to the North of England, it has material from all over the British Isles due to its origins as the collection of the Society of Antiquaries.

Although the Museum is best known for its Roman collection, its prehistoric and Anglo-Saxon collections are also of international renown. The former includes the largest and most significant collection of prehistoric rock art in Britain, as well as material from the Neolithic and Bronze Age periods. The Anglo-Saxon material includes examples of almost all the monuments known from the period, as well as good representations of the crosses and decorative motifs. Significant pieces include the Rothbury Cross, which is the earliest Christian rood surviving in the country, and the Alnmouth Cross, which has the only clearly attested Irish name on an Anglo-Saxon artefact.

As the main museum for the World Heritage Site of Hadrian's Wall, its spectacular Roman collection includes the material evidence for the Roman Empire's most north-westerly frontier. This includes artefacts relating to almost every province of the Roman Empire and the military units and civilian populations of these provinces. As one of the largest collections of Roman inscriptions and sculptural stones in Britain, the Museum includes many important pieces such as the Birth of Mithras from Housesteads, with the first depiction of the Signs of the Zodiac in Britain. The smaller artefacts include many internationally acknowledged masterpieces, such as the Aesica Brooch, the South Shields Bear Cameo, and the Aemilia Finger Ring, which may be the earliest Christian artefact to have been found in Britain.

It is to Dr C.I.C. Bosanquet's credit that the Shefton Museum of Greek Art and Archaeology was established.

The Natural History Society's collection was also starting to overflow, but it took until 1884 before the Society was able to move to its present magnificent premises, designed in 1878 by John Wardle and known ever since as the Hancock Museum, after the noted naturalists John and Albany Hancock. In 1958, a 99-year agreement was signed between the University of Durham and the Natural History Society that the Hancock would be run by the University, who would be responsible for the building. In 1992, the management of the Museum was passed to Tyne and Wear Museums who now operate it on behalf of the University.

The Antiquaries, in the meantime, had continued to occupy the Keep and the 13th-century Black Gate. In the 1930s, their council began to be concerned that medieval buildings run by volunteers were not ideal for a collection of international importance and began discussions with the University of Durham. Plans were well advanced when war broke out in 1939 and the idea was put on hold. In the 1950s, Dr C.I.C. Bosanquet, Rector of King's College and a keen antiquarian, revived the project with the help of Professor Ian Richmond. A place was found for the collection in the building next to the Arches, which had been built in 1949 as a coke-testing station by W.B. Edwards and Partners for the Department of Physical Chemistry. Dr David Smith, a graduate of

Brian Shefton had joined the staff of the Department of Classics in 1955 and Bosanquet put a sum of £100 at his disposal in order that he might acquire artefacts to aid the teaching of a new course in Greek Archaeology. The next year another £100 became available, and the collection in a cupboard in Eldon Place began to grow. In 1957, a Greek vase came on the market at £260 – a sum beyond the Department's own means. Dr Bosanquet appealed to the National Arts Collection Fund and others, and the vase was acquired. A special case was built and it was revealed to the public in the University's Hatton Gallery, but then had to be put away again because there was no museum.

The opening of the Percy Building in 1958 provided the opportunity for a small museum to be fitted out, with the aid of R.B. Holland of the Fine Art Department. Members of the public could ask for access if they wished. The acquisition of objects continued apace as Professor Shefton took advantage of a range of local and national funding opportunities, supported by Dr Bosanquet. When the Classics Department moved to the Armstrong Building, space was found in the old Chemistry Laboratories on the first floor and the new Museum of Greek Art and Archaeology was opened in

1993. The name of its founder was added to the name of the Museum in 1998, and the running of the Museum was transferred from the Classics Department to the staff of the Archaeological Museums in January 1999.

The Shefton Museum of Greek Art and Archaeology now consists of some 1,000 inventoried objects, mostly acquired between 1956 and 1984 through purchase, gift or loan. It is the only museum of its kind actively collecting north of Birmingham. It is also the only major, permanently displayed, publicly accessible collection of Mediterranean artefacts between Manchester and Edinburgh. In 1998, Professor J.P. Barron of Oxford University, in his assessment of the collection, referred to it as 'the careful assembly of mainly small objects, made piecemeal by a formidably knowledgeable and keenly discerning scholar'. He went on to say that 'it cannot be too much stressed that this is a collection of international importance, in this country the most important beyond the British Museum, the Ashmolean and the Fitzwilliam'.

As well as its fine collection of Greek pottery and Etruscan bronzes, the Shefton Museum has a range of sculpture on long-term loan from the Wellcome Institute. One fine figure of Nike is now known to have belonged to John Ruskin and features in several of Ruskin's sketches

and diary or letter entries. Many of the other pieces have interesting histories, including the enormous porphyry foot from second-century Roman Egypt which belonged to Lord Bessborough and Thomas Hope before entering the collection of Sir Henry Wellcome.

The Archaeological Museums, although small in size, have always 'punched above their weight' and have a high level of achievement in research, publication and conservation, being particularly renowned for their outreach and educational work. Although both play a part in teaching and research throughout the University, both have a much wider role, locally, nationally and internationally. The Museum of Antiquities was the first museum in the country to mount a full exhibition on the internet and now has one of the most active museum websites in Britain, attracting over 1 million virtual visitors per year. One of its many excellent IT/education projects was short-listed for the Gulbenkian Museum of the Year Prize in 2004, a first for a university museum. However, the Shefton Museum is hard to find and the Museum of Antiquities building is decaying and bursting at the seams. We all look forward to once again combining with the Natural History Society's collection in the Great North Museum – the next exciting chapter in the history of the museums at Newcastle University.

Lindsay Allason-Jones

THE HATTON GALLERY

Described in recent years as 'one of the most impressive exhibition spaces in Britain', (Andrew Graham-Dixon, *The Telegraph*), the Hatton Gallery has been at the heart of cultural life in the North East since the early 20th century.

Its origins however lie as far back as 1837, when the 'North of England Society for the promotion of the Fine Arts in their Higher Departments, and in their Application to Manufactures', was founded. The Society planned to establish a school of art, a permanent collection, exhibition programme and library devoted to art. In 1888, the Society was amalgamated with Durham College of Physical Science, and two years later Richard George Hatton, a painter and designer, was appointed as second art master. A keen advocate of William Morris's Arts and Crafts Movement, Hatton established the (Newcastle) Handicrafts Company, which introduced students to a wide range of crafts including metalwork, enamelling, woodcarving and embroidery. A new building, the King Edward VII School of Art, was opened in 1912 and, in 1917, Hatton became its first Director, remaining in the position until his death in 1926. The gallery within the School was named after Hatton in recognition of his contribution.

Top left: The Anglo-Saxon Rothbury Cross

Centre left: Statuette of Nike that once belonged to John Ruskin

Right: The entrance to the Hatton Gallery, named for the first director of the School of Art, Richard Hatton

Below: J.A.M. Whistler, Billingsgate, 1859, etching

The exhibition space in the Hatton Gallery

Under Hatton, the Gallery had begun to show exhibitions in what is now the front room since 1919. A collection of artworks also began to take shape with donations from Professor Hatton himself, who gave his Indian miniatures and his copy of Burgkmair's *Triumphal Procession*. At the same time, the Charlton family donated to the University a collection of over 1,000 paintings, drawings and prints by John, Hugh and William Henry Charlton.

Collecting accelerated in the early 1950s, when Lawrence Gowing was appointed Head of Fine Art and Director of the Hatton. Using funds from a bequest by Joseph Shipley, a local industrialist, Gowing, together with the art historian Ralph Holland, instituted a programme of acquisitions. Works ranging from the 14th to the 19th century were collected with the purpose of assisting teaching and illustrating developments and techniques in painting, drawing and printmaking. Amongst the works Gowing bought for the collection were a *Portrait of a Young Man with Statuette*, attributed to 16th-century Italian painter Tiburzio Passarotti; *A View of Tivoli* by Gaspard Dughet, the pair to which hangs in the Art Gallery of Toronto; two 14th-century altarpieces depicting Saints Francis and John the Baptist and Saints Bartholomew and John

the Evangelist, and a large altarpiece by Domenichino of *The Descent from the Cross*.

At the same time as expanding the collection, the Hatton Gallery was home to a programme of exhibitions that showed the latest developments in art and design. Several leading radical artists, including Richard Hamilton and Victor Pasmore, were working in the Fine Art Department and experimenting with new approaches to making and exhibiting art. It was in Newcastle that Hamilton began to develop his interest in combining art and popular culture, a journey that would lead to the early forms of Pop Art. In 1955, Hamilton organized the landmark exhibition *Man, Machine and Motion*, which explored the relationship between man and machine. The following year, Hamilton and Pasmore produced the ground-breaking show, *An Exhibit*. With no formal, visual subject, the exhibition consisted of a system of Plexiglas panels, hung vertically and horizontally, which visitors had to negotiate their way through.

Hamilton was also responsible for the acquisition of the most outstanding work in the Hatton's collection, the *Merzbarn* by German émigré artist, Kurt Schwitters. Originally constructed in a barn in the Lake District during 1947–8, the *Merzbarn* was Schwitters's final, and in his own estimation 'greatest', piece of work (letter

Domenichino (1581–1641), Descent from the Cross, oil on canvas

from Schwitters to Ludwig Hilbersheimer, October 1947). Measuring 2.5m by 4.5m, it is the only surviving example of his Merz constructions, built using found objects and personal debris, including the rose of a watering can, twigs and a china egg. The wall was unfinished on Schwitters's death in 1948 and remained untouched and relatively unknown until Hamilton sought to rehouse it. Under his direction, the wall was documented in its original Elterwater site, before being moved to Newcastle in 1965 and incorporated in the fabric of the Hatton Gallery building.

Between the 1950s and 1980s, the collection of modern and contemporary British paintings was expanded by gifts from the Contemporary Art Society, including works by Francis Bacon, Walter Sickert, Patrick Heron and William Roberts. In addition, several important bequests were made including the Bosanquet Collection of European textiles dating from the 16th to the 19th century and the Hall Bequest of Baxter and Victorian prints. The most significant acquisition of recent years was the gift of almost 100 items of West African sculpture from the painter and collector Fred Uhlman. Like Schwitters, Uhlman had fled Germany after the rise of the National Socialist Party, eventually being interned with Schwitters on the Isle of Man. The collection of carvings, masks and items of jewellery mainly originates from former French territories, particularly Mali and the Ivory Coast. Whilst some of the sculptures were everyday objects used in domestic life, the majority were connected with religious rites and beliefs, including ancestor worship, propitiation of spirits and divination.

Today the Gallery operates principally as a temporary exhibition space, presenting a wide variety of art exhibitions including shows evolving from the permanent collection and major national and international touring exhibitions. Whilst the Gallery is now managed independently of the Art School, close links are maintained with annual undergraduate and Master's degrees shows, and exhibitions of work by research Fellows and staff. In recent years the Gallery has also collaborated with a diverse range of academics within the university, commissioning artists to produce new painting, sculpture and new media work in response to developments in subjects as wide-ranging as Neuroscience, English and Politics.

Lucy Whetstone

02

A New Century

Into the New Century

The royal visit of 1906 may fittingly be seen as the culmination of the early history of the two university colleges at Newcastle. By the early 20th century, they were well-established academic institutions. The University of Durham Act of 1908 provided them with a more settled status. The University now comprised two divisions, Durham and Newcastle, with the Newcastle element still in two separate colleges. They continued to benefit from the support of local businessmen and industrialists, who played leading parts in administration and fundraising, but were generally content to leave academic matters in the hands of academic staff, especially the professors. It was not until 1935 that lecturers acquired any formal participation in College government.

Armstrong College was still involved in sub-degree work, providing courses for such groups as railway clerks and Poor Law officials. Although this continued into the inter-war years, two developments reduced its scale. In teacher training, the proportion of non-degree students, initially a majority, gradually dwindled until the Education Department effectively only recruited degree students. In 1909, an amicable demarcation agreement with the city's Rutherford College saw Armstrong College shed much of its sub-degree technical teaching. At the same time, staff and student numbers continued to grow.

This progress came to an abrupt stop in 1914 with the outbreak of war. The principal concern of the College of Medicine became a continuing supply of doctors for the armed forces. Armstrong College was hit hard by the immediate requisition of its principal buildings to form an emergency military hospital. For the next few years the College contrived to work in makeshift premises. Its original parent, the Lit and Phil, provided one refuge, and other accommodation was given in the Hancock Museum and the College of Medicine.

When peace came, more normal conditions returned, but the Newcastle colleges suffered from the economic problems that beset the region during the inter-war years. In 1920, professors at Armstrong College waived salary increases in order that junior staff salaries could be improved. An Appointments Board, created in 1919 to facilitate student employment, had to be suspended on financial grounds in 1924.

Generous gifts allowed some improvements. Cecil Cochrane gave 20 acres of new playing fields, and George

Left: Edward VII arriving at Newcastle in 1906, where he officially opened Armstrong College

Below: Emergency military hospital in Armstrong College: World War I

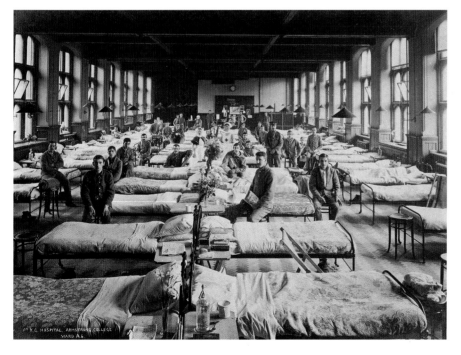

Henderson a substantial sports pavilion, at Cochrane Park. Cochrane, a leading industrialist, financed a major new Students' Union building for both colleges, opening in 1925. Henderson, a prominent local business leader, paid for the first hall of residence for male students of both colleges, which opened in 1932. Elsewhere in this book, individual subject histories show continuing academic expansion even in the inter-war years, a considerable success story in difficult circumstances.

In the mid-1930s, an unexpected crisis in the College of Medicine sparked major changes at Newcastle. What was initially a confrontation between two strong-minded individuals over internal financial proposals escalated into a major row that involved both colleges, external bodies, including the General Medical Council, litigation and a great deal of unwanted publicity. Eventually the situation deteriorated so much that, in 1934, a Royal Commission was appointed to enquire into the University's administration. Its report was followed by the University of Durham Act of 1935 which introduced major changes. The two Newcastle colleges were united into King's College, governed by a mainly non-academic Council and an Academic Board on which all professors sat. The old status of the College of Medicine was recognized by Medicine being the senior faculty and the new Dean of Medicine being given unusually wide powers within the new unified college. A Rector became the head of King's College, alternating with the Warden of the Durham colleges in the University vice-chancellorship.

The new King's College was by far the biggest single element in the reformed university structure. A purely academic Senate, representing both Newcastle and Durham, still governed academic activities for the University as a whole. To its credit, the reformed Senate never divided simply between its Durham and Newcastle members on any matter. Subject departments were grouped into eight faculties which advised Senate on their own areas of interest. Lord Eustace Percy took office as the first Rector in 1937, an admirable choice both because of his local family connections and his own distinction as politician and author. King George VI opened the new Medical School early in 1939, but the united college had scarcely time to bed down before the outbreak of war in 1939 presented new difficulties.

Norman McCord

Below: Grey's Monument as seen from Grainger Street

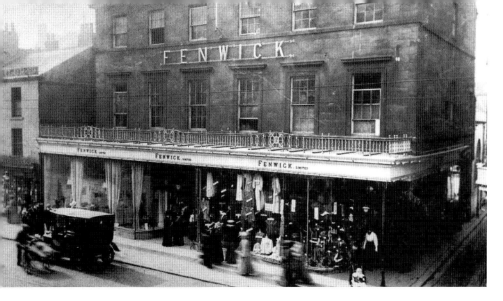

Above: Fenwicks Department Store sale in 1905

NEWCASTLE IN A NEW CENTURY

In 1900, Newcastle was among the best-known cities of its size anywhere. The Tyne was one of the world's great ports, and Newcastle was the nerve centre of its activities. Shipping companies, the coal trade and a huge variety of commercial and professional activities were concentrated here. Among them was a remarkable organization whereby the enormously swollen population of the city and neighbouring communities was fed and supplied with an increasing variety of goods from all over the world. The city was a major industrial centre, with the great Armstrong Whitworth company, which employed well over 20,000 workers, as a principal showpiece.

Newcastle provided a large and constantly increasing array of retail and recreational activities. Department stores such as Bainbridges, Binns and Fenwicks were accompanied by suburban shopping centres and innumerable corner shops. Newcastle United's first First Division game in 1898 was watched by 20,000 spectators at St James' Park, the capacity of which was raised to 55,000 nine years later. The city's confidence was illustrated by the annexation of a second ring of suburbs in 1904 – Fenham, Benwell, Walker and part of Kenton.

Right: Women munition workers on their way to work during the First World War

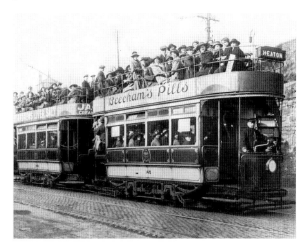

More far-sighted observers already discerned danger signals. The economic base of the city and the surrounding region depended heavily on a limited range of interests – coal, iron and steel, engineering, shipbuilding – linked in a spiral of mutually reinforcing growth. If these should falter, prosperity would be seriously threatened. At Armstrong's there were already attempts to broaden the company's output by expansion into new fields such as car production. The outbreak of war in 1914 brought a continued concentration on the region's staple industries, and there was no substantial structural innovation. During the war Armstrong's built 47 warships, armed another 62 and repaired or refitted 521, as well as supplying enormous quantities of aircraft, guns and munitions.

War brought other problems. Recruitment into the armed forces was substantial and so were the casualty lists, as examples from local schools demonstrate. Rutherford School had over 830 old boys in uniform, of whom over 150 were killed, Dame Allan's School 625 serving and 84 killed. The North East had always been a region of low female employment, but war pressures brought many women into new activities, including munitions factories and public transport. Shop and office work had largely been male preserves before the war, but this also changed, with some long-term effects remaining after 1918.

In the inter-war years, the region's concentration on mining and heavy industry realized pre-war forebodings. Some important coal markets had been lost and the world was no longer hungry for warships and munitions. Despite valiant attempts at diversification, Armstrong's declined in the late 1920s, forced into a shotgun marriage with Vickers in which the Tyneside flagship company was much the junior partner. After a brief post-war boom for the North East, there came years of increasing unemployment, culminating in the tragedy of the worst Depression years of the early 1930s, which burned deeply into the region's mentality. During the preceding period of expansion and success, workers in the principal regional industries had been relatively highly paid and highly regarded. Now, many thousands found themselves suddenly unemployed and poor. Unlike some other local communities such as Jarrow, Newcastle's diverse employment provided some protection from the worst of the depression, but there were wide variations even within the city. Industrial suburbs like Elswick were among the region's black spots, while other suburbs such as Jesmond and Gosforth escaped more lightly.

The Depression was only one part of the region's diverse experiences in these years. The industrial sector was not uniformly depressed. Some sectors, including heavy electrical engineering, continued to prosper. Most North East workers remained in employment at a time when declining prices were improving wages' purchasing power. During the later 1930s, economic recovery was substantial. The developing but cautious official regional aid policies played a relatively small part in this. Much more effective were the global economic recovery and revival of the region's staple industries brought about by rearmament programmes.

Against the deprivation of the worst Depression years is the equally notable feature that the inter-war years saw social improvement on an unprecedented scale, even in this hard-hit region. Wartime experience had brought massive increases in official activity, and some of this continued into post-war years in ways that

Above: Unemployed workers' protest during the inter-war depression

Left: Commemorative photograph of Newcastle United FC 1909–10 season

Right: An aerial view of terrace housing, South Shields

improved such services as public health, housing and education. In 1920, Newcastle Council took over nine mothers and babies' welfare centres, originally founded by voluntary initiative. National subsidies encouraged new housing provided by both public and private agencies. Newcastle Council had built only 454 houses between 1890 and 1920, but it built 8,130 in the 1930s. This represented a substantial minority of the 22,160 new houses built there in that decade.

The Public Assistance Committee of the Council, which replaced the old Poor Law Union after statutory reform in 1929, spent £340,000 in 1932, and improved the old workhouse infirmary, now Newcastle General Hospital. Patients admitted were 3,048 in 1930, 6,695 in 1936; operations performed were 596 and 2,722. Infant mortality in the city dropped from 96 per 1,000 in 1923–5 to 89 in 1935–7, and there was substantial improvement in other health statistics. The other major Newcastle hospital, the voluntary Royal Victoria Infirmary, also saw expansion. An appeal in 1927 raised £143,000 (including a £75,000 gift from Lord Runciman) for new buildings there.

The provision of recreation for the city and neighbouring communities also increased. Fifteen new cinemas were built between 1931 and 1939. From 1921, working men's clubs in the area, which expanded greatly in post-war years, owned their own Federation Brewery

in Newcastle. Transport improved, with bus and trolley-bus services contributing significantly to the mobility of Newcastle citizens and access to Newcastle facilities available to many people in surrounding districts. In summer months, huge crowds from Newcastle used the suburban electric railways to visit nearby coastal resorts.

By 1939, great inequalities of wealth, comfort and opportunity still existed here, but there had been a continuing expansion of efforts, by both official and voluntary agencies, to tackle social problems. There had been a significant attack on the slums that had disfigured the region, including Newcastle, for generations, even if much remained to be done. When the Second World War began, the great majority of local inhabitants were enjoying a higher standard of living than in 1920, or in any earlier period.

One aspect of the economic recovery of the 1930s remained dangerous: the absence of any major reconstruction of the region's industrial base. The rearmament programmes were a godsend to the North East's ailing heavy industries, but reinforced reliance on them. Wartime pressures involved a renewed concentration on coal, steel, engineering and shipbuilding, and provided little opportunity for substantial modernization and replacement of equipment. The inter-war years had provided a complex mix of deprivation, social progress and continuing economic imbalance which left serious problems to be tackled by later generations.

Norman McCord

Below: A postcard of Newcastle from the turn of the 20th century

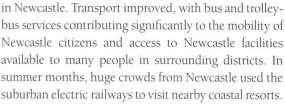

WAR MEMORIAL &
S. THOMAS CHURCH,
NEWCASTLE-ON-TYNE.

1ST N.G. HOSPITAL. ARMSTRONG COLLEGE
WARD C.I.

MEDICINE BETWEEN THE WARS

'It is inevitable that an account of the College of Medicine between the Wars should concentrate on the "Hutchens Affair".'
E.M. Bettenson

'I have waited twenty years to get that bugger Hutchens out.'
Stuart McDonald, Professor of Pathology

The row that split the College of Medicine within a few years of its foundation was purely an internal affair, resolved without rancour or recrimination. That which overshadowed much of the period between the wars divided not only the College but also the wider medical and academic communities in Newcastle and beyond.

Its repercussions reached high offices of State and, ultimately, the Crown. Yet it led to the reordering of academic affairs in Newcastle and Durham to the lasting benefit of both.

The Great War had inevitably brought hardship to the two Newcastle colleges. Armstrong, commandeered as a military hospital, had survived only through determination and an ability to improvise in borrowed premises. The College of Medicine continued to function, although restricted by the surrender of some of its space to Armstrong College and by staff losses due to enlistment. The University of Durham Medical Gazette reflected moods of patriotism and sadness, with exhortations to enter the King's service and lists of the

In the First World War, Armstrong College became a military hospital and the Hatton Gallery served as a hospital ward

Lord Londonderry with Sir Robert Bolam, Head of the College of Medicine

its target, insufficient to enable the College of Medicine to undertake urgently needed developments. Its existing accommodation could not cope with the numbers of returning ex-service students or the expansion demanded by the enlarging scope of medical services. It borrowed to acquire the now available site opposite the Royal Victoria Infirmary, but was faced with the arduous task of raising funds for a new building.

During the post-war years the College was led by Professor Robert Howden, a distinguished anatomist. Sir Cecil Cochrane, the Treasurer, was a genial and generous benefactor, who himself provided new playing fields and the Students' Union building. Both men were getting on in years and Howden was very deaf. Raising funds for a new building and driving through its construction would require vigorous leadership beyond their capabilities, and both were nearing retirement.

Howden was succeeded in 1927 by Sir Robert Bolam, a dermatologist and former Professor of Medical Jurisprudence. A man of energy and ability, he was a prominent figure in local and national medical politics and had served two terms as Chairman of Council of the British Medical Association (BMA). Domineering in character, he attracts sobriquets of decreasing generosity as the story of his leadership unfolds – manipulative, duplicitous, ruthless, mendacious – yet there is no doubting his commitment to what he saw as the good of the College. Cochrane was succeeded by Sir Joseph Reid, a businessman from the newspaper world with a reputation not unlike Bolam's. They made a formidable pair, committing themselves with relentless vigour to restoring financial viability and raising funds for the new building. Seeing little prospect of increasing income, they set about imposing economies – a 25 per cent reduction in expenditure was the declared aim – mainly at the expense of staff. A particular target was the Department of Bacteriology and here we meet the third of the principal *dramatis personae* of our story.

H.J. Hutchens, Professor of Comparative Pathology and Bacteriology, stood apart from his colleagues. Older than most, he had qualified in 1899 from Oxford and St Bartholomew's Hospital, London. He had served in the Boer War and had been awarded the Military Cross. He lived out of town, which was unusual, and he also had a home in Surrey where his wife lived with their invalid son. His department was in Armstrong College, separated from the Medical School in Northumberland Road.

dead, wounded and decorated from amongst those students, graduates and staff who did so.

By the end of the war the College of Medicine faced multiple problems, compounded by the unwieldy Durham administration. Most civic universities obtained their charters near the turn of the century and, had they been independent of Durham, together the Newcastle colleges might have done likewise. As it was, the link with Durham, although valuable in the early years, was now an encumbrance. The Newcastle Corporation's financial support was niggardly, which displeased the University Grants Committee (UGC) and adversely affected its own dispensations. An appeal, launched jointly by the colleges, achieved less than half

Although liked by students, he was not popular with colleagues, and events were to reveal a tendency to obtuseness, stubbornness and a singular capacity to misconstrue. Unlike the younger heads of department, Hutchens refused to accept the cuts.

As with a hurricane, it took the coincidence of prevailing elements to generate the storm. Feelings of victimization, disaffection with authority, above all incompatible personalities – these provided the backcloth to the 'Hutchens Affair'. It had all the ingredients of a C.P. Snow novel and we are indebted to E.M. Bettenson for his masterly account of it.

Hutchens's department provided a public health laboratory service additional to its teaching function. Under Bolam's proposed economies, not only was Hutchens to lose members of staff, he was also to relinquish responsibility for the service laboratory. He took his grievance to the BMA, thus spreading word of the dispute and infuriating Bolam. He engineered the establishment of a Committee of Enquiry, weighted against Hutchens, which determined that he be asked to resign on terms to be accepted within days, or withdrawn. Hutchens stalled, pleading an unavoidable delay in dealing with the matter; his way of saying he was waiting to hear if the Association of University Teachers (AUT) would back him. The dispute dragged on until the College Council eventually lost patience and in February 1931, nearly five years after the start of the troubles, moved to dismiss him. There was a snag: his formal appointment by the College was to a lectureship, his professorial title having been conferred by the Dean of Durham, Warden of the University. By now, only the Senate of the University had the power to dismiss him and it resolutely detached itself from any involvement. Mr (sic) Harold John Hutchens, Lecturer, was given six months' notice by the College.

Meanwhile, the circle of those involved in the dispute was widening; factions supportive of Hutchens or against Bolam were declaring themselves, the latter including members of Armstrong College and the City Council. Of particular significance was the emergence of a group to become known as 'the young clinicians'. They were members of the Royal Victoria Infirmary (RVI) staff and part-time teachers in the College who had become increasingly disenchanted with Bolam's

Top left: Northumberland Road College of Medicine. When it first opened in 1883, it was the most up-to-date medical premises in the country

Above: Final agreements between Hutchens and the University for the £342 18s 0 annuity

Right: Construction of the new Medical School on Queen Victoria Road

Below: Programme for the 100th birthday Celebration of the College of Medicine

CELEBRATION of
the HUNDREDTH
ANNIVERSARY of
the FOUNDATION
of the
UNIVERSITY OF DURHAM
COLLEGE OF MEDICINE

at Newcastle upon Tyne

THURSDAY AND FRIDAY,
4th and 5th OCTOBER, 1934.

style of management and his failure to nurture the academic aspirations of the College.

The AUT saw Hutchens's notice of dismissal as a threat to the sanctity of tenure. A writ was issued on 15 October 1931 – *Hutchens v. The University of Durham College of Medicine and Sir Robert Bolam*. Hutchens's counsel was Norman Birkett, chosen less for his expertise in the field than for his ability to match Bolam in contumely and belligerence. But the case collapsed ignominiously.

By now, the Court of Governors of the Medical College, a body with overarching though seldom exercised authority, had begun to take notice. It included several influential figures in legal, educational, business and civic affairs. They approached Lord Londonderry, Chancellor of Durham University, expressing their concerns about the running of the College and demanding another enquiry. The new enquiry was entrusted to Sir Amherst

Selby-Bigge, Secretary to the Board of Education. Although criticisms of Bolam's actions and attitudes were voiced, he, as usual, subverted proceedings with the support of senior colleagues, including Stuart McDonald, Professor of Pathology, he to whom is attributed the less than endearing reference to Hutchens quoted above. Sir Amherst's report, to the dismay of many, was almost entirely favourable to Bolam.

The reformers were persistent. Seeking to increase their influence, they had nine of their number added to the membership of Court by the legitimate device of paying £25 to become 'contributory Governors'. The ever-watchful Bolam, just before the register closed, had 33 of his friends and relations likewise installed. Again he had bested his adversaries; but his triumph was short-lived. The university community up and down the country was now aware of the crisis. There was deep disquiet in Newcastle about Bolam's 'bought votes'. 'Exposure of new College of Medicine scandal', proclaimed the Newcastle *Evening Chronicle* headline. Such was the ferment that Lord Londonderry, in consultation with the Chairman of the UGC and the Chancellor of the Exchequer, successfully petitioned the Crown for the appointment of a Royal Commission.

The Medical School on Queen Victoria Road, now the George VI Building

The main concern of the Royal Commission was the organization and management of Durham University and its constituent colleges. Hutchens became a secondary consideration, although the drama surrounding him was not played out. He still refused to resign, and when his belongings from his old department were sent to his home in Surrey, his wife refused to accept delivery. The findings of the Royal Commission were highly critical of the University administration and of the part played by Bolam. Its recommendations, incorporated in the University of Durham Act 1935, were far-sighted. On the First Appointed Day in 1937 two separate and largely autonomous divisions of Durham University were established, the College of Medicine and Armstrong College uniting to form King's College, the Newcastle Division. Twenty-six years later, the sound constitution of our University as we know it today would be firmly grounded in the recommendations of the Royal Commission. The reformers had achieved their objective. Hutchens, ironically, was still there. It was not until 1938, six years after he had last performed his professorial duties, that he formally resigned on terms decided by the new Rector of King's College, Lord Eustace Percy.

In spite of the distraction of these years of conflict, the College continued to go about its business of teaching medical students, whose numbers steadily increased, rising from 245 to 432 over the period 1927 to 1936. The College responded to developments in medical science and practice, although the pace of change did not compare with that of today. Many of the inter-war years were blighted by economic recession, and the voluntary and municipal hospitals were always hard-pressed. Advances such as the widening availability of blood transfusion and the introduction of sulphonamide drugs brought general benefit, but the history of the College is written in the achievements of talented and dedicated individuals, many of whom receive mention in other chapters. Two who played a particular part in shaping the future of the College were Frederick Nattrass and James Spence, both prominent among those urging reform and determined that Newcastle should be on the map in the field of research. They were to become the first full-time clinical professors to be appointed. Nattrass campaigned for changes in the undergraduate curriculum, a cause vigorously championed by the students, although it was to be some years before major revision was achieved. The establishment of a Post-Graduate Committee in 1924 had started a tradition of postgraduate medical education in which Newcastle remains at the forefront. Spence's legacy was a transformation in the care of children, which extended far beyond Newcastle.

A staunch supporter of Bolam, opposed to Nattrass and Spence yet sharing their academic ambitions for the

College, was George Grey Turner, a renowned surgical pioneer and clinical teacher. He did much to enhance the growing reputation of the College until his call to the Postgraduate Medical School in Hammersmith as the Foundation Professor of Surgery. In the field of obstetrics, Farquar Murray, appointed to the Chair in 1935, introduced the first 'Flying Squad' in England. Sir Thomas Oliver, President of the College from 1926 to 1935, was one of the world's leading figures in the field of industrial health.

These are but a few of the individuals who moulded the College in these difficult years and secured its strength and reputation. The achievements of Sir Robert Bolam should not be diminished by the unworthiness of his conduct in the Hutchens affair. He enabled the assimilation of Dentistry as an academic discipline within the College and encouraged Sir Arthur Sutherland to subscribe to the building of the Dental School and Hospital in the RVI precinct. Sutherland also provided £100,000 for the building and equipping of the new Medical School for which Bolam and Reid had striven so assiduously. Its closeness to the RVI facilitated what was to become a fruitful and enduring partnership. The planned opening of the building in 1938 by Mr Neville Chamberlain had to be deferred because of the Munich Crisis. The following year, on 21 February, the ceremony was performed by King George VI in the looming shadow of the Second World War.

David Shaw

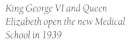

King George VI and Queen Elizabeth open the new Medical School in 1939

THE UNION SOCIETY

This is not a complete history of the Union Society, but focuses instead on two periods in its history when both authors were heavily involved in Union Society affairs, namely the early 1950s and the first years of the 21st century.

A signally generous act in 1925, now widely known to be due to Cecil Cochrane, was the gift of money to construct a building to house the joint Armstrong and Medical Students' Society. Bettenson explained that this endowment allowed the removal from the Armstrong College *Calendar* of the blunt sentence, 'The Students' Union is still very inadequate.' Because of the ever-increasing expansion in student numbers since the Second World War, and despite some additional new space leased from the University in 1963 under a 'peppercorn rent', this same sentence could now well be reinserted in appropriate University documents today.

Care of the 1925 building is vested in a Board of Trustees appointed by the University Council. These Trustees are only responsible for maintaining the fabric of the original building, with the help of money provided annually by the University. The Union Society also has a Board of Trustees and, through a Management Committee, operated for many years all desirable student services, untrammelled by the costs of the building. The Management Committee no longer exists, but the current system of operation hardly differs from days gone by.

The Society building of 1925 was a great boon to the campus. Now a Grade II-listed building, it has changed

little, although the fabric now needs serious attention. Inside the building, in the 1950s, women went to the right and men to the left, and in these different directions both had their common rooms and other facilities. Gender separation was, however, by no means total. The sexes could first meet at the 'hot seat', near the entrance: a raised wooden form with central heating pipes running underneath and therefore very comfortable in the winter! There was a 'waitress-served' mixed dining room on the top floor, heavily used by students. On the floor below lay the Oak Room to which academic and senior administrative staff repaired to eat and drink. And deep below in the basement lay the Bun

JEFF BALE (1968–73 UNION PRESIDENT)

AGRICULTURE / 1971–2

The year I was President was a time of great fervour in student politics, with regular demonstrations and the ultimate weapon – the 'sit in'. I arrived in my office one morning aware of 'trouble at Lancaster'. Apparently, students had occupied the admin block. The telephone rang and it was Henry Miller, the Vice-Chancellor. 'Jeff, have you heard about Lancaster? That fool Charles Carter (Lancaster VC!) has made a silly announcement and the students are sitting in. What's it like here – any problems?' I wasn't aware of any unrest, but the VC suggested that I go over for a drink to discuss matters at 11.30 that morning.

I made my way to Kensington Terrace, climbed the stairs to the first floor and turned to the right along the corridor. The VC's office was on the left, his PA (Shirley Fallaw) directly across the corridor, in an office that had a wall about a metre high, and then plain glass all the way to the ceiling. As soon as I started to walk along the corridor, I saw a man crawling along the floor on all fours. It was the Registrar, Ernest Bettenson. He must have heard me approaching, because he looked over his shoulder and grinned. 'I'm just creeping up on Miss Fallaw', he said. I was bemused, but said nothing. Maybe university senior managers act like this all the time? I 'booked in' with Miss Fallaw and was immediately shown across to the VC's office, where I was given my first, as well as the largest and strongest gin and tonic I have ever encountered.

The VC wasted no time. 'Had the *Evening Chronicle* on the phone. They've heard about Lancaster and want to know if there's going to be trouble here.' 'No, no', I said. 'Newcastle students are just fine. It's the professors who cause all the problems!' It was ever thus, I suppose.

Room, where eating and drinking were more informal, mightily so on Saturday evenings, when the extrovert Billy Weeks from Agriculture (who else and from where else?) led the singing of raucous, bucolic and evermore salacious songs as floods of beer were consumed.

Even in the early 1950s, a large proportion of students had an ex-service background: past colonels, redundant 'fliers' and ex-Navy men mixed well together and with boys fresh from school. It was a happy place! But the building's decoration was appalling, not having been touched since before 1939. At that time, the Union was still governed by the Union Management Committee (UMC). To persuade the Bursar to agree to the release of the 'Painting and Decorating Reserve', solely for decorating purposes, was a triumph of collective minds (the UMC less the Bursar) over matter (the Bursar): but released it was. So 1953 was

momentous: Elizabeth II was crowned, Hillary and Tensing conquered Everest, and King's College Union Society was painted from top to bottom, inside and out! To the Bursar's delight, the Painting and Decorating Reserve (and much else) was restored by the President placing an impost of one half-penny on each pint of beer sold in the Union Society, but resulting in the President's arraignment before the Annual General Meeting months later for 'scandalous profiteering'!

More than 50 years on, has the Society changed? It has, but not beyond recognition. The student body has increased roughly sixfold since the early 1950s, but the Union Building is still the same size it was in 1963. This physical restraint must have had a limiting effect on Society membership, but, as with the entire University student body, membership is now more diverse than at any other time. With over 150 groups, student societies and Athletic Union clubs are still the backbone of the Society. Many continue to grow and flourish, but fierce rivalries between student groups have diminished and collaboration is the name of the game today – of course, the 'agrics' still display the same fierce individualism as they have always done, an individualism to which nailed-down metal furniture is only a partial solution! Since the inauguration of Northumbria University, friendly rivalry between the two students' unions has blossomed, perhaps best seen in the annual hotly contested Stan Calvert Cup, for which many sports teams from both universities compete – Newcastle, of course, is dominant!

Although intensely important to those directly involved, governance of the Society is not an enthralling issue to the Union membership generally, but it is important. Student bodies throughout the land had Students' Representative Councils (SRC) for many years. At Newcastle, an SRC was formed in 1900 to deal formally with the Board of Professors and to represent

DOUGLAS BRADLEY

CHEMICAL ENGINEERING / 1949–53

Other memories included walking up the steps of the Union Building to be faced, almost always, by an attractive girl student sitting in a provocative pose on the radiator under the window that faced the steps. There was an annual election for 'Miss Hot Seat' – I don't know if this ritual still continues.

Halls and Digs

Above: Henderson Hall

Right: Ethel Williams Hall

KATHLEEN FARDEY / GEOGRAPHY / 1933–6

I lived out at Fenham. It was quite a long way and we had to walk because it was one penny on the tram. We weren't allowed to smoke at Fenham. There was a lot of wood and I suppose there was a grave danger of fire. We all used to hang out of our windows with our fags.

We used to go to the Odeon. The first half dozen rows you could get in for a shilling. That was a lot of money to us in those days. After that we used to go to one of the Carrick restaurants. We would have tea there, which would cost about 1/6d and if we went really wild it was 1/9d. That left 'B' all for the rest of the week! No matter what the weather was doing – whether it was chucking it down or snowing – we had to walk.

RONALD TATE / LAND USE STUDIES / 1965–9

I spent my first undergraduate year (1965) in Eustace Percy Hall. Electricity supplies were restricted to a 5 amp two-pin circuit, enough to supply a transistor radio. It was easy to tell which neighbour was using an illicit toaster when the whole wing's lights dipped.

Many engineering students were resident, and they decided to test the plumbing. By posting lookouts at all the entrances and having colleagues positioned at each toilet, on a given signal, they simultaneously flushed them all. The site sloped towards the entrance where a rose garden provided an attractive setting and where the warden and his family had their residence. The result was that all the manholes, set amongst the rose garden, lifted, and a temporary pungent lake was created. The roses seemed to thrive that year.

MOIRA MCKENNA / GENERAL DEGREE / 1971–4

In 1972, we became some of the first tenants of Esther Campbell Court, where I remained for the next two years. I remember the shower room, with the sloping floor that didn't slope quite enough and always seemed to be under an inch of scummy water (!) and the hexagonal bedroom off the lounge, which required ingenuity to furnish. One of my flatmates got her artistic sister to paint a tree on the lounge wall – a feature admired by all our visitors. It was a lovely flat – we even liked the fluorescent nylon curtains, a different colour for each bedroom: Day-Glo orange in mine, if memory serves!

Some of our first efforts at self-catering were quite memorable. I recall an occasion where we decided to cook savoury rice for a house party. In the mid-70s, rice was not the staple fare in UK households it is now and I don't think any of us had ever eaten it at home, let alone cooked it. In measuring out the quantity, we did not take into account the fact that it swells considerably during the cooking process... I'm sure you can picture the results. I think we were eating rice at every meal for the next week!

Left: Richardson Road   Above: Leazes Terrace

LINDSEY PILKINGTON / PHYSICS / 1972–5

We were the first occupants of Richardson Road. Everyone was allowed to paint their lovely clean white rooms, so the majority went for shades of brown – it was the 70s! I remember you could access the next-door flat through the fire escape in the showers – so, surprise surprise, the male flats soon realized they could break the glass and spy on adjacent female flats in the shower! Whoever designed those? Mind you, the ensuing shower parties were great fun!

HUW JONES / HISTORY / 1980–3

I lived in 'Trendy Hendy', a 40p bus ride away. Far nicer than the Leazes, but still with a reputation for being old-fashioned due to its mostly male inmates. Formal dinners still saw most wearing gowns. My grant just about covered the hall fees of £4 a day in 1980 for half board – bargain! Living out was more fun but rather chancier and depended on the area and landlord. Mine in my third year was a delightful old widow in Heaton. Most of my friends lived there or towards Sandiford, Fenham or, for the harder cases, Benwell.

ALEX LEUNG / ELECTRICAL AND ELECTRONIC ENGINEERING / 1980–3

I lived on the second floor of Lake House, Leazes Terrace, facing the football ground. Other residents used to come to my room on Saturdays to have a glimpse of the matches. Living in Leazes Terrace was quite an experience due to its open shared kitchens, providing unlimited social interactions. We had such a great time, playing, studying (sometimes), cooking (setting things on fire), partying and drinking, of course.

JANET JONES / MODERN LANGUAGES / 1966–70

Along with many others, I was housed in Whitley Bay from 1966 to 1968. The landladies were great and long-suffering and it was good to be by the sea. However, the downside was the lack of evening entertainments once students had made the 30-minute journey to the coast. So a group of us rented the top floor of a club in Whitley Bay and set up a bar with entertainments. Great fun, especially when you called time and no one took any notice.

all students in matters of policy. The SRC remained a separate entity from the Union Society until 1981–2, much later than in all other English universities. Thankfully this historic division then came to an end and Newcastle students became like those of other universities in pursuit of their legitimate affairs.

This merger was surely a major development, as was the decision during the 1990s to do away with the presidential system and to have a 'flat' outcome of power once Sabbatical Officers were elected. In 2006, however, a presidential system returned! But through all the governance changes, the Society has continued to flourish. Student-run activities have been immensely impressive over the years. *The Courier* now has a readership of over 12,000, is published in full colour and has in recent years broken some national stories. The Newcastle University Theatre Society (NUTS) puts on many annual productions and is well respected at the Edinburgh Festival. Newcastle Student Radio broadcasts on FM and the internet throughout the university year. Perhaps most impressive is the Student Community Action Newcastle (SCAN), which is now regarded as one of the leading action groups in the UK. And the themes of equality and fees are still very much at the heart of student politics.

The Union Society did not suddenly come into existence in 1925. The 1893 *Calendar* for the University of Durham College of Physical Science, Newcastle upon

Tyne, is a rather more succinct document than any university equivalent of recent times, and contains a calendar *sensu stricto*, surrounded by information relating to aspects of College activities, ranging from the names of Council to those forming the 'Plumbers' Technical Class Committee'. Also listed were College societies: the Musical Society, the Athletic Union and the Union Society! Although rather overburdened with vice-presidents compared with the size of the Management Committee of the time, the Society's basic governance organization seemed not dissimilar to that in existence in 1953.

Although there have been some changes over the years, much has remained the same. The Society's debating programme is as important a facet of the Union today as it was in earlier times. In 1893, the debating programme comprised 'Individualism and Socialism', 'The Englishman of the Future' and, on Ladies' Evening, a debate entitled 'Ought Women to Confine Themselves to Domestic Duties?'; then thrown in for good measure, a visit from the Durham Union Society to debate 'Vivisection'. The convenor of debates, with a little luck, could probably get away with this programme today. And much else of value in this Union Society will change little in the future: so be it.

Duncan Murchison and Tom Gorman

Student newspapers Union Sauce *and* The Courier

Below: Posters for the Union Society debates in the 1960s

Left: The Union Society library

Members of the Officers' Training Corps on exercises

THE MILITARY CONNECTION

The University of Durham has had links with the military for well over 100 years. The volunteer contingents established in the late 1850s were closely tied in with individual colleges, many of which had a company composed of their students and, on occasion, staff members.

More formal links emerged with the establishment of a Military Education Committee (MEC). In 1908, with the formation of the Senior Training Contingents (forerunner of the Officers' Training Corps), any university with a contingent was required to appoint an MEC to oversee the military aspects and to exercise an 'academic' overview. Durham MEC, later Northumbrian Universities MEC (NUMEC), had that role and now oversees the activities of Northumbrian Universities Officers' Training Corps, Air Squadrons and Royal Naval Unit. These service units serve all five North East universities (Durham, Newcastle, Northumbria, Sunderland and Teesside) and the Military Education Committee, on which all five are represented, provides an internal university contact and maintains a liaison with each university and the military units.

THE OFFICERS' TRAINING CORPS

As early as 1859, volunteers from Durham University paraded with the Newcastle upon Tyne Volunteer Corps, and one company of infantry was composed of students. In 1883, the Corps became the 3rd Volunteer Battalion Northumberland Fusiliers and was involved in the Boer War; again one company was made up from University students.

In 1908, with Haldane's Army reforms, the volunteer companies became university contingents of the Senior Division of the Officers' Training Corps, known as the Senior Training Corps. Durham University was one of the first to form a contingent in the Senior Division. It comprised four companies, one of which was from Armstrong College. Members were trained to take up Special Reserve or Territorial Force Commissions, although this was not mandatory. They subscribed 2s 6d, enlisted for three years and received free uniforms.

During the First World War, the contingent continued to recruit and train, and individual members served in a variety of regiments. The pages of *The Northerner*, the Armstrong College magazine, contain numerous obituaries of those killed and wounded, and list many gallantry awards. It is worth noting that the University, which was training contingents countrywide, supplied over 2,000 commissioned officers, of whom 350 were killed and 300 received decorations for gallantry.

In the inter-war years, the contingent remained very popular and, again, *The Northerner* of the time reports successful camps at Shorncliffe, as well as parades and social events. The professional staff were mainly officers who had fought in the Great War. Two colonels had a major impact on the contingent through their leadership and organizational ability and both were Durham academics. One was Lieutenant Colonel Macfarlane Grieve MC (Highland Light Infantry), Commanding Officer from 1927 to 1935, having previously served as Adjutant from 1919 to 1927. The second was Lieutenant Colonel W.D. Lowe DSO, MC (Durham Light Infantry). Many contingent members were ex-servicemen taking advantage of grants, provided by the Government, to go or return to university and take a degree. Terms of service were very similar to those in 1914, but add-ons were somewhat less generous. It cost 10s 6d to join and the only free kit was a khaki shirt, collar and tie!

The approach of war in the period up to 1939 made an increase of interest in the contingent inevitable and, in 1939, it had a battery of field artillery, an infantry company, two machine-gun platoons and a field ambulance company. In 1940, the contingent was placed on a war footing, membership for male undergraduates was made compulsory, and it became part of the Home Guard. Personnel carried out guard duties at local positions of importance. As in the First World War, individuals entered the Forces and their officers' training at university stood them in good stead when it came to officer selection. In 1941, the strength was 832, comprising:

Infantry:	*446 Newcastle*	
	112 Durham	
	83 Sunderland	
Artillery:	*36 Newcastle*	
Medical:	*155 Newcastle*	

Numbers rose in 1941–2 to 964 and in 1942–3 to 1,160. Again there were inevitable losses, but as ever bravery was abundant, one example amongst many being Lieutenant Harry Faulkner-Brown, who was awarded the Military Cross for outstanding gallantry at Arnhem. (He subsequently taught Architecture at the University and became a member of the MEC.) After 1945, reorganization came, and with it another name change: the Senior Training Corps became the Officers' Training Corps (OTC). The OTC was to be officered by professional Army officers supported by Territorial Army officers, with the universities in the form of the

Tim Goggs, killed during a landmine accident in Afghanistan, was awarded the George Medal in 1992

Military Education Committee keeping a watchful eye on proceedings. The succession of commanding officers presents an imposing list of high-quality officers, as does the roll of honorary colonels, which includes Lord Ridley and the Duke of Westminster.

The OTCs in the early post-war days were viewed as part of the National Service procedure and, in 1948, were made part of the Territorial Army (TA). This move was to try and enhance the attractiveness of volunteer service against the background of National Service. The scope of the OTC activities was widened to include technical elements and, in 1949, part of the Women's Royal Army Corps was included. In 1955, the contingent was again renamed, this time to Durham University Officers' Training Corps, with its prime objective being to prepare students for commissioned service. With the emergence in 1963 of the University of Newcastle upon Tyne, there was a final name change to the Northumbrian Universities Officers' Training Corps (NUOTC).

Even in times of peace there have been local conflicts, several of them major ones. NUOTC members have served with distinction and some have made the ultimate sacrifice. It is with pride we should note the posthumous award of the George Medal to Tim Goggs for outstanding bravery during mine-clearing operations in Afghanistan.

THE AIR SQUADRON

The idea of university air squadrons was first suggested in 1919 by Lord Trenchard. Their aim was 'to encourage an interest in flying and to promote and maintain liaison

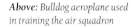
Above: Bulldog aeroplane used in training the air squadron

Far right: Naval Unit at Neptune Staircase, Banavie Lock on the Caledonian Canal

with the universities in technical and research problems affecting aviation'. In 1925, the first two squadrons were established at Oxford and Cambridge. They were designed to assist those who wished to take up aeronautics as a profession, and those who, while not making aviation their career, desired to give part-time service to defence in the non-regular Air Force.

In 1937, permission was given for suitable third-year students to be commissioned as pilot officers in the regular Air Force and to fly current front-line aircraft. However, in 1939, the university air squadrons were disbanded (only to be reinstated a year later), and a further 20 new squadrons, of which Durham was one, were established. This squadron drew students from Durham, Newcastle and Sunderland, and concentrated on pre-service training for potential officers, with flying restricted to the occasional air experience flight.

Towards the end of the war, a number of air squadrons were disbanded, but Durham survived. It has had something of a gypsy existence, starting life in the early wartime years at Woolsington, now Newcastle Airport. In 1945, it moved to RAF Usworth, near Sunderland. When that station closed, the squadron moved to RAF Ouston and, on its closure, to its present home at RAF Leeming in North Yorkshire. Initially equipped with five Tiger Moths, they were replaced in 1951 by five Chipmunks, which gave 23 years of valuable service before being substituted for five Bulldogs. They in turn have been replaced by the Tuton two-seat training aircraft.

In 1963, when the University of Newcastle came into existence, Durham University Air Squadron was renamed the Northumbrian Universities Air Squadron (NUAS), with the squadron motto being 'Knowledge gives Wings'. The squadron has a reputation not only for outstanding professional achievement but also for its successful sporting and social activities. The Annual Dinner and trophy presentation is a sparkling occasion and, attended by staff, squadron members past and present and guests, is one of the student military highlights of the year. Throughout the years, NUAS has produced first-class officer men and women, a number of which have reached the highest ranks in the service. As in the NUOTC, many squadron members gave their lives in the Second World War, and the furnishings of the Norman Chapel in Durham Castle are dedicated to their memory.

UNIVERSITIES ROYAL NAVAL UNIT

Northumbrian Universities Royal Naval Unit was formed in 1995 and is based at HMS *Calliope*, adjacent to the new Millennium Bridge and the lively Newcastle Quayside. It is one of 14 units located in university towns and cities throughout the United Kingdom. It recruits undergraduate volunteers for the duration of their studies and offers a unique opportunity to sample Royal Navy life.

Students do have a life on the ocean wave, gaining sea-time and experience on HMS *Example*, the unit's fast patrol craft. The main objective is to recruit high-calibre students who have the potential to be society's future leaders and opinion formers, and to assist students who aspire to a career in either the Royal Navy or Royal Navy Reserves.

Air Commodore I.H. Forster OBE

Refugee Students at Newcastle

This essay was prompted by the wish to record the circumstances in which ten free places were offered to refugee students from Nazi Germany and Austria in January 1939 by King's College – Newcastle Division of the University of Durham – and to trace as far as possible the careers of the students who benefited from this generous offer.

The idea of admitting refugee students to King's College appears to have begun with a circular letter from the Regius Professor of Physics at Cambridge addressed to the Medical School in July 1938, suggesting that each medical school in the United Kingdom should take one refugee student. At Newcastle, a Council meeting in January 1939 accepted a proposal by Lord Eustace Percy that up to ten free places should be offered to refugee students, 'provided that the College will not thereby be involved in any additional teaching'. The Royal Victoria Infirmary, in respect of medical students and the University of Durham – not only King's College – agreed to the proposal. Given the small size of both divisions of the University of Durham at the time, and the much smaller *per capita* funding of universities by the Government compared with post-1945, the offer was a generous one.

The Students
Dr Wolfgang (Erich) Brassloff
(BA Economics, 1943)

Brassloff was born in Vienna in 1921, and forced to leave in 1938. He obtained a free place at the Quaker boarding school at Great Ayton, Yorkshire, passing the school certificate examination in the summer of 1939. He started studies at King's College in History, Economics and Politics, but although designated as a refugee, he was interned in May 1940 and later transported to Canada. He was released in the autumn of 1941, after the intervention of Lord Eustace Percy, and took up his studies again. He graduated in 1943 and then worked at the Labour Research Department (founded by Sidney and Beatrice Webb) for two years. He returned to Vienna and obtained a doctorate in 1953 for a thesis on the English Civil War. In 1960, he returned to Britain, taking a post as lecturer, eventually becoming Professor at Salford University. He has written widely in the fields of international economics and on employment and unemployment.

Erwin Knoepfler (BArch, 1943)

Knoepfler was born in Hungary in 1909. As a left-wing student in the 1930s, he was forced to flee to Austria, and then to Czechoslovakia. He and Fritz Wachs (see below) were the only non-Czech citizens to receive visas through the British Committee for Refugees from Czechoslovakia, which also secured them places at King's College. They came to Britain, with a refugee transport that had to be routed through Poland and Sweden, in March 1939. Knoepfler retained his Hungarian passport and was thus not subject to internment as an enemy alien in May 1940. After qualifying, he lived in Glasgow for a time, but spent most of his working life as an architect with Northumberland County Council at Newcastle. He died in 1993. His son, Mark Knopfler, a well-known rock musician and founder of Dire Straits, was awarded an honorary doctorate of Music in 1993.

Dr Hans Kronberger, FRS, CBE, BSc, PhD
(BSc Physics, 1944)

This famous nuclear physicist was born in Linz, Austria, in 1920, and emigrated to the UK in 1938. He was supported by the Quakers, who had arranged his arrival and (probably free) place in Newcastle. They gave him £1 a week. Out of this he paid for his room, food and books and was proud that he was able to save enough to buy a bicycle. He was interned in 1940 and sent to Australia, returning to the UK in 1944, where he completed his studies at Newcastle.

An impressive list of awards accompanied a distinguished career with the Atomic Energy Authority, where he designed reactors and developed the Kronberger mass flowmeter to measure the specific heat of corrosive gases. He was a member of the United Nations Scientific Advisory Committee and the International Atomic Energy Authority in Vienna. Kronberger was consulted by the Israeli government on the desalination of seawater by atomic energy. When he arrived in Israel, the Prime Minister sent her personal car to the airport to meet him. But his personal life was beset by tragedy: his family perished in the Holocaust and both his wives died from brain tumours. He himself committed suicide in 1970.

Professor Malcolm M. Martin, formerly Mencer
(MBBS with Honours 1945, MD 1952)

Martin was born in Vienna in 1920 and left in 1938 to live with an aunt in Newcastle. He served in the British

Above: Professor Malcolm Martin

Above right: Erich Orton

Erich Orton, formerly Immerwahr
(BA French, 1942, MA 1949)

Born in Berlin in 1921, he came to Britain in 1936 through the generosity of his Danish godmother and enrolled at King's College in 1938. When the war stopped funds from Denmark, the College gave him a free place and enabled him to earn some money by teaching German; it also helped to get him released from internment.

In 1943, he joined the Army as a signaller in the Royal Rifle Corps, changing his name at the Army's insistence. After a year, he taught German to officers of the future British Military Government in Germany and served in Education Control in Germany. In May 1945, as he was walking across a bridge in Hamburg, he suddenly realized that the woman coming towards him was his mother, from whom he had not heard for six years. She had been bombed out in Berlin and lived in Hamburg. His father died in the Holocaust.

After demobilization in 1947, Orton took a post as Modern Languages teacher at the Royal Grammar School, Worcester, and later became Head of Modern Languages there. He wrote a number of language courses and TEFL (Teaching English as a Foreign Language) textbooks.

Army until the Dean of Medicine secured his leave of absence to continue his studies. As an undergraduate, he won several scholarships. His many awards and appointments, including a Leverhulme Research Fellowship at Middlesex Hospital, London, eventually led to his being appointed Professor of Paediatrics and Medicine at Georgetown University, Washington DC, in 1967. He has now retired from the Chair of Endocrinology there. He is a member of ten American medical societies, as well as the New York Academy of Sciences, and visited Newcastle in 1995.

Professor Friedrich Ignaz Mautner
(BSc Mathematics, 1943)

Mautner was born in Vienna in 1920. He was interned in Canada in 1940, but returned to King's College in 1941. He became a highly regarded mathematician, first working with Schroedinger who, with Dirac, had won the Nobel Prize for Physics in 1933. He later went to Princeton and worked with Von Neumann, who formulated Games Theory. In the 1950s, he was a professor at Johns Hopkins University, Baltimore, teaching his last class there in 1963. He spent several years on extended leave in France and is believed to have lectured at the University of Orsay. His later positions and work are unknown. Up to 1963, Mautner was concerned with mathematical logic, rings of operators in Hilbert space and the differential geometry of unified field theory.

Peter Sieber (BSc Electrical Engineering, 1943)

Born in Vienna in 1921, he, his brother and mother came to Britain in 1938. After matriculating within 12 months of arriving in Britain, Sieber was given a free place at Newcastle. He was interned and sent to Canada, but was released in 1941 and returned to King's College. After graduating, he joined the Royal Navy. This was believed to be impossible for an 'enemy' alien at the time, but Sieber actually obtained a commission, probably the only refugee from Austria to do so. He served as an electrical officer in operational and experimental mine-sweeping. In 1945, he was transferred to the Naval Intelligence Division and served with the British Naval Gunnery Mission in Germany. He was one of the first refugees to be naturalized after the war.

Sieber founded and became managing director of a number of successful firms specializing in advertising and marketing support for technical and scientific products. He claims that his engineering background, rather rare in advertising, was invaluable to him in his business life.

Fritz Wachs (BSc Civil Engineering, 1941)

Born in Vienna in 1911, he was politically active against the Austro-Fascist government and had to leave Austria immediately after the Germans marched in on 13 March 1938. He lived for a year in Brno, Czechoslovakia, and left a few days before the German occupation, travelling via Poland and Sweden to Britain. He had already studied Civil Engineering in Vienna, so he entered the second year of the course at King's College in 1939. In May 1940, he was interned and shipped to Canada. After his release in January 1941, he returned to Britain and completed his course, graduating in June 1941.

When enemy aliens were allowed to join the fighting services, Wachs joined the Royal Engineers in 1943, and fought in Holland and northern Germany. After the war, he was an interpreter with the Allied Control Commission for Austria in Vienna. From 1947, his professional life was spent as an engineer in the Austrian Government Service. Wachs died in Vienna in May 1997.

Kurt Wendtner (BSc Chemistry, 1944)

Born in Vienna, he became a refugee because of his membership of the *Sturmscharen*, a Catholic youth movement. After graduating, he went to London, where he is believed to have become a teacher. Friends of his report that he suffered from a spinal illness in Newcastle and that he died young.

Professor Frederic Wolf (MBBS, 1946, MD 1957)

Wolf was born in Berlin in 1920 and came to England in 1939, where he attended Bryanston School, Dorset. He obtained a free place in the Medical School, King's College, in 1939. Interned in 1940, he was released in 1941.

From 1950 to 1952, he was a squadron leader in the RAF Medical Branch. Since then he has held some of the top medical posts in the US, including Professor of Medicine (Emeritus 1991) at the George Washington University School of Medicine, and President of the Institute of Drug Development, where he has acted as a consultant to the US government on the problems of drug development and the power of the pharmaceutical industry.

He has been Visiting Professor for lengthy periods in China, South Africa and New Zealand, has given numerous seminars in Britain and Europe, and has written for scientific and medical journals in Britain, the US and Germany.

Frederic Wolf

Conclusion

Four of the ten students obtained University appointments, three became full professors (in the US), another former student became a Fellow of the Royal Society and appeared in an Honours List. One became a successful businessman and two became teachers. An architect (in local government service) and an engineer (in Austrian government service) complete the list. The University can thus be very gratified by the outcome of its generosity.

All the former students whom it has been possible to contact personally expressed their appreciation in general terms, and above all to the late Lord Eustace Percy and other members of staff for particular acts of kindness and help on their arrival and stay, and especially, during the internment period.

Taken from an article by Margaret Jones, previously published in *Arches*, based on research by Dr Herbert Loebl

Agriculture and Forestry before the Second World War

Although Professor Johnston of Durham University lectured on Agricultural Science in Newcastle in 1845, it was to be 45 years before the foundation of a permanent Agriculture and Forestry presence in the city. Johnston was a prolific author and publicist, but he died before the foundation of Durham College of Physical Science at Newcastle in 1871, and remained a lone agricultural scientist amid a host of theologians in Durham.

His lectures in Newcastle were given to the Farmers' Club at the Lit and Phil, but with the repeal of the Corn Laws and improvements in the transport of American wheat, agriculture sank into a prolonged depression in the 1870s. Attempts to promote its introduction as an academic subject at Newcastle found little favour until Northumberland County Council Education Committee, together with other northern county councils and the Board of Agriculture, worried by the effects of the depression, decided to give money to the Durham College of Science to found the Department of Agriculture and Rural Economy. They endowed a Chair of Agriculture, which was quickly filled by Professor Sir William Somerville. The Department, founded in 1891, was a place of learning for degree and diploma students, but also somewhere for farmers to be advised on modern practices and shown new ways of improving their businesses.

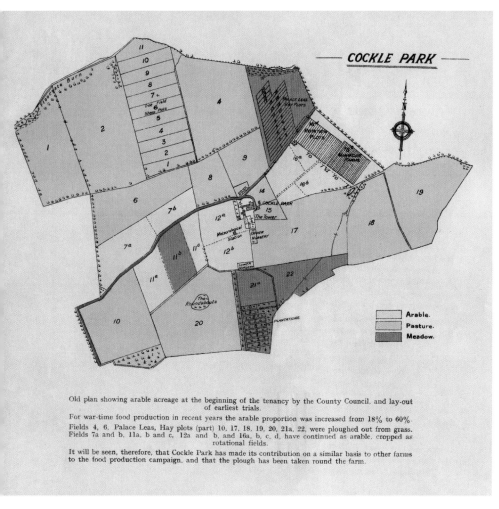

COCKLE PARK

Arable.
Pasture.
Meadow.

Old plan showing arable acreage at the beginning of the tenancy by the County Council, and lay-out of earliest trials.

For war-time food production in recent years the arable proportion was increased from 18% to 60%.

Fields 4, 6, Palace Leas, Hay plots (part) 10, 17, 18, 19, 20, 21a, 22, were ploughed out from grass. Fields 7a and b, 11a, b and c, 12a and b, and 16a, b, c, d, have continued as arable, cropped as rotational fields.

It will be seen, therefore, that Cockle Park has made its contribution on a similar basis to other farms to the food production campaign, and that the plough has been taken round the farm.

Top: Cockle Park Farm. Experiments were on pasture in Tree Field, on old land hay at Palace Leas and on crop rotation in Backhouse Field

Above: Sir Thomas Middleton, Head of Agriculture 1899–1902

From 1891 to 1896, Somerville and his colleagues, as well as teaching, ran experiments at farms to demonstrate how improvements could be made without increasing costs. In 1896, there were 46 separate experimental centres on commercial farms across the four northern counties. Somerville found the lack of permanent research and demonstration facilities restrictive for both farmers and students, and he convinced Northumberland County Council to lease the farm at Cockle Park, north of Morpeth. On the farm, in 1896, he began long-term demonstration-style experiments. These experiments were vast by modern standards as they were designed for farmers to be taken on to plots where 20 of them could stand and discuss what was happening. Somerville's successor, Sir Thomas Middleton, added the long-term Hanging Leaves experiment on grazing which showed that a mixture of sheep and cattle gave twice as much animal growth than sheep on their own. Both men succeeded in

establishing a vibrant new department with some of the best research facilities in Britain.

Their replacement, Douglas Gilchrist, was to remain until his untimely death in 1927, and his 25-year reign was to bring Newcastle and Cockle Park to the fore nationally and internationally. In Mid Tower Field, he introduced an experiment on longer-term rotational grass, and the success of this is immortalized in the Cockle Park song (sung to the tune of 'Hark the Herald Angels Sing'):

Basic slag and wild white clover,
They're renowned the whole world over,
Gilchrist's mixtures fine and rare,
Smoked by farmers everywhere.

The last is poking fun at the Cockle Park species-rich grass seeds mixtures (still on sale 80 years after their introduction) by likening it to a pipe smoker's tobacco mix. On the poorest land on the farm, Gilchrist's method increased the hay yield sixfold, and Sir George Stapledon, in 1944, after paying tribute to the earlier workers at Cockle Park, said: 'It was Gilchrist who was nearer the heart of the matter, for it is to Gilchrist that we must give the chief credit of having brought all the factors together: the phosphate, the wild white clover, the sensible seeds mixture, the greater needs of the farmer – all together in the ley.'

The growing reputation of the Department attracted students to the degree and also farmers and others to the six-term diploma (two terms each year so that students could go home in spring to get the farm work done!) and the six- and ten-week courses, called Squeakers and Tweakers respectively, which lasted into the 1930s. Fame brought visitors from all over the world; over 40 countries were named in the visitors' book by the start of the Second World War. The supreme accolade was the visit, in 1925, of Sir John Russell, the Director of Rothamsted Experimental Station in Hertfordshire, to see the Palace Leas meadow hay experiment.

Gilchrist's death did not, however, end his impact, for he had not only founded much of continuing value, he also donated his extensive book collection to the Library and it remains available today in Special Collections. He was not the only 'friend' that benefited the Department. Clement Stephenson, a local vet and the Honorary Veterinary Adviser to the Department, generously contributed half the cost of a new building (now occupied by Architecture) in the emerging

reported extensively in the local press. The close relationship between the academics, their students and the graduates led to the formation of an agricultural students' association, initially with the memorable acronym DCSNASA (Durham College of Science at Newcastle Agricultural Students' Association), only marginally improved today as UNAS (University of Newcastle Agriculture Society), with a senior and junior branch. The senior society invited notable speakers to their meetings, and the proceedings were published in volumes whose name was to change repeatedly to reflect the evolving stature of academic life in Newcastle, but which for much of its existence was the *Journal of King's College Agriculture Society*.

Above: The Medieval Tower at Cockle Park, 1830

Left: Clement Stephenson, a local vet, paid for half the cost of a new building for Agriculture (today occupied by Architecture) in the quadrangle

The stature of the farm as an experimental station required the presence of a permanent 'record keeper', a post that was filled in 1916 by Cecil Pawson, but was never able to retain staff for any length of time. It seems to have been the booby prize, handed down to a graduate with nowhere to go. One good, or bad, feature of the post was that the holder had a flat in the Medieval Tower at Cockle Park, the University's oldest property, from which former tenants had watched the advance and retreat of marauding Scots. Professor Gilchrist, like his two predecessors a Scot, was the first of that nation to live peaceably in the Tower, in the upper flat.

quadrangle. This was to be the Department's home for nearly 50 years, though entry was delayed when it and the adjoining Hatton Gallery were used as the Northern Field Hospital during the Great War. During that war, the Department moved out to St George's Terrace in Jesmond, a highly advantageous situation for Professor Gilchrist, who lived in the same street, as now do many of the more affluent undergraduates!

Other friends were the Duke of Northumberland, Lord Allendale, Lord Eustace Percy, Viscount Ridley and Charles Bosanquet of Rock, who all played, with Northumberland County Council Education Committee, a central role in the development and expansion of the Department. The Council contributed by adding Paradise Land, an ironic Northumbrian appellation for a wet and difficult area, to Cockle Park and, in 1907, the Department took over the management of 900 acres of Chopwell Woods, to add to its Cockle Park woodlands. These woodlands, and others visited during farm walks, were to become even more important during the timber shortages of the Great War that led to the formation of the Forestry Commission.

From the outset, publication and popularization of the results of the Department's research was a priority, and an annual report of results from Cockle Park was produced until the outset of the Second World War. Academics went out regularly to speak to farmers' groups all over the country, and these meetings were

Pawson was to find favour in Gilchrist's eyes and for many years functioned as his assistant, in spite of never completing a first degree. One of his duties was to carry the Professor's notes, in a file bound with red tape, into the lecture theatre and to lay them out: a sort of warm-up act prior to the main event. Pawson was to remain at Newcastle for his working life, finally in the 1950s writing his account of the work at Cockle Park farm. He was very much a gatherer and reporter of the work of others, rather than an innovator, but a lucky find at Ogle Castle of 18th-century letters between George Culley and Robert Bakewell, the two men responsible for the creation of the Border Leicester breed of sheep and for developing the rules for breed improvement, was to provide Special Collections with wonderful archive material and Pawson with a DSc and a Chair of Agriculture.

After Gilchrist's death, the Department went through a fallow period. This coincided with the Great Depression of the 1930s and severe unemployment on

Gilchrist and Pawson (wearing trademark bonnet) at Cockle Park

Tyneside. Agricultural prices even fell below those of the late Victorian depression. With no new ideas at Newcastle and no great figure to fight Agriculture's corner, the Department hovered near to extinction. Both the Board of Agriculture and the various county councils became disillusioned with the services provided, and as the latter had themselves created local colleges at Newton Rigg, Houghall and Kirkley Hall, Newcastle's role was questionable. The saving factor was to be the threat of another war. The advisory service was expanded, and the Head of Department, Professor Hanley, moved to the Ministry of Agriculture and to the relative safety of Cumbria. Robert Wheldon, who had joined the staff in 1915 as an 'emergency appointment', took over leadership in 1940, though he had effectively run the Department for much of the time since Gilchrist's death. Now, with his hands untied, he produced a second flowering, though this was to be

based more on laboratory analysis than the farm research of Gilchrist's time. New appointments were made and the science laboratory work expanded greatly to cope with the deluge of requests for help. Sidney Collins had begun work in 1900 in what was called Agricultural Chemistry, the subject Professor Johnston had been promoting half a century before, and was to provide valuable data on the quality of the animal feeds from the Cockle Park experiments. He was succeeded by Brynmor Thomas who, like Pawson, was to rise through the ranks to a personal chair. He oversaw the laboratories throughout the Second World War and sowed the seeds for the third great flowering when Mac Cooper was to drag husbandry into a brave new world and David Armstrong was to found a world-leading centre of animal nutrition research.

Robert Shiel

03

Faculty of Humanities and Social Sciences

ARTS AND HUMANITIES

The study of arts and humanities had an uncertain start in Newcastle. This was not because these subjects lacked support within the region, since among the sponsors of the College of Physical Science there were Newcastle institutions that had long acted as centres for scholarship and education in the humanities: the Literary and Philosophical Society (founded 1793) and the Society of Antiquaries (founded 1813). But when, in 1871, the

Right: Owen Seaman, 1861–1936, the first lecturer in Literature

Left: The Architecture building, which began life as the Agriculture building at the end of the 19th century

executive committee responsible for developing the College set out its proposals, it recognized that scientific teaching had to take precedence.

Despite this decision, teaching in arts was required. The School (later College) of Medicine had long demanded a preliminary examination in arts; in 1867, indeed, it had only narrowly fought off a suggestion from the General Medical Council for a compulsory examination in Greek. The new courses in the College of Physical Science equally called for preliminary instruction in subjects such as History, English and foreign languages. Alongside these demands there was clearly a call for day and evening classes from schoolchildren, primary school teachers and governesses in the city. Most of this work was inevitably at a fairly elementary level – it was only in 1896 that the age of admission to the College of Science was raised from 15 to 16 – but Dean Lake, as Warden of the University of Durham, saw the need for academic appointments to support this teaching. In 1872, and again in 1880, he offered a number of posts in arts subjects to the College on the basis of a £20 retainer and two thirds of student fees. These were all short-lived, though the Rector of Gateshead, with the title of 'Professor of History', proved to be an extremely popular lecturer on the Norman Conquest.

Despite these hesitant beginnings, a base was slowly being built up. In the 1880s, the Newcastle School of Design, originally set up by the Pre-Raphaelite William Bell Scott, was incorporated in the College of Science and, in 1888, a lectureship in literature was established in Classics from which all subsequent teaching in Classics and English is directly descended. This was filled by Owen Seaman, later to be editor of *Punch*.

The great leap forward for the arts came in 1889 with the proposal that the University of Durham College of Physical Science should establish a day-training college for teachers at sub-degree and degree level. This not only gave the College an assured stream of income, but meant a steady supply of students for arts subjects. The College responded with a series of appointments. Seaman became Professor of Literature in 1890 – a title that included both Ancient and Modern – and other appointments were made which were to play a major part in the College over the next two decades, notably Albert Latham in Modern Languages and, on Seaman's resignation in 1893, James Wight Duff in Classics. By 1895, the teaching strength was such that the College was able to introduce a Bachelor's degree. But this was a BLitt and not a BA. To the evident frustration of the Newcastle staff, the University refused to grant the College's degree equal status and titling to that of the Durham-based degree because it lacked a compulsory Greek element. From Durham's viewpoint this was understandable, since most of its graduates were intending ordinands and the bishops, deeply suspicious of the quality of non-Oxbridge graduates, were unlikely to accept any seeming diminution in the linguistic rigour of the Durham BA. But, as Wight Duff repeatedly warned in his annual departmental reports, the status of the BLitt degree – even with Honours – was widely misunderstood; as a result he and his colleagues were often involved in preparing their BLitt graduates for external London BA degrees.

Numbers of students were still, by modern standards, extremely small: there were 12 finalists for the BLitt in 1898–9. And staff numbers were equally minuscule: in 1904, for example, Classics was staffed by Professor Wight Duff, English by Professor Charles Vaughan and Modern History by a single lecturer, who had succeeded Professor Frewen Lord, a barrister whose impressive lifestyle encompassed a suite of rooms in the Grand Hotel. With such small numbers, relations between staff and students took intriguing forms: the fiery Vaughan, for example, though disregarding women students in class, organized dinners to teach his students appropriate table behaviour.

Over the early years of the 20th century, pressure built up for a Newcastle-based BA degree. In 1906, the City Council used its absence as an excuse to withhold any increase in its grant to the College, whilst an influential Treasury report in 1907 argued that the

standard of the Newcastle BLitt was fully equivalent to the BA, which was, by now, being awarded in numerous English universities. The whole issue then became entangled with the complex politics of what became the University of Durham Act of 1908, which formally established the two divisions of the University of Durham. The Newcastle division was at last able to offer a BA degree, though, still with an eye to potential episcopal disapproval, this right was subtly formulated by allowing Durham-based graduates, whose course of study had included Latin and Greek, to append the words in *Litteris Antiquis* to their title.

Both pass degree and Honours courses in arts now emerged at Newcastle. In 1912–13 there were 97 students reading for an arts degree, of whom 22 were Honours candidates. Staffing numbers were strengthened to meet the new demands. Professor Reinhold Hoernlé, who later moved to Harvard, was appointed to a Chair in Philosophy in 1911 and Albert Latham, whose silken curled moustache so entranced his students, was given a Chair in Modern Languages. And at last the Chair of History was revived and occupied by F.J.C. Hearnshaw. Thanks to a regional economic depression, progress was not always smooth before the First World War, but by 1914 much had been achieved, including full integration into the College of the King Edward VII School of Fine Art, which received a Royal Charter in 1912.

The Great War forced the dispersal of arts departments across the city as the University's own premises were requisitioned. Most of them moved to the Bolbec and Neville Halls where they had the great advantage of being able to use the library of the Lit and Phil. Nevertheless,

Above: An assessment of students' artwork in the late 1950s by (left to right): Ralph Holland, J.R.M. McCheyne, Kenneth Rowntree, Geoffrey Dudley and Victor Pasmore

Below: *The interior of the Library of the Lit and Phil*

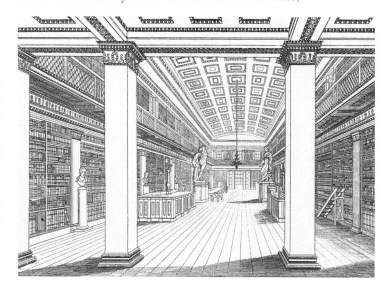

even in this period of disruption, initiatives were being taken. The need for reinforcing Modern Languages teaching was pressed strongly by the Principal, although his efforts were not aided by the internment of a lecturer in German as an enemy alien. A lecturer in Spanish was appointed in 1914, and Russian was made available through the employment of a Mr Orloff of the University of Petrograd. Most impressive of all, a Chair in Fine Art was established in 1917, its first holder being Richard Hatton, whose name is now commemorated in Fine Art's Hatton Gallery.

After the war, more courses and more departments arrived. Thus in the 1920s, Fine Art and Music became available in the BA degree; Geography was established as a department in 1927, and its single lecturer accommodated in a hut, whilst Romano-British archaeology was started in 1931. Teaching of Norwegian and Swedish was also inaugurated just before the war. Numbers of students in arts rose steadily through the 1920s; by the end of the decade, a quarter of the College's students were arts-based. But development was increasingly hindered by the restrained finances of the College resulting from the economic depression of the time. One of the more unfortunate effects of this was that the establishment of a promised chair in Music was postponed by Senate in 1928. In consequence W.G. Whitaker, who for nearly 30 years had taken a major role in developing musical studies in the University and region, left to become Principal of the Scottish Academy of Music. Nevertheless, by the time that King's College had come into being with the University of Durham Act of 1935, many of the main characters who were to dominate arts life in the College for the next 20 or more years were in post: G.B.A. Fletcher and Ian Richmond in Classics, Duncan Mennie in German, C.M. Girdlestone in French – and W.L. Renwick of English, who famously warned that 'a university is not a nursery home for weaklings'.

The post-war years saw a gradual expansion, with some very distinguished scholars arriving in Newcastle, among them John Butt, Peter Ure and Barbara Strang in English, together with William Burn and Geoffrey Barrow in History. Even that listing, however, is eclipsed by Fine Art's galaxy of teachers in the 1950s and 1960s, which reads like a catalogue of the major figures in British art of the period: Lawrence Gowing, Roger de Grey, Richard Hamilton, Victor Pasmore, Kenneth Rowntree and Leonard Evetts.

NICK POTTS

FRENCH / 1957–61

What is often not appreciated nowadays is just how few cars there were on the roads back in the late 50s. Statistics of the time showed that cars numbered about one per ten head of population, while today the figure is one for every two people in the UK. One very noticeable vehicle was seen frequently around the French Department and the Union in the late 50s and was operated by a consortium of us

within the Department. It was a 1935 Austin London taxi, which, at over 20 years old at the time, was lovingly cherished by us, whose money was very limited, whose engineering knowledge was barely embryonic and whose technical facilities were zero. Pre-war cars still abounded on the roads, but there were few like Henry the taxi, which used to drive down, from the French Department in the Victorian house on Kensington Terrace to the Union at lunchtime, bursting at the seams with waving students and friends. On occasions even the august figure of our Professor Girdlestone was known to join us. Henry was taken to Europe on a long vacation jaunt, and we observed that eyebrows were raised much higher in Paris, Lyons and Barcelona by our stately passage than in Newcastle.

Denis Matthews playing in Hull in 1974. He was appointed Professor of Music in 1972

In 1963, the Robbins Report demanded a sudden and large-scale expansion of university teaching. Newcastle's arts numbers rose to 1,217 by 1967–8 but, for a variety of reasons, the Arts Faculty of the now independent University of Newcastle upon Tyne was not given the increase in students that its application numbers merited or which its competitor universities achieved; this was to cause problems in ensuing years. But expansion was at work and the quality of students was steadily improving. This was reflected in the Faculty of Arts by the development of the former multi-subject BA General Degree. Under Tony Taylor and his energetic successor Jerry Paterson, this degree expanded until it absorbed nearly a quarter of arts entrants, allowing combinations of subjects hitherto impossible within the Joint Honours BA. In 1976, it was retitled Combined Honours in recognition of the academic transformation of the degree. Among other developments, Music was finally able to appoint as Professor in 1972 the distinguished pianist Denis Matthews and a Department of Archaeology appeared belatedly on the scene – belatedly because its teachers, many of them internationally famous scholars, had hitherto been scattered across the University in Adult Education, Classics, History and English.

After the headlong expansion of the 1960s, the following decades saw a series of cuts throughout the University. Disadvantageous funding regimes and inopportune resignations or retirements (which allowed disestablishment of posts) hit the Arts Faculty particularly badly, and its relative size meant that constituent departments lacked the necessary critical mass successfully to carry the cuts. A crisis point was reached in the early 1980s, when the economies demanded of the Faculty could no longer be spread across the whole range of departments without widespread damage to core teaching. The Faculty managed to fight off a proposal to close Music, thanks to its well-established level of support across the University and city. But Scandinavian Studies was lost and so was Philosophy, the latter a particularly painful blow because the subject had a long and distinguished history at Newcastle, and had excellent students and teachers.

Despite these losses, other departments whose future had looked uncertain revived and flourished, allowing student numbers in arts to rise to some 1,560 by 1990–1. Divinity, now rebadged as Religious Studies, managed to attract various forms of outside funding to keep afloat. Changes in school curricula threatened Classics after Fletcher's retirement in 1969, but the Department, under David West and Trevor Saunders, boldly expanded its Ancient History teaching and controversially, but successfully, began teaching Latin and Greek *ab initio*. Modern Languages was equally threatened by weaknesses in the subject within schools, but under Professor Tony Lodge, and using the new language laboratories established by Derek Green, the departments developed innovative courses for instilling linguistic competence, and moved into new and popular areas of study including Film. Demand for History and English studies remained very high, at both undergraduate and graduate level, and their departments were able to attract such high-quality staff as the Shakespearean scholar Ernst Honigmann and the historian John Cannon. When the new demands for expansion arrived in the later 1990s, the Faculty was thus well placed to play its part.

Richard N. Bailey

CLASSICS

While I was being interviewed for a lectureship in Ancient History at Newcastle in early 1972, the lights went out. As a result of the miners' strike electricity was cut on a rota basis. So there I was in Kensington Terrace, late on a gloomy February afternoon, surrounded by candles, being asked questions from shadowy shapes on the other side of the table. I had a clue about the generosity of spirit of the University when they selected me, despite the fact that I was a Herefordian by birth and in just the previous week Hereford United had beaten Newcastle in one of the greatest of FA Cup upsets. On that dank winter's day, I little realized that I was joining a Classics department with a vivid history and a dynamic future.

Greek and Latin had been part of the curriculum at Newcastle ever since the appointment of the Reverend J. Bulmer in 1874. Between 1889 and 1893, Classics

Top right: Fletcher's collection of antiquarian editions of Classical texts, now housed in Special Collections in the Library

Below: Professor J. Wight Duff who was Head of Classics from 1893 for nearly 40 years

teaching was carried on by Owen Seaman, who was later to become a famous editor of the satirical magazine *Punch*, and whose gloomy attitude to life is supposed to have provided A.A. Milne with the model for Eeyore in the Winnie the Pooh stories. Classics and, indeed, the arts as a whole, were really entrenched at Newcastle by Professor J. Wight Duff, author of one of the most influential histories of Latin literature, who held his chair at Newcastle for nearly 40 years from the late 1890s; the fine library holdings in Classics were largely based on his efforts. The next Professor, S.K. Johnson, a distinguished editor of the Roman historian Livy, was only in post for a short time before he disappeared mysteriously while walking in the Austrian Alps. His successor in 1937 was G.B.A. Fletcher, a punctilious Latin scholar, who dominated Classics for 30 years. Fletcher's manner could be forbidding to colleagues. But there was another side to him; few know that in retirement, without prompting and without fanfare, he provided the funding for some of the Easter Lectures for Young People at Newcastle.

Classics at Newcastle was for many years the natural home for Roman archaeology. Sir Ian Richmond, the great Roman archaeologist, spent 21 years in Newcastle before becoming the first Professor of the Archaeology of the Roman Empire at Oxford. That same Oxford professorship was later to be held by Martin Harrison who, as Professor at Newcastle, created a separate Department of Archaeology in 1972.

The early 1970s was a very exciting and innovative time. Traditional Classics training in schools was in crisis. Newcastle, with David West and Trevor Saunders at the helm, was one of the first university departments in the UK to open up its Honours degrees to students who came with little or no training in Latin or Greek. The Department was prepared to teach them from scratch. Not only that, but members of the Department became some of the best-known figures in the country, touring schools and conferences, and providing support and encouragement to teachers and pupils at a time when the outlook for the subject in many places was less than clear. John Lazenby created the first Single Honours degree in Ancient History in this country, which enabled Newcastle to tap into a pool of talent among young people who were fascinated by the ancient world, but in many cases had little or no chance of studying it at school. Nearly all Classics departments have a similar approach to degree courses now, so it is important to remember just how innovative and critical the initiatives of Newcastle classicists in the 1970s and 1980s were.

Classics at Newcastle has survived and flourished, and continues to thrive, by being nimble on its feet and responding to new demands and situations. Most remarkably, the seed sown by James Longrigg, the scholar of Greek medicine, has burgeoned in recent years into a major centre for research and teaching in ancient medicine, led by Professor Philip van der Eijk.

A previous Vice-Chancellor once remarked in the middle of one of those spending crises that regularly hit universities, 'Gee, I'd close Classics down if they weren't so darn good.' It was a joke, but also a sincere compliment.

Jeremy Paterson

POLITICS

The academic study of politics has a pedigree that stretches back to the ancient Greeks but, as a modern university discipline, it is a relative latecomer. In Britain in the 1950s there were a few prominent centres for the study of politics, such as Oxford, the London School of Economics and Manchester, but in most other universities, if Politics was on the curriculum at all, it was represented by two or three lecturers in departments of History or Economics. So it was at Newcastle. Before 1955, Politics was taught within the Department of History but, in that year, two members of that department, John Brown and Ted Hughes, became the founding members of the Politics Department. They were joined in 1963 by Tim Gray, who was appointed Assistant Lecturer immediately after his graduation from the University of Durham. However, the survival of the fledgling department was soon thrown into doubt. Ted Hughes left to become the University's Director of Adult Education and John Brown moved to a Chair at Swansea, leaving a youthful Tim Gray as the Department's sole representative.

The University decided the Department should survive only if a suitable candidate came forward to fill the readership in Politics. Fortunately, one did. In 1965, Hugh Berrington was appointed Reader and Head of Department. The appointment of Vincent Wright, who was to become a distinguished scholar of French and European politics, restored the Department to its full complement of three staff. Hugh remained Head of Department for the next 29 years, and it was under his leadership that the Politics Department developed into one of the most successful in the UK. Hugh also became a leading figure in the subject nationally. The many offices he held included Chairman and President of the UK Political Studies Association and Chair of the Politics and International Studies Panel for the 1996 Research Assessment Exercise. In 2005, he received a Lifetime Achievement Award from the Political Studies Association for his scholarship and his other services to the discipline.

In the early years the Department, given its small size, was able to offer only joint degrees combining Politics with Anthropology and Economics, and later with Social Administration. With the appointment of several additional staff, including Alan Beith, Ben Pimlott, David George, Rod Hague, Ian McLean, and Peter Jones, the Department, in 1973, was able to launch its Single Honours degree in Politics. In the previous year, it had established the BA in Politics and History, which became the most popular of its Joint Honours degrees. Further appointments, notably those of David Goodman, David Hine and Ella Ritchie, enabled it to offer innovative BAs in Politics and East Asian Studies, and Government and European Community Studies (later renamed Government and European Union Studies), and a joint degree with Philosophy. Until the 1980s, the efforts of the Department were very much focused upon undergraduate teaching. The Department was able to grow only by taking advantage of opportunities to recruit undergraduates in increasing numbers, which the University then matched with increases in staff. That strategy proved effective: nowadays, at any one time, nearly 400 Newcastle undergraduates are reading for Single or Joint Honours degrees in Politics, taught by 19 full-time staff.

The introduction of devolved funding at the end of the 1980s enabled the Department to recruit part-time teachers to assist with the delivery of its undergraduate

Hugh Berrington, Head of Politics 1965–94

Alan Beith, who gave up an academic career to become the Liberal Democrats' MP for Berwick-upon-Tweed

programmes, so enabling some of its full-time staff to develop postgraduate studies in Politics. In 1990, it established MA programmes in European Union Studies, International Studies, and International Political Economy. During the same period, Tim Gray threw his energy and enthusiasm into developing the Department's PhD programme, with marked success. Each year, the University now has around 100 postgraduate students reading for either MAs or PhDs in Politics.

The Department has always numbered distinguished researchers amongst its staff, but its need to grow from its small beginnings and its consequent emphasis upon student recruitment meant that, early on, its energies were devoted more to teaching than to research. That emphasis changed during the 1980s, and the development of the Department's research standing is reflected in its performance in successive national Research Assessment Exercises: after a disappointing start, it was awarded a grade 3 in 1989, grade 4 in 1992 and 1996, and a grade 5 in 2001. So it now ranks amongst the best research departments in the country. The Department's research profile was enhanced by the foundation of an East Asia Centre in 1982, directed initially by David Goodman and then by Reinhard Drifte, and by the award of a Jean Monnet Centre of Excellence (for EU studies) in 2000 directed by Ella Ritchie. The staff of the Department have contributed importantly to research in all major areas of the subject: political philosophy; international relations and global politics; the politics of Britain, Europe and the EU; the politics of Africa, the Middle East and East Asia; political behaviour and the psychology of politics; and public policy, particularly environmental policy.

Like other academic departments at Newcastle, Politics ceased to be an independent unit when the

University was restructured in 2002. It is now part of the School of Geography, Politics and Sociology. It aims to retain and develop its strength in its own subject area, while exploiting the interdisciplinary opportunities opened up by restructuring. With a recent influx of able and committed young staff, it is well placed to achieve those aims.

Peter Jones

HISTORY

When the College of Physical Science was set up in 1871, tuition in the arts was only a minor element of a curriculum dominated by applied science. The ecclesiastical roots of the parent institution, Durham University, determined that Divinity and Church History were privileged alongside Classical Studies. Quite naturally, the teaching of History in the new college perfectly reflected this rationale. In 1879, alongside Greek and Latin Literature, students reading Honours took classes in Ancient History, Roman History and English History from Richard I to Edward III. Given that knowledge of history was judged to be an essential attribute of those applying for medical scholarships, or studying for the Licence in Theology, such demand undoubtedly helped to raise the profile of the subject.

However, retaining qualified staff proved to be somewhat problematic. The appointment of Reverend J. Atkinson to teach English History and Literature in 1872 lapsed three years later, and the appointee to the new Chair in Modern History in 1880 had scarcely taken up his post when he left. Reverend W. Moore-Ede, whose post carried a stipend of £120 per annum, lectured on the Norman Conquest for a mere 12 months and thereafter History classes are said to have 'collapsed under his deputy'. Charles Stamford Terry's tenure was rather more enduring, even though he was initially engaged to teach classes in English Constitutional History on Saturday mornings and obliged to secure his salary from the students' fees! Fortunately, his efforts were eventually rewarded with a lectureship in 1902.

The admission of women to all classes, except for Divinity, was an important innovation and, in 1895, the College achieved a perfect gender balance of first-year history students. At that point in time, the College still had no arts degree, and as the BLitt degree did not attract government funding, this continued to act as a drag on development. Nevertheless, at the turn of the century

NEIL MURRAY

ENGLISH AND PHILOSOPHY / 1967–72

My new course was in English and Philosophy with some Politics. For the first time I began to realize the benefits of a seriously good library. My tutors included Alan Beith, the future MP for Berwick, and Karl Britton of Philosophy who had been a student of Wittgenstein. Mike Brearley, the future England cricket captain, also lurked within the Philosophy Department.

the Department of History benefited from the skills of a new lecturer, Walter Frewen Lord, and a livelier programme of studies. The College hoped that Frewen Lord would energize the study of Modern History, and duly awarded him a professorship in 1902. In the event, however, when Frewen Lord departed in 1903, it was left to his successor, Frederick Bradshaw, to modernize a curriculum still heavily steeped in religious and constitutional affairs by adding some courses on the 19th century. Visits to local historical sites and the establishment of a flourishing branch of the Historical Association typified his dynamic approach.

After 1911, when Armstrong College had finally secured the necessary agreement to offer a BA degree, Professor Holtham Vickers and Bradshaw offered new classes on 'The Contemporary History of the British Empire' and 'The History of Modern Europe', a reflection no doubt of the tense political climate. As war beckoned, European studies assumed centre stage and students were actively encouraged to study Joint Honours in History and Modern Languages. With the College premises occupied by the War Office, the History staff and their 94 students were relocated to Neville Hall. Despite the difficulties, the move heralded a number of key developments, including the introduction of classes in Local History and the launch of a History Society that still survives. In 1920, the Department appointed its first female members of staff, E. Tesh and M. Deansley, while the acquisition of a dedicated History library was largely due to Professor Vickers' indomitable efforts to secure sponsorship and a large donation of books.

Professor J.L. Morison, who succeeded him in 1922, expected his Honours students to read Latin and French as well as Economics, Political Economy and a demanding programme of British and European History. In 1925, it was his good fortune to secure the services of the young Alfred Cobban. Even at that early stage, Morison judged that Cobban's research was extremely 'promising'; and so it proved, for Cobban's classic studies of Edmund Burke, Jean-Jacques Rousseau and the French Revolution continue to be essential reading for students today. The war brought new challenges and further staff changes, notably the appointment of William Laurence Burn in 1943. A barrister, as well as an accomplished historian, Burn was popular with his students and respected by his colleagues, not least because of the scholarship invested

in his seminal study of the mid-Victorian generation, *The Age of Equipoise*.

In the post-war period the curriculum was modified in line with the growth of Social and Cultural History and assumed a global geographical remit. Since the 1960s, the History staff, individually and collectively, have helped to secure the University's reputation and push forward the intellectual boundaries in all of the established fields. Some took up temporary residence as holders of James Knott and Earl Grey Research Fellowships, before moving on to high-profile positions at Cambridge, Oxford, Edinburgh, Yale and elsewhere. In the ranks of eminent British historians we can note the contribution of Geoffrey Barrow, Alexander Murray, John Derry, Norman McCord, John Cannon, Bill Speck, Bernard Porter and Martin Pugh. Landmark publications in the field of European History have been published by, among others, Norman Hampson, Euan Cameron and Bob Moore.

In the 1970s and 1980s, American history was promoted under the expert guidance of Professor Tony Badger. It is this field which has yielded Newcastle's most famous student, Paul Kennedy, whose book *The Rise and Fall of the Great Powers* has been hailed as a masterpiece, and secured for him the Wolfson Prize and a professorship at Yale. In a fine tribute to the tutor who had inspired his undergraduate years, Dr Joan Taylor, Kennedy donated most of the prize money to establish travel awards for History students at Newcastle.

Joan Allen

Paul Kennedy's book, which earned him the Wolfson Prize

Paul Kennedy with Dr Joan Taylor and Margaret Butler

Above: Norwegian students in 1984

Far right: Vice Chancellor Laurence Martin unveiling a plaque marking 100 years of Teacher Education at Newcastle

Centre: Dorothy Heathcote, celebrated internationally for her work in drama education, was awarded an honorary doctorate by Newcastle in May 2005

EDUCATION

A hundred years of Teacher Education at the University were celebrated in 1990, despite the anxiety that government dislike of Education departments might bring them to an end. Yet they sprang from a wish to improve the quality and status of elementary teachers by attaching their training to institutions of university rank. The first 20 pupil teachers at Newcastle's College of Physical Science enrolled for a two-year course in September 1890. Complementing their professional studies by attending ordinary classes in various undergraduate programmes, most students were soon staying to complete a degree. Their presence highlighted the College's limited non-science provision, and so stimulated the teaching of arts and humanities, and the introduction of a degree in Letters.

The original training centre was among the first six established in England. Its principal (and 'Master of Method') Mark Wright, formerly head of a Gateshead school, became in 1895 the country's first holder of an established Chair in Education. Lacking conventional academic qualifications, he was awarded an MA by Convocation acting on a Senate resolution. His department also took a lead in one of the first programmes to challenge the assumption that the subject knowledge of teachers in secondary schools made any training unnecessary.

A capacity for successful innovation was demonstrated early and has persisted. The 1959 appointment of a lecturer in Speech and Speech Pathology was, nationally, the start of a university base for training speech therapists and, at Newcastle, of a major centre for teaching and research in Applied Linguistics. In Education, the Commonwealth bursars recruited in 1960 were the beginning of a national centre for overseas teachers and administrators, who have come over the years from some 50 countries. The year-long course for Norwegian teachers of English

began in 1962. Chosen by the Norwegian Ministry of Education, which also annually appoints an additional specialist tutor to accompany them, students undertake a year's study of English language, literature and institutions.

The necessarily wide curriculum offered to initial trainees prompted a lecturer from the 1930s to call it 'extending one's ability to conceal ignorance'. Provision for experienced teachers also grew substantially. Following the post-war decision to link all teacher training colleges with a local university, the Institute of Education created at Newcastle in 1948 both validated qualifications in six colleges from North Tyneside to Cumberland and also offered its own qualifications. Giving up the headship of the Department to lead the Institute, Professor Brian Stanley inspired a widening range of specialist advanced diplomas for seconded teachers. These gained appeal for non-graduates when it became possible to be awarded a BPhil through a further dissertation by part-time study. The BPhil was recognized as a first general degree for salary purposes. By 1986, when a steep national drop in secondments forced (as elsewhere) a large switch to evening courses, around 300 successors of the first 20 trainees were matched in number by experienced teachers on advanced courses.

As elsewhere, however, falling demand for teachers had upset the Institute's outreach role. Ken Rockett, who succeeded Brian Stanley in 1972, compared his inheritance to changing horses just before the Light Brigade charged. His successor, Colin McCabe, reported to the Vice Chancellor in 1983 on his part in closing three colleges, the BEd degree and, finally, the Institute itself.

Back in 1920, Godfrey Thomson became Mark Wright's successor to the Chair of Education. For Northumberland, Thomson developed the country's first group intelligence tests with the declared purpose of 'helping children of intelligence' from humble backgrounds not to be overlooked. Contributing more generally to a research base for the art and science of teaching slowly became a departmental priority. Early in the 1980s, a Centre for Evaluation and Management was created, its title reflecting major policy preoccupations, and Carol FitzGibbon developed a system for enabling schools and colleges to assess their own examination performance, which became widely adopted nationally as being fairer and more constructive than Government-imposed monitoring. She and the Centre later moved to Durham University, but a strong departmental emphasis on applied research produced a wide range of policy- and practice-based investigations, many of them funded by the Research Council or by government agencies. In the first national reviews of research performance, and especially in the more precise national assessments beginning in 1992, educational research at Newcastle showed up very well.

The training centre created in 1890, with Mark Wright at its head, became a College department in 1905, located in the main building until it moved to adjoining houses in Leazes Terrace. Department and Institute, installed by then in the Joseph Cowen Building, combined in 1972 to form a School of Education, which also included a sub-department of Speech and the Centre for Physical Education and Sport. Extra space in what had belonged to Newcastle Breweries provided a rather palatial boardroom and a warren of passages, prompting stories of finding remains of unfortunates who had failed to find a way out. The uncertainties of adapted accommodation were also evident in the Sports Centre's Kings Walk Building, which consisted of a former Victorian ballroom, a restaurant and brewery garage. But by the time the Sports Centre at Claremont Hall opened in 1984, the scope of its activities would have astonished the two ex-Army instructors in physical exercise and drill, appointed some 80 years before.

By then, both the Centre and Speech were full departments within an Education Faculty that also included Lifelong Learning (the old Extra-Mural Department). By then, too, the Institute had closed. In the University's 2002 restructuring, Lifelong Learning

A student on teaching practice in a junior school

was transferred to Sunderland and the rest of the Faculty became the School of Education, Communication and Language Sciences. Communication is obvious common ground, the strength of Language Sciences is recognized, and the traditional commitment to Teacher Education is complemented by substantial non-vocational undergraduate teaching.

Anthony Edwards

ANNE PICKERING

EDUCATION / 1969–70

Father Towers was the Catholic chaplain and a great character. He used to begin each academic year with a series of cheese and wine parties to which he invited all students who gave their religion as Roman Catholic. He held the 'Sebastian' discussion groups on Thursday evenings. Sebastian was an imaginary student whose life was told as a serial, and the moral dilemmas he encountered were discussed earnestly each week. The issues would probably seem very naive to the students of today, but for us this was what university life was meant to be like!

In the Education Department, my tutor was Mrs Berrill. In March 1970, the students of education year were invited to a residential conference in Otterburn Towers. I had a problem in that I had an interview for a teaching job back in Cramlington. I did not have a car and public transport was not easy. Mrs Berrill drove to Otterburn to collect me, took me for lunch in the Senior Common Room and drove me to Cramlington! I am sure that was not in the job description!

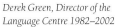

The visit of the President of the British Academy to the Language Centre in 1985

The Language Centre

The initial impetus for the creation of the Language Centre in 1968–9 was the arrival in the University of the first language laboratory and the realization that more needed to be done to meet the English language needs of the University's overseas students.

Initially the 'Language Laboratory' – in 1972 renamed the 'Language Centre' as the fledgling department increased its activities – was used by students of the foreign language departments to listen to tape recordings of the languages they were studying and by overseas students trying to improve their English. The appointment of the first lecturer in English as a Foreign Language in 1970 and confirmation of Allan Andison as the first Director of the Language Centre in 1972 produced a flurry of new developments. Courses in remedial English were established for the overseas students, and classes designed to support the learning of modern foreign languages by students and staff of the University ran at lunchtimes and in the early evenings. Within two years, two further laboratories had been established in the Claremont Bridge Building to cope with this; there was also an additional demand

Derek Green, Director of the Language Centre 1982–2002

from overseas students for remedial classes in English, resulting from Senate's resolution in 1972 that the proficiency in English of all overseas postgraduate students should be tested during registration.

From the start, the Language Centre adopted a very entrepreneurial attitude to all its activities. The main problem in providing courses in English for the overseas students was that they were all in their regular subject classes for much of each day – the engineers often for about 30 hours a week. This meant that the Centre's classes had to be held in evenings and lunchtimes, and students' progress was often slow. The Department sought to solve this problem by teaching as many of the overseas students as it could in an intensive course called the 'Pre-Sessional' in July and August. Newcastle was one of only two universities to start a Pre-Sessional in 1974. Today – 30 years later – almost all UK universities do so. Since the first Pre-Sessional started with just under 30 students in 1974, numbers have grown until they have topped 300 in some recent years.

By the end of the 1970s, the Language Centre was already generating some of its own funding by running courses for foreign governments, such as the course for Saudi teachers, summer schools for the British Council and later – from 1985 onwards – in an attempt to support the University's recruitment of overseas students, summer schools for students of Korean, Japanese, Taiwanese and Thai universities.

Following the appointment of its first lecturer in Modern Languages in 1972, the Centre became involved in the degree teaching of Russian and, by the 1980s, in the teaching of modern European languages to non-specialists. In the early 1980s, the establishment of the degree in East Asian Studies by the Department of Politics involved their students in a year's study in an Asian country, and this led to the provision of courses in Japanese, Chinese and Korean by the Language Centre.

On its incorporation into the Faculty of Arts in 1982, the Department joined with the then Department of English Language and Linguistics to offer a taught Master's for overseas teachers of English. Throughout its history, the Centre had sought to innovate by the use of equipment to support the teaching and learning of languages. This led to the acquisition and use of satellite television equipment and networked computers in the 1980s. In 1989, it added its own Master's course in Software Design (later renamed Media Technology) to allow the Department to communicate its growing

expertise in the use of technology for language teaching. The equipment in the labs had to be watched carefully. In the early 1980s, the Centre was burgled one day at around noon, and the robber was seen making his escape with a very expensive tape recorder. When the technician, Kevin McErlane, went in hot pursuit, the thief turned and threw the recorder at him. Kevin returned to the Centre, triumphantly bearing the recorder, only to be rebuked by his boss for not having caught it before it hit the pavement!

An important theme within the TESOL (Teaching English to Speakers of Other Languages) degrees was the development of facilities for the self-directed learning of languages. The Centre had always provided these but, in 1997, the University helped the Centre to create a superbly designed and equipped Open Access Centre on the ground floor of the Old Library Building. This was a stunning achievement – the result of much study and many visits to see other such centres in the UK and abroad – and was admired by colleagues and students in and far beyond Newcastle.

Another signal success – unique to Newcastle at the time of its inception – was the establishment of Master's degrees in Chinese–English Translating and Interpreting, which recruited about 20 postgraduate Chinese students each year. The fields of translating and TESOL also yielded a number of successful PhD students. In 2000, the process turned full circle when the University decided to move the teaching of modern foreign languages, the Master's and PhD programmes into academic schools, leaving the Language Centre to provide language-learning facilities and a multifaceted English Language programme for the foreign students.

Derek Green

Left: The modern, fully-equipped Open Access Centre opened in 1997

Right: The Percy Building, where the English department is situated

ENGLISH

In 1898, a Chair of English was founded in the College of Physical Science in Newcastle. It was one of the earliest such chairs in the country, and in 1909 was named after Joseph Cowen, a prominent local liberal newspaper owner and Member of Parliament. Colleges in Newcastle already taught Medicine and the Science and Engineering appropriate to local industries. In dignifying the study of the vernacular language and literature, among other chairs in the arts, the University put in place the last of the three elements that came to mark a major civic university. The chair has been held by a series of distinguished literary scholars and, in 1964, a separate Chair of English Language was founded.

Those teaching English at that time were apprehensive about the separation from Durham in 1963. They feared the loss of the library holdings in Durham, and worried that arts in Newcastle would be overwhelmed by more dominant disciplines. In the event, with the increasing popularity of English degrees in post-war decades, the School has held it own. It currently teaches close to 700 undergraduate and 150 postgraduate students.

To begin with, there was one degree, Honours in English Language and Literature. Separate degrees in English Literature and in English Language were added in the 1960s and Linguistics in the 1970s. The literature studied in these decades was almost exclusively that of Britain and Ireland. Anglo-Saxon was compulsory, as were Chaucer, Shakespeare and Milton. The rest was covered by 'period' papers from the 17th to the 20th century.

Gradually horizons started to expand. The tramp through the 'periods' was modified by 'special author' and 'special topic' courses; the teaching of American literature was formalized; film courses were introduced; and the first step towards bringing creative writing into degree courses allowed third-year students to submit a folder of their own creative work. In the 80s, the new 'Literary Theory' started to terrify the first years. On the language/linguistics side, courses in the structure and history of English were supplemented by more specialized courses, including sociolinguistics, semantics and pragmatics, computational linguistics, and phonology and morphology.

In courses taught mostly by lecture, with few seminars, the students' most significant teaching experience in the week was the regular tutorial, which allowed students to choose the topics they studied from week to week. This sometimes led to a scramble for books and hasty reading by tutor and students; but when it worked, it encouraged open-ended exploration of intellectual ideas. Numbers were small enough for first-year groups to perform a mini-Shakespeare play, for annual cricket matches with Durham, and a staff-student pantomime at Christmas. The students threw themselves into drama, 'Lit Soc', and producing their own magazines.

Modularization of courses in the early 90s was a watershed. This allowed staff to teach in their specialized areas of research and coincided with a major expansion in the areas coming under the remit of English courses. The concept of 'post-colonial literatures' gave a specific focus to the study of writing in English worldwide. Taking a similar global view, the language side developed research expertise in a wide range of languages, including endangered Native American languages. Notable recent additions to our courses have been in creative writing, children's literature and digital cultures.

Recent developments have been closely linked to the University's geographical situation. The innovative Tyneside Linguistic Survey established in the 60s has

been given a new lease of life in the Newcastle Electronic Corpus of Tyneside English, a major resource for the study of language in the North East. Language study has been enhanced by the transfer of staff from the recently closed Durham Linguistics Department. Together with linguists in other schools, the staff in this area form one of the largest language/linguistics groupings in the country. The introduction of modules on children's literature coincided with the opening in Newcastle of Seven Stories, the Centre for Children's Books.

To avoid the 'pick and mix' aspect of modularization, English modules in Newcastle are arranged in bands by period or topic to give structure to students' choices. The result is some brilliant work in modules in both the traditional and the new areas. Nevertheless, there is no denying that modular courses in universities, built upon the abandonment of the chronological teaching of History in schools, can result in confident claims that John Donne was a Victorian!

So what is the current ethos? Tutorials – though larger than before – survive in the first year. Thereafter, teaching is by module and the richness of the student's experience probably depends on the success of the module seminars in enabling the discovery and sharing of ideas. The rise in postgraduate numbers means that staff time is directed more than ever towards postgraduate teaching and supervision. As for the undergraduates, if staff (whose numbers have risen but not in proportion to the rise in student numbers) do not always have as much time for them as before, the students themselves (without grants and facing huge debts on graduating) take jobs that reduce in turn the

Above and top: Interior and exterior of Seven Stories, the Centre for Children's Books

Left: The English Society Committee at their fancy dress ball

CREATIVE WRITING

Jackie Kay performing at BALTIC

Creative Writing is perhaps the fastest-growing discipline in English studies, and Newcastle is firmly in the vanguard. Our North-East Literary Fellowship is one of Britain's oldest and best-respected residencies. Past Fellows include Anne Stevenson, Barry Unsworth and Jo Shapcott. The Fellow, who holds the post for two years, is appointed to encourage the creativity of students in both Newcastle and Durham Universities. Poets, novelists and playwrights work with students, both individually and as part of the syllabus. Out of this hothouse environment came Neil Astley, founder of the North East-based Bloodaxe Books, the largest poetry publisher outside London.

In the early 90s, poet Desmond Graham introduced a poetry workshop into the syllabus, and ten years later the first Poetry MA was offered. This has blossomed into an MA in Creative Writing, with separate pathways in poetry, prose and script. Our Creative Writing PhD is a highly innovative degree.

Writers now teaching at the School of English Literature, Language and Linguistics include poet and novelist Jackie Kay, novelist and playwright Margaret Wilkinson, poets W.N. Herbert and Jack Mapanje, and film-maker Tina Gharavi. There are regular readings by visiting and local writers, and Bloodaxe co-hosts with English a prestigious series of lectures on contemporary poetry. These are published annually, alongside an anthology of the best work from the MA.

Also housed in the School is the archive of poet Barry MacSweeney; and our strong interest in the link between creative writing and health is commemorated in the best-selling Poetry Cure, a recent anthology edited by Cynthia Fuller and the late Julia Darling.

amount of time they have for the staff. Counterbalancing this is the increased opportunity for research or project work in the modular courses, in particular the Extended Study, in which students work one-to-one with a supervisor on a topic of their own choosing. We still have excellent academic results from enthusiastic students, who graduate with well-rounded CVs and many of whom go on to postgraduate work at Newcastle and elsewhere.

Claire Lamont

ENGLISH LANGUAGE

Newcastle's considerable contribution to English Language studies was largely the work of three outstanding scholars. The first is Allen Mawer, who succeeded David Nichol Smith as Professor of English in 1909. Afterwards remembered by students as possessed of a cavernous voice and having 'no use for literary flowers', he pioneered the modern study of English

place names in this country. Towards the end of his period at Newcastle, he published, in 1920, his *Place Names of Northumberland and Durham*, which was immediately recognized as bringing a philological rigour to a subject that had hitherto been the province of popular etymology. From that work flowed the establishment of the English Place Name Society in 1923, whose county publications are now a mine of historical, sociological and other information. Mawer went on to become Provost of University College London; his former department is now once more actively involved in place-name research and teaching.

The second figure is Harold Orton. From the time of his appointment in 1921, the Spenserean scholar Professor C.L. Renwick had been determined to include the study of Northumbian dialect in his department and eventually managed to recruit Orton in 1928. Within a year, departmental reports commented enthusiastically both on the involvement of students in collecting material and on the collaboration with the Physics

Barbara Strang, who became Professor in 1964. One of her major projects was the Tyneside Linguistic Survey

Department in experimental phonetics. Renwick himself even personally financed the purchase of an oscillograph. Orton's first major work was on the *Phonology of the South Durham Dialect* and appeared in 1932; it represented a huge step forward in the modern study of dialects. He left Newcastle in 1939, but the work begun here eventually yielded his classic *Survey of English Dialects*, which emerged in the 1960s.

The third member of this triumvirate is Barbara Strang, who came to Newcastle in 1950 and became Professor of English Language and Linguistics in 1964. From a background in conventional philology, early on she began to develop a unique integration of descriptive and historical approaches to the study of English Language, which became the hallmark of the Newcastle department. Her two books on *Modern English Structure* (1962) and *A History of English* (1970) rapidly became standard works, and her reputation began to attract a large number of postgraduate students from home and overseas to work in her department. Through the 1960s and 1970s she built up, and inspired, a strong group of linguists and medievalists. Among them were staff whom she recruited to her Tyneside Linguistic Survey – another pioneering work that brought the new insights of sociolinguistics to the study of a modern urban dialect; that material is now once more being used within the Department's research. Totally committed to Newcastle and the region, she once replied to an

VALERIE JONES

ENGLISH / 1974–79

One of the wackier requests I received was to do the research for a play to be produced at the University Theatre. The topic was life in Newcastle in 1876, the target audience was school kids and there was money to be had for it!

I dragged two impoverished flatmates into the scheme and we spent fascinating hours in the Library, reading back copies of the *Newcastle Journal* (or was it *Chronicle*?) from 1876. The adverts were as revealing as the news. 'Dr Kings Pills' would cure both diarrhoea and constipation, and to speed-walk you could buy 'Amazing Spring Boots'. They made a real pair of spring-soled boots for the production and one unfortunate actor had to risk his neck bouncing Zebedee-like across the stage.

invitation to take up a dazzling senior post in southern England that 'I would only come if they let me live in Northumberland'. For students and new colleagues alike the first response to her was one of awe. But soon awe gave way to admiration and then to great affection. After her sudden death in 1982, one student recalled her teaching as being among the most inspiring events of his life.

Richard Bailey

ANTHEA FRASER GUPTA

LINGUISTICS / 1969–73

I didn't spend much time in the pubs, partly because I had a heavy theatre habit to support. Every October I would begin the year by buying a booklet of Northern Arts vouchers, which got students what at the time seemed like a huge reduction on theatre and concert tickets. I went to the theatre or a concert most weeks. Northern Sinfonia, Royal Shakespeare Company, Scottish Opera, People's Theatre, Aeolian String Quartet ... and the Playhouse, right on campus, had plays AND lunches.

The General Degree with Honours was a pioneering programme that allowed students to find out what they liked. I came with an interest in Religious Studies and Sociology and ended up with a degree in Linguistics and Archaeology. I received help from Richard Bailey and Barbara Strang. They actually invented an ad hoc course for me to do – not many people actually enjoyed Linguistics.

MODERN LANGUAGES

Languages in Newcastle have always been combined with other disciplines. The 1921 University handbook states that 'business men are beginning to appreciate men who are at the same time men of knowledge (with, for example, a good grasp of one or more foreign languages) and men of character'. Languages began in 1880 with Gustave de Poitiers lecturing in French, followed in 1885 by a lecturer in German. In the late 1880s, the French lecturer, one Signor Catoni, also taught Spanish and Italian. By the 1890s, language teaching began to incorporate literary studies. The first Professor, appointed in 1910, was Albert Latham, who had started teaching French in 1893, succeeded by Cuthbert Girdlestone in 1926. By the 1940s, there were

The Merz Room where the film archive is housed

four French lecturers and two German lecturers. One of these was Duncan Mennie, who had spent the war years seconded to the BBC. He introduced Scandinavian languages in 1945, at which time the old Department of Foreign Languages split into separate departments: French and German/Scandinavian. Mennie became Professor of German in 1959.

With the expansion of the university system in the 1960s, Languages moved to the new Claremont Buildings. Philip Yarrow (1963–85) headed eight French staff; German/Scandinavian was the largest department with ten staff, supported by the German academic exchange service; Spanish had four staff; and Portuguese was introduced in 1965, supported by the Portuguese Instituto Camões. During the 1980s, the departments moved to the refurbished Old Library. French began to diversify the traditional language–literature mix with modules in history and politics. Peter Evans, who succeeded George Cheyne as Professor of Spanish, and Phil Powrie (French) introduced cinema studies in their two departments, and a general European film course for students in all languages. Scandinavian fell victim to 1980s cuts, but the three departments developed considerable strengths in linguistics, with five staff under Tony Lodge, who was appointed Professor of French in 1985. Spanish built on Peter Bradley's historical research on 16th-century Peru with an increasing focus on Latin American studies. Jens Hentschke worked on the modern history and politics of Brazil, while Vanessa Knights developed interests in Latin American cultural studies, as did Chris Perriam. He had succeeded Peter Evans as Professor of Spanish in 1995, and, like him, carried on developing Spanish cinema studies.

The separate departments became a single school in 1994 under David Place, who was Head of School followed by Phil Powrie, Colin Riordan, and Elizabeth Andersen. The School of Modern Languages grew in a number of ways. Previously department-specific initiatives – such as the teaching of interpreting in French – spread to the other languages, as members of the School began working more closely together. School-wide introductory modules were started in a number of disciplines, such as film, linguistics and literature. New degrees combining languages with other disciplines were offered in Business and Management Studies, Film, Law, Linguistics and Politics, as well as a very popular three-language degree.

Students using the interpreting labs

The student intake went up in this period from 70 to 170, putting an end to the rather more intimate feel of Modern Languages in previous decades. Gone now the days when Dave Place and Phil Powrie regularly took groups of students trudging across the Lakeland Hills to forge bonds; but then gone, too, the famous occasion when they led an unsuspecting group of weary walkers off the wrong side of Helvellyn!

The School absorbed Language Centre staff working in East Asian languages, attracting large numbers of East Asian students to a professional MA in Translating and Interpreting. The Centre for Research into Film was established, also running a successful MA, and attracting Research Council funds for a large project on film adaptations of the Carmen story. Similar funds were given for Colin Riordan's innovative work on nature and environment in modern German literature. This project, which investigated how German literature contributes to attempts to reconcile the conflicting demands of industrialization and the natural environment by reshaping conceptions and perceptions of nature, caught the mood of the 21st-century pre-occupation with human environmental impact, and showed the ways in which literature affects and is affected by global issues.

At the turn of the millennium, the very masculine bias evidenced by our opening paragraph, already mitigated by the fact that many more female students had been attracted to languages since the 1960s, was further mitigated by the appointment of three women professors: Florence Myles (French linguistics), Maíre Cross (19th-century French literature and gender), and Rosaleen Howard (Latin American language, ethnicity and gender). And the Eurocentric bias of languages, taught since the 19th century, has shifted as the School has opened out towards East Asian languages and cultures.

Phil Powrie

LAW

The first degree in Law offered by Armstrong College was the BCL (Bachelor of Civil Law), originating in the late 19th century. This was a second degree after an arts degree, for which no teaching was offered, the candidates being expected to get through the very wide syllabus by themselves. Records show that most candidates were clergymen. In the words of the late Professor D.W. Elliott, Head of Department and Dean of the Faculty of Law throughout the 1960s: 'Once an adequate stock of sermons for all occasions had been composed, [they] found that time hung heavy on their hands. The cure of souls in a country parish evidently did not provide mental roughage to prevent intellectual constipation, so they would amuse their declining years by studying law.'

Before 1922, there was no Department of Law either at Durham or at Newcastle, but there was a lecturer in Law in Armstrong College: Mr C.B. Fenwick, who later became a judge. He did not teach Law students – since BCL students received no tuition – but lectured on legal subjects to students of other faculties, such as Economics. By the Solicitors' Act 1922, one year's attendance at an approved law school was made compulsory for non-graduate articled clerks, and the Law Society subsidized this vocational law teaching. Armstrong College was approved for this purpose in 1923, and from that year onwards there has been a Department of Law at Newcastle, latterly known as the School of Law.

Bill Elliott, Head of Law 1960–89

Left: Newcastle Law Courts, where many Newcastle graduates have sat as judges or appeared as Counsel

Below: *The University's Law Library*

The first Head was Mr E.C.S. Wade, later Downing Professor of the Laws of England at Cambridge University and joint author with Godfrey Phillips of the classic *Constitutional Law*. He was assisted by a lecturer, in Accounting, and also by Dr John Charlesworth, later a county court judge, author of *Charlesworth on Negligence* – a practitioner's standard – and, later still, Chancellor of the Chancery Court of the Palatine of Durham. 'Dr John', as he was affectionately known, did not give up his lectureship until shortly before his death in 1957. Overlapping his final years of service were: J.B. Clark, a Chancery barrister of incisive intellect and great distinction, later to become Professor of Law and Head of Department in 1976, and editor of the classic *Theobald on Wills*; and E.J. Heath, a Roman Law specialist, who published *Torture as a Method of Proof*, a topic of some currency in recent times.

By this time Professor Charles Ryder was Head of Department. He is remembered for maintaining particular rigour in the teaching and assessment of students, whilst being scrupulously courteous to all. In 1960, he left for a post at University College London. He was replaced by Professor D.W. (Bill) Elliott, an academic of formidable intellect and presence, who had a profoundly beneficial influence on the standing and character of the Law Department through his exceptionally strong research in criminal law and his outstanding quality as a teacher. In 1963, two more formidable intellects joined: I.S. Stephenson and John Mickleburgh. Together, and with later colleagues such as J.D.R. Adams (now a circuit judge), the late Jim Stephens and Joan Mathesson (once affectionately dubbed by the students as 'the Bonnie from Clyde'), the Law Department staff earned tremendous respect from students.

In 1971, the flamboyant, unconventional and deeply clever Harry Calvert joined as the second Professor of Law, specializing in public law in various guises. His expertise on Northern Ireland's constitution led him to advise the Heath government at the famous

Sunningdale Conference on the future of the province. Calvert went to Cardiff in 1976 and was replaced by Professor Anthony Ogus, who was pioneering interdisciplinary research in law and economics and who introduced the BA in Law and Economics (later, the BA Accounting and Law). Ogus secured a major research project for the University on conciliation in family disputes. Bill Elliott retired in 1989, followed by J.B. Clark in 1992.

The 1990s saw a new breed of Professor of Law with Michael Purdue, Tim Frazer, Mark Thompson and Mike Allen. The School's research in areas such as environmental law, competition law, land law and criminal law was enhanced by the respective contributions of these professors. Frazer was the last Dean of Law when separate faculty status was withdrawn in 1995. Allen was Head of Department through a difficult six-year period in which funding was severely curtailed, but he maintained the collegiality for which Newcastle is still renowned today.

From 1923, Law teaching was offered to articled clerks in preparation for the Law Society's exams. Wade advocated the institution of a Law degree, and straight away ran into university politics in the form of a rival bid for Law Society funding from the Durham colleges. The Law Society refused to fund Law teaching at Durham, preferring to build on the Newcastle provision. University departments in those days were expected to pay their way, and without the Law Society's support Durham could not institute an LLB programme.

Despite setting up the LLB in 1925, it was not until 1928 that two students matriculated in the Faculty of Law: Messrs Alan and Baker duly passed their Finals in 1931. No further graduations occurred until 1935, when three men graduated. The poor enrolment was apparently due to a compulsory arts first year, making the degree four years long. The Law Department staff were nonetheless engaged with teaching the articled clerks, who, except in wartime, never fell below 30, until the course for them was finally wound up in 1962.

Rising numbers and some 15 years of operation led to the degree becoming an Honours degree just as the war broke out. In 1943, the entire graduate year were women, all four of them, but by 1947, the course was heavily taken up by ex-servicemen. There were about 40 undergraduates, 11 graduating that year. Graduating numbers steadily rose to around 35 in 1969, 50 in 1976 and 75 in the 1980s. They are now at 150 rising to 180.

Life in such a small faculty was apparently relaxed. For example, the minute book for 1930 contains a terse note to the effect that a Faculty Board Meeting was called at a set time, but as no one but the Dean turned up, the meeting could not be held. In 1923, the University Registrar convened a committee meeting in 'the Law Department, Armstrong College'. Wade wrote hurriedly back saying that the Law Department consisted of his room, and when he was in it with the door shut there certainly wasn't room for anyone else.

The list of premises occupied by the Law School is long. Starting in the Mathematics lecture rooms, and then the top of the tower of the Armstrong Building, the Department moved to the house in Eldon Place where Robert Stephenson lived, before he built the High Level Bridge; this is now demolished and Claremont Tower stands on the site. The School ousted the then Lord Bishop of Newcastle from his house in Kensington Terrace, only to be ousted by the Registrar. Bizarrely, there was a church, where the University Theatre now stands, which was used by the School as a lecture hall, with the pulpit as the lecturer's podium. The Percy Building became home for some years and, from 1968 to 1977, floors 9 and 10 of the Claremont Tower. Grand expansion plans took the School to Windsor Terrace, where it is still located with 23 staff and nearly 600 students, although a move back to the Armstrong Building is under consideration.

Ashley Wilton

Right: Mid-morning coffee break in the School of Art's entrance hall, *pen and ink drawing with watercolour by Hilary Williams 1957–61*

Below: The sculpture studio in the School of Art

FINE ART

It might be said that the place of an art school in a university lies 'in the uneasy seam between science-fact and space-fiction' (Reyner-Banham). The remarkable achievements of Fine Art at Newcastle have come in part from embracing such seeming contradictions to produce a fusion of scholarship and practice aimed at the rational exploration of the function and values of art.

The early history of what was to become the Edward VII School of Art and Design can be traced back to the far-sighted efforts of the North England Society for the Promotion of the Fine Arts to establish an art and design school in Newcastle in the 1830s. Then, as in the following century, the forms of British art education were moulded by an awareness of international cultural developments, and the prefatory notice to the Society's first exhibition signals a belief in the need for home institutions to rise to the challenge of progressive European models of practice: 'The originators of the Society had … felt the reproach that in England the taste of the public generally was inferior to that of our continental neighbours even with respect to high art, but more especially with regard to its application to manufactures.'

In 1839, in order to further their educational aims, the Society entered into discussions with the newly formed Council of the School of Design at Somerset House and the outcome, in 1842, was the appointment of the Pre-Raphaelite William Bell Scott as Master of the Newcastle School of Design. Over the next 20 years, Bell Scott struggled, against a background of local

ART SCHOOL REMEMBERED

BETTY HJERSING / ART / 1936–9

How good those years at the Art School were! We had such a wonderful time. We girls vying with each other with clothes we designed, and I even wove the tweed for one. We passed all our exams, in spite of sometimes skipping lectures for the 'flicks'.

There were Saturday hops, dances, glamorous balls, Rag Revue, *Union Sauce* (College newspaper and source of gossip). In the Union, we were segregated and met for coffee in the Bun Room in the basement, or tea in the refectory upstairs. The bar was for men only. Super toasted egg-and-tomato sandwiches upstairs were only 4d. Happy, happy days!

JEAN NICHOLSON / FINE ART / 1945–8

I went up to study Fine Art at Newcastle when I was 17, in 1945. It was a delight to me in every way. At the end of my first year, Professor Raine retired and Robin Darwin, grandson of Charles Darwin, arrived as Professor, straight from the Army. He had a large black moustache and drove an ancient Rolls Royce, which was delicately painted to look like wickerwork. We all swooned! After doing a stint in Newcastle, he went on to the Slade School of Art, and became very influential in the art world. He was terrific, starting off by calling all students together and telling us we were the most constipated group he had ever met. I have to say he was quite right!

JOHN A. WALKER / FINE ART / 1956–61

The fact that the University awarded a BA Hons degree in Fine Art was unusual at the time. The staff included some of the most prestigious names in British art: Lawrence Gowing, the Director, was a painter, scholar and curator; Victor Pasmore, the Master of Painting, was one of Britain's leading abstract, Constructivist artists; Richard Hamilton, his chief assistant, was a versatile artist, designer and intellectual, soon to become known as a 'father of Pop Art' (he later taught Bryan Ferry of Roxy Music fame), and three art historians: Quentin Bell (a direct link to the Bloomsbury Group), Ralph B. Holland and Ronald A. Davey. Altogether there were about 15 staff and 150 students.

The art education we received was predominantly influenced by modern art from Post-Impressionism onwards, but contained an unresolved mix of historic academic practices (such as life drawing and still-life painting) and modern practices (such as basic design). Much of the history of art taught was unrelated to making art and there was almost nothing on the profession of being an artist and the art business. During the late 1950s, there was also a powerful external influence – American Abstract Expressionism. There was little in the way of interdisciplinary contacts with other university subjects. The curriculum could have benefited from the inclusion of photography and film; nevertheless, it was probably one of the most progressive and sophisticated available in Britain at the time.

Margaret Clark and John Walker c.1959. They met at art school and married in Newcastle in 1961

A FRESHER IN THE FIFTIES

The Festival of Britain in 1951 was supposed to cheer us all up after years of wartime austerity: I attended the futuristic South Bank junketings just before making my way to Newcastle where - by the skin of my teeth - I had obtained a place in the Fine Art Department of King's College (precursor of Newcastle University). It was my first taste of independence and my first experience of living in the north-east which seemed an exciting place compared to my previous parental home in industrial south Yorkshire. Despite my sense of liberation, Tyneside still bore many signs of its wartime deprivations: rusty bridges; bombed-out vacant lots; draughty stray trams (from Gateshead?) still rattling laboriously through soot-blackened streets; many foods still rationed and cigarettes - especially cheap Woodbines in packets of 5 - obtainable only occasionally by favoured customers from 'under the counter'.

At the time of my arrival, the art school was undergoing a transition: Lawrence Gowing (a doyen of the pre-war Euston Road school) had recently been appointed professor and would soon replace the older guard of painting tutors like Roger de Grey and Christopher Cornford with some of his London contemporaries such as Victor Pasmore, Quentin Bell and - in due course - Richard Hamilton. Professor Gowing was a big, bear-like but inspired principal who was handicapped by a pronounced (and slavering) stutter. I remember on my first day at registration he proffered me his left hand in order to accept my entry documents. Misunderstanding the gesture, I grasped it warmly with my own left hand to give him a cordial shake. "Ne-ne-ne-NO!" he spluttered, "I only we-we-we-wanted your pe-pe-pe-PAPERS" - evidently anxious to deny any suggestion that a secret fraternal greeting was intended.

Despite his apparent cumbersomeness, he painted with great delicacy (and wrote several monographs in an equally perceptive and elegant style). At about that time he was undertaking a number of important portrait commissions. There was a story prevalent in the Fine Art Department (perhaps apocryphal?) that on one occasion he was painting the chairman of ICI who had driven up in his Rolls Royce from Billingham for a sitting. The professor volunteered to help him park the Roller somewhere near the Arches. As the captain of industry backed it into a suitable space, Lawrence shouted directions: "Come on-back-back-st-st-sT-ST-ST-ST-STOP!" he eventually exploded as the back-bumper crunched into the masonry.

In those days, first-year students alternated between weeks in the painting school, the design studio and in the subterranean sculpture department. The painting course initially consisted almost entirely of drawing and painting empty wine bottles. They were lined up, several rows deep, on trestle tables around the walls of the studio: one chose as interesting a group as presented itself then set about a somewhat monotonous still-life study. Very occasionally a tutor would look in to offer guidance or encouragement. Most of us used oil paints (acrylics had still to be introduced) and a heady smell of turpentine pervaded the building. At the end of each day, brushes were cleaned-off in a sludgy bucket of paraffin positioned near the exit. On one occasion Christopher Cornford accidentally stumbled backwards into one of these glutinous receptacles and Roger de Grey, passing the opened door, was heard to enquire in his immaculate Etonian drawl: "Oh, Chris, why on *earth* have you got your foot in that *filthy* bucket?"

Design was taught in the big room above the Arches under the general supervision of Leonard (Len) Evetts, a well-known ecclesiastical stained-glass maker and the author of a standard analysis of Trajan-column letter-forms. Much time was spent by us tyros cutting out little pieces of coloured paper to make collages resembling church windows or drafting Roman inscriptions in pencil. He had a particular propensity for pink, we discovered. Often he would lean over our handiwork saying: "I think a bit more pinky-winky wouldn't go amiss just here."

Down in the Stygian basement we modelled (and occasionally cast) small clay mannequins under the supervision of Murray McCheyne and his assistant Geoff Dudley.

I found it a cold, dispiriting place and always wore my scarf (the college one, naturally) as essential protection. Once, on one of his infrequent rounds, Mr McCheyne demanded: "Take off your muffler, laddie, and stop dropping y'sweetie papers a-roond" Objecting to the first instruction and denying the second (I couldn't afford sweets!) I ignored both - and abandoned sculpture as an option at the earliest opportunity.

We were a motley crew, the class of '51. I remember particularly Adrian Henri who was even then sizing-up the available crumpet - he went on to be a sensitive painter in the Gowing mould and a leading Merseyside poet; Ian Stephenson who became a senior Royal Academician (and whose work was featured in a Baltic two-person show in early 2006); Guernsey-man Richard leFeuvre who retired a few years ago as a faculty leader at the University of the South West; Derwent Wise who evidently enjoyed working in the catacombs a great deal more than I, since in due course he succeeded Murray McCheyne as the Department's Head of Sculpture; plus a quietly-spoken, amiable (and rich) Californian from Hollywood called Madison Win Han who told us his father was a 'Dentist to the Stars'. David Mercer was a year or two ahead of us and was already making a reputation as a writer. Another revered senior student was George Wall, generally regarded as an outstanding artist amongst his peers: after graduation he soon became Head of Painting at Coventry School of Art. These last two both died tragically young.

Most of the female intake were cloistered in the Ethel Williams Hall in Longbenton (all novices expected back to their rooms by 10.00 o'clock) but there were no equivalent places offered to newly-arrived male students, so most of us had to be consigned to boarding-houses in Whitley Bay. I remember handing over my ration book to the buxom, motherly Mrs Bishop who - as landlady - provided bed, breakfast and evening meal on weekdays and full board at weekends for (as I recall) a little under £15 a week. The food was plain but wholesome - but woe betide those who arrived late for meals! I shared lodgings with two other King's students (Marine Engineering and Science) plus a couple of permanently-resident elderly misfits who didn't seem to have a home of their own. The wizened Mr Bishop rarely appeared. Constantly coughing up phlegm, he crouched disconsolately over a stove in the kitchen - apparently victim of gassing during the First World War. Their tall Edwardian terrace-house was just off the promenade near Cullercoats. The baleful sound of the lighthouse foghorn - just round the corner - is indelibly linked in my memory of those early seaside years.

Segregated as we effectively were from female student company (it was a miserable three-quarter hour 'bus journey from Newcastle and we were required to return to the coast by 7.00 o'clock prompt for evening meals that we just couldn't afford to miss) the social life of we male scholars was severely restricted. Far from the glittering lights of Bigg Market and the fleshpot of the Union's Bun Room, we huddled in freezing garrets listening to jazz on wind-up gramophones or haunted the numerous costal cinemas (some of them fleapits with bench seats for 6d = 2½p) watching - warm and dry, at least - the flickering black-and-white images of other, more exotic, locations.

What did I learn during this first encounter with higher education? Mainly from more talented fellow-students, the limitations of my own creative abilities and the realization that I would need to garner what skills I could muster to scrape an eventual fair degree. Warm admiration of the indomitable Geordie spirit. A muffler-protected love of the windswept Northumbrian coastline. A keen enthusiasm for Vanbrugh's architecture - his (then) ruined and deserted masterpiece at Seaton Delaval (just up the coast) became a regular place of pilgrimage. A taste for of spam fritters and chips - then a gastronomic luxury for the impecunious but now almost impossible to find. And - despite the fleas - a lifelong devotion to the movies.

Michael Dawson, Ludford Mill, Ludlow, SY8 1PP - 2006

MICHAEL DAWSON / FINE ART / 1951–4, 1956–8

In those days, first-year students alternated between weeks in the painting school, the design studio and in the subterranean sculpture department. The painting course initially consisted almost entirely of drawing and painting empty wine bottles. They were lined up, several rows deep, on trestle tables around the walls of the studio. Very occasionally a tutor would look in to offer guidance. Most of us used oil paints (acrylics had still to be introduced), and a heady smell of turpentine pervaded the building. At the end of each day, brushes were cleaned off in a sludgy bucket of turps positioned near the exit. On one occasion Christopher Cornford accidentally stumbled backwards into one of these glutinous receptacles and Roger de Gray, passing the opened door, was heard to enquire in his immaculate Bloomsbury drawl: 'Oh, Chris, why on earth have you got your foot in that filthy bucket?'

Down in the Stygian basement we modelled (and occasionally cast) small clay mannequins under the supervision of McCheyne and his assistant Geoff Dudley. I found it a cold, dispiriting place and always wore my scarf (the College one, naturally) as essential protection. Once, on one of his infrequent rounds, Mr McCheyne demanded, 'Take off your muffler, laddie, and stop dropping y'sweetie papers!' Objecting to the first instruction and denying the second, I ignored both – and abandoned sculpture as an option at the earliest opportunity.

We were a motley crew, the class of 51. I remember particularly Adrian Henri who was even then weighing up the available crumpet – he went on to be a sensitive painter in the Gowing mould and a leading Merseyside poet; Ian Stephenson who became a senior Royal Academician. David Mercer was a year or two ahead of us and was already making a reputation as a writer.

What did I learn during this first encounter with higher education? Mainly from more talented fellow students, the limitations of my own creative abilities and the realization that I would need to garner what skills I could muster to scrape an eventual fair degree. Warm admiration of the indomitable Geordie spirit. A muffler-protected love of the windswept Northumbrian coastline. A profound appreciation of Sir John Vanbrugh's architecture – his (then) ruined and deserted masterpiece at Seaton Delaval just up the coast became a regular place of pilgrimage. A taste for spam fritters and chips – then a gastronomic luxury for the impecunious but now almost impossible to find. And – despite the fleas – a lifelong love of the movies.

Left: J.R.M. McCheyne, who was in charge of Sculpture, and Victor Pasmore, Master of Painting

Above: An art workshop in the School, 2004

parsimony and central government scepticism, to widen the scope of the School in a spirit of experiment and individuality, liberal ideas and general culture. That spirit survived into the 20th century with the School continuing to flourish as part of King's College, University of Durham.

The period of the 1950s and 60s saw the emergence of the Department of Fine Art as a major force in the art world. Those who were brought together to teach or who visited the Department first under Professor Lawrence Gowing and then under Professor Kenneth Rowntree included many of the most significant names in late 20th century art. Victor Pasmore and Richard Hamilton, who together provided the impetus for a dynamic revision of art education in England, were in company with Quentin Bell (who was on staff); David Hockney, Sydney Nolan and Joe Tilson, who exhibited at the Hatton and were visiting lecturers; Eduardo Paolozzi, who was an external examiner; and Terry Frost and Robert Medley who were Fellows of the School.

The Basic Design course developed by Pasmore and Hamilton had as its model the teaching of the Bauhaus, and their sense of the need for a response to European Modernism was complemented by their contacts with the post-war American avant-garde. One outcome of this internationalist thinking was the emergence of a generation of distinguished artists with a highly evolved and sophisticated understanding of the new art of the time. They included Noel Forster, Ian Stephenson, Roy Ascott, Mark Lancaster, Eric Cameron and Sean Scully.

Another aspect of Hamilton's commitment to the idea of a basic language of form was predicated on the belief in underlying consistencies in the material world. This sense of the relevance of natural science to the work of visual artists is evident in his extensive use of D'Arcy Thompson's *On Growth and Form* as a source for design exercises. Similar concerns are evident in the work of many contemporary artists who show an interest in genetic engineering and the structures of DNA, an area of continuing importance at Newcastle.

The range of intellectual disciplines with which visual artists have been engaged since the 1970s has generated an unprecedented range of practice. Debates in the fields of anthropology and psychology, as well as more generally in the area of cultural theory, are found in the work of Susan Hiller, the most recent distinguished practitioner to hold a Chair in Fine Art at Newcastle. Hiller's association with BALTIC – committed as it is to exhibiting the best of contemporary art – suggests that Fine Art's face is still determinedly turned outwards.

As new forms of expression proceed from interdisciplinary exploration, the future of Fine Art practice seems certain to reach out further to digital technology and the natural sciences. In the complex interdisciplinary world of today's universities, science-fact and space-fiction have never been closer partners.

Gavin Robson

Above: The School of Architecture

Above right: Planning and research take place in the Claremont Tower

THE SCHOOL OF ARCHITECTURE, PLANNING AND LANDSCAPE

The School of Architecture, Planning and Landscape (SAPL) was established in 1999 through the merger of the Department of Architecture and the Department of Town and Country Planning. Since then its mission has been 'to develop an inter-cultural and multi-disciplinary approach to creating and sustaining places which enhance the quality of life for the present and future generations'.

PIET RUTGERS

TOWN AND COUNTRY PLANNING / 1969–73

Professor Ian Melville had a unique way of teaching us about our environment: a series of field trips in the Tyne Valley under the heading 'Clues and Places'. The object of the exercise was for students to observe natural and manmade features and deduce why a farm, path, railway, hedgerow, stream, quarry or village was sited where it was and how it related to other aspects of the environment.

The format of the trips was an early morning bus ride from Newcastle into the valley; at designated points we would disembark, one at a time, with a route map, hand drawn by Professor Melville. For the next five to six hours we would simply walk the route through fields, farms, villages, woodlands and make copious notes and sketches of what we observed. At the end of the day the bus would materialize in a village square or at a designated pub. The next week's classes would be devoted to student presentations and discussions about the what, where and how of the land-use pattern of the Tyne Valley.

In following this mission, the School has become an internationally renowned centre of excellence in the field of the built environment. SAPL has consistently striven to be a major player in research, teaching and consultancy, capitalizing on the unique juxtaposition of its main areas of interest: architecture, town and country planning, landscape and urban design. Amongst the common themes that link them are: a focus on the built environment, the professional nature of many of its taught programmes, and the theoretical, philosophical and policy orientation of its research.

Although Architecture was taught in the University throughout the inter-war period, the Department of Architecture was not created until 1938, with the first Chair of Architecture being established in 1943. Its first incumbent was Wilfrid Bythell Edwards. A part-time course in Town and Country Planning had been offered in the Department of Architecture, but a new Department of Town and Country Planning was created in 1946. The first chair was held by Jo Allen, who had previously been the Head of the School of Architecture at Leeds. From 1951, Landscape courses were developed within the Department of Town and Country Planning. This initiative was led by Brian Hackett, later Professor of Landscape Architecture.

In more recent times, effective links between the two departments started in the 1980s with the introduction of a 'fast-track' route, allowing BArch students to take the postgraduate Planning degree, and thus become dually

The Architecture Design Project (above) and the Planning Consultancy Project (left)

qualified as architects and planners. In the early 1990s, the MA Urban Design (MAUD) degree was developed, drawing on the expertise of staff in both departments.

RESEARCH

Great care has been taken to create an environment in which research can prosper because of its importance for academic standing and income generation. For the next Research Assessment Exercise in 2008, the aim is to improve upon the high degree of success that was achieved in 2001, when Landscape was graded 5*, Planning 5 and Architecture 4.

SIR TERRY FARRELL

ARCHITECTURE / 1956–61

I came to Newcastle in 1956. The Architecture Department then had 150 students. I gather that this is now the number of students in the first year – and that the intake is 50% female. There was only one woman in the whole School when I was there. However, Alison Smithson was at Newcastle before me, and of course with her husband, Peter (also an alumnus of Newcastle), went on to become very well established.

The playwright Alan Plater was also studying Architecture with us. Each year had to put on a sketch and compete with the other years and there was a prize for the best act. In the first year I organized ours – it was a spoof of a TV detective series and I think Alan Plater acted in it. We won a couple of bottles of whisky.

Research is organized through a number of research groupings: Global Urban Research Unit (GURU), Tectonic Cultures Research Group (TCRG), Centre for Environmental Appraisal and Management (CREAM), Landscape Research Group (LRG) and Applied Research in Architecture (ARA). Although each member of academic staff is associated primarily with one group, movement between groups is encouraged in order to take account of emerging research agendas and to capitalize on funding opportunities.

Research also benefits from its connections with some of the University's new research institutes, bringing together researchers from different schools to work on larger projects. SAPL has links with the Institute for Public Policy (IPP), the Institute for Research on Environment and Sustainability (IRES), the Newcastle Institute for Arts, Social Sciences and Humanities (NIASSH), the Informatics Research Institute (IRI) and the Institute for Ageing and Health (IAH). These links demonstrate the breadth and relevance of the School's research.

The School operates a sabbatical policy of up to six months, when academic staff can devote their time to developing new ideas, seeking funding as well as writing and publishing. Equally, staff are encouraged to apply for fellowships that can give them longer periods of time to dedicate to research.

Research is one of the cornerstones of the School, but does not exist in isolation from other activities. SAPL has fully embraced the University's policy of 'teaching being informed by research'. At both undergraduate and postgraduate levels, every effort is made to introduce the results of both theoretical and applied research into the taught programmes. Consultancy work can also benefit from research. Growing professional and public awareness of the quality and range of research has resulted in the School being approached to undertake specific commissions in this country and other parts of the world. These include town centre management (linked to the School's Market Towns research), a visitor perception survey for the Northumberland National Park (linked to the research of CREAM), the appraisal of government-funded initiatives at the local level and the reconstruction of Iraqi cities (both linked to the research of GURU).

The School has one of the largest groups of doctoral students in the University. In 2004, it reached a peak of 110. The students are drawn from many parts of the

The design studio for SAPL postgraduates

Institute (RTPI). Other degree programmes have a strong relationship with the built environment professions, for example the MA in Urban Design and MSc in Digital Architecture.

Although the professional bodies provide a framework for the development of degree programmes, the School has its own Teaching and Learning Committee that responds to directives issued by the Faculty and University. It also has links to QUILT (the body responsible for 'Quality in Teaching and Learning' within the University).

At the present time, there are 1,004 students registered on undergraduate and postgraduate programmes. This number is likely to grow as the University expands, and every measure possible is being taken to maintain an effective staff–student ratio. The School has a budget for bringing in professional expertise to supplement what is available from the permanent staff. In this way students can be assured of receiving the strongest grounding in both theory and practice.

The School has a strategy to maintain and develop its strong tradition of professional education. Through the boards of studies, end-of-year reviews, feedback from external examiners and local advisory boards, every effort is made to keep the content of degree programmes relevant to the professional arenas in which students will operate. Given the ever-changing nature of professional work environments, the guiding pedagogic principles remain 'knowledge, understanding, skills and ethics'.

globe, including South-East Asia, the Indian subcontinent, Africa and the Middle East, as well as some from the UK and Europe. The quality of published research and the engagement with overseas research have contributed to the School's reputation and encouraged students from other countries to pursue their doctoral studies here. This international mix of students adds to the dynamic research environment in SAPL.

The School's research seminar programme is open to both academic staff and research students. The lively debate that these seminars generate has done much to help integrate students into the School's research environment and heighten awareness of the variety of work being undertaken. Current PhD topics include: sustainable urban form and accessibility; urban sustainability and renewable energy technologies; urban spaces in a contemporary urban environment – urban design approach for Saudi cities; landscape planning and environmental control in hot arid cities; hospital planning – the role of planning guidelines and norms; the visible and invisible heritage in historical areas of Mexico.

The School offers a wide range of undergraduate and postgraduate taught degrees, many of which are accredited by professional bodies. The School has had a long association with: Architects Registration Board (ARB), Royal Institute of British Architects (RIBA), Institute for Historic Building Conservation (IHBC), Landscape Institute (LI) and Royal Town Planning

THIRD STRAND

Since its reorganization in 2002, the University has developed a more proactive approach to generating income through consultancy work. SAPL's contribution to this is based on its research and professional practice expertise. To date, this has included work for private clients, government-related bodies, such as the Countryside Agency, contributions to national panels of enquiry and the development of partnerships with external practices. This provides a rich source of information to feed into teaching and research.

Of particular importance is the *Journal of Environmental Planning and Management* (JEPM), which is owned by the School and edited in house. It evolved from its predecessor *Planning Outlook*, but, under the editorship of Professor John Benson (who sadly died in 2004), it blossomed into an internationally acclaimed publication that generates substantial income for the

School. JEPM is one of a number of journals edited in the School: *Planning Theory, Landscape Research* and the e-journal *Surveillance and Society*.

Although there has to be a balance between the time devoted to consultancy, teaching and research, Third Strand activity does provide a valuable source of income that can be reinvested in the School. It has provided money for new teaching posts, investment in IT, the retention of staff on short-term contracts and support for ongoing research.

New Horizons

Internationalization lies at the heart of the School's vision for the future. As part of an ongoing strategy to position itself globally, it is investing heavily in the promotion and delivery of high-quality teaching, research and consultancy, often in partnership with other universities, government bodies and private organizations.

Built environment disciplines have much to gain from participating in the wider world. Degree programmes that draw on the experiences of other countries will be better informed and offer more challenges for students. Equally, the development of international networks will enhance the quality and relevance of research.

The international profile of the academic staff has been transformed in recent years. Seventeen are drawn from other parts of Europe (Belgium, Finland, France, Italy, Spain), Africa (Kenya, Sierra Leone, South Africa), Asia (Iran, Pakistan, Turkey), Australia and the United States. These staff are exerting an important influence on the development of existing and new degree programmes, as well as bringing new perspectives to research.

SAPL has an ambitious recruitment policy. Working with the University's International Office and its agents, staff are visiting overseas countries and meeting with potential students. School publicity, including its website, is updated on a regular basis, and a virtual open day will soon be available via the Web and on CD-Rom. A new degree programme, MSc Architecture, designed for the overseas market, was introduced in 2005/6 and a new research Master's degree, reflecting the research work of the Tectonic Cultures Research Group, is being developed with a target market that includes Europe and North America.

The School is also committed to recruiting home-grown, high-achieving undergraduate and postgraduate students for both taught and research degrees. The aim is

to have a blend of home and overseas students; a mixture of different cultures, traditions and ideas to create a stimulating academic environment, while providing the best long-term publicity about the quality of the learning environment: word of mouth.

Reputation and relevance are central to the future prosperity of SAPL. Reputation is based on the quality of its activities in teaching, research and consultancy. New business will be generated as a result of published work and the plaudits of former students and clients. The measure of the School's future success will be its ability to deliver well-educated students to the built environment professions, and the relevance of its research and consultancy work to government, agencies, academe and clients at home and abroad.

Tim Shaw

Architectural students sketching at Tynemouth railway station

*St Paul's Girls School
W6
March 6*

*Dear Whittaker
I was too overwhelmed by the singing of your Bach Choir to thank them properly so I write to ask you to do so for me.
I did not know before that so small a body of voices could produce such a wonderful volume of tone. But this is only one of their many virtues. Even more important is their clearness of diction and beautiful quality. But my greatest delight was in their flexibility which rivalled that of a first rate orchestra – I know no other body of singers who equal them in this.
Accept my warmest congratulations and thanks and ask them to do the same.
Yrs Ever
Gustav Holst*

Top: A letter from Gustav Holst to Whittaker, praising the Bach choir

Above: Programmes from the Bach Choir performances

Left: William Gillies Whittaker, who founded The Bach Choir in 1915

MUSIC

Music has played a vital part in the life of the University for over 100 years. The first in a long line of distinguished teachers and scholars was Charles Sanford Terry, who joined the staff of the College of Physical Science in 1890 as Lecturer in History, contributing to the musical training of teachers and directing the newly established College Choral Society. The Society's third annual concert on 1 June 1895 included W.G. Whittaker at the organ (he was a student in the early 1890s) and the musicologist and composer Sir John Stainer in the audience. According to *The Musical Times*: 'This excellent Society can show a good record of earnest and artistic work … unaccompanied songs were sung with real delicacy and artistic refinement. The band numbered 40 performers, and the chorus consisted of about 100 voices, a proportion of vocal and instrumental that is not always attained by similar societies.'

When Terry moved to Aberdeen in 1898, he was replaced by his lifelong friend and fellow Bach scholar William Gillies Whittaker. According to C.E. Whiting in *The University of Durham* 1832–1932, Music at Newcastle 'is almost entirely due to the work of Dr W.G. Whittaker … Owing to his training, the Armstrong College Choral Society has been able to attack very successfully what might otherwise have been considered very ambitious programmes.'

One of Whittaker's most important contributions was the founding of the Newcastle Bach Choir in 1915, which rapidly acquired a national reputation, not only for its pioneering performances of Bach, but for its championship of other British music. Whittaker was on friendly terms with many leading composers, including Holst, Vaughan Williams, Bax and Howells. A highlight of this period was the Choir's acclaimed German tour of 1927, including several performances of Whittaker's own challenging setting of Psalm 139.

The Great War had an impact on the College Choral Society, but numbers rose rapidly after it ended, and 1920 saw the inauguration of a College orchestra. Programmes normally ended with a couple of Whittaker's renowned folksong arrangements, followed by Terry's setting of the College Song, *Carmen Novocastrense*.

Whittaker was supported by another fine musician, W. Henry Hadow, who, as Principal of Armstrong College from 1909 to 1919, was anxious to improve the status of Music within a science-based college. Whittaker eventually left in 1929 to become Gardiner Professor of Music at Glasgow and Principal of the Scottish National Academy of Music. He was replaced, after the brief temporary appointment of Patrick Hadley, by Sidney Newman, described by the *North Mail* as 'fair-haired and slightly chubby … He speaks in public very diffidently but writes on music authoritatively'. Newman was, like his predecessor, a demanding choral director, who, in rehearsals, would often ask choir members to sing their line on their own!

Newman also left to take up a Scottish chair, this time as Reid Professor at Edinburgh, and he was replaced at King's College in 1941 by the distinguished musicologist Jack Westrup. Although his period at Newcastle was short, leaving in 1944 to take up chairs first at Birmingham and then Oxford, he made his mark as a warm, enthusiastic teacher. His successor for nearly 30 years was Chalmers Burns, who had worked with Whittaker at Glasgow and had studied conducting under Sir Henry Wood. Chalmers oversaw the introduction of the BA

The Gilbert and Sullivan Society's production of 'Ruddigore' in 1959–60

Honours course in Music in 1948; he fostered a regular series of chamber music concerts and frequent visits by members of the Dolmetsch family, the famous musicians and instrument-makers, with whom he was closely associated.

Denis Matthews, appointed to the first Chair of Music in 1971

As an orchestral conductor, Chalmers was a great Brahms enthusiast. Mike Smith, who led the second violins in the University Orchestra from 1958 to 1961, recalls performing most of the symphonies, and also the Requiem in which, at one stage, he was the only viola – quite a challenge as the violas are divided for much of the work! Rehearsals always began with Chalmers tucking his long hair behind his ears and hitching up his trousers. In those days some instruments, especially the brass, were often missing; performances frequently ground to a halt – usually a cue for the conductor to turn round and address the audience. Derek Downes led the orchestra for the Gilbert and Sullivan Society, founded in the early 50s, whose Saturday afternoon performances on a makeshift stage in Kings Hall brought out the local landladies in strength in a magnificent array of headgear.

In the early 1960s, when the Music Department was based in the Old Assembly Rooms on Kings Walk, there were just ten students and three lecturers in the

*Music students using the modern,
well-equipped recording studio*

Department – a far cry from our current annual intake of 90 undergraduates, plus numerous postgraduates.

Throughout the first 80 years of Music at Newcastle there had been no professor. This changed in 1971 with the appointment of Denis Matthews to the first Chair of Music, something that the then Vice-Chancellor, Henry Miller, regarded as his greatest achievement. Denis had a fine career as a concert pianist, but no formal academic credentials; he was, however, a brilliant lecturer, provided of course that he was within a few feet of a piano, preferably the ornate Steinway, originally built for an ocean liner, that lived in his room in the Armstrong Building. Those who were lucky enough to hear Denis's renowned public lectures will understand why his inaugural lecture had to be repeated by popular demand. He had a wonderful turn of phrase, but it was his ability to play a vast range of music, including long chunks of the Ring cycle, from memory that was quite awe-inspiring.

The 1980s were a turbulent time for Music at Newcastle. Reduced university funding led to a proposal that the teaching of Music should be discontinued. The Vice-Chancellor was inundated with protest letters from 'Disgusted of Gosforth' and the Department survived.

Denis Matthews had placed practical music-making firmly within the curriculum, but now the theoretical importance of music within its cultural context became central to the Department's teaching, while the appointment of Richard Middleton to the Chair of Music, in 1998, heralded a broadening of the music studied and a massive expansion of both staff and student numbers. New degree programmes were developed in Popular and Contemporary Music and in Folk and Traditional Music, the latter one of the many areas of collaboration with The Sage Gateshead. The International Centre for Music Studies, as the Department is now called, has just led a successful collaborative bid to become a Centre for Excellence in Teaching and Learning in Music and Inclusivity. This involves £4.5m funding over five years, allowing us to enlarge accommodation and expand the curriculum. Now with some 300 students studying a comprehensive mix of musical styles and genres, it is a far cry from W.G. Whittaker's one-man show, yet he would still recognize the important contribution of the University to the vibrant musical life of the North East.

Eric Cross

THE BUSINESS SCHOOL

The 'new' Newcastle University I joined in 1967 as an Economics lecturer was of course a much older establishment, but recent construction was giving it a new feel, just as the old buildings still provided a sense of history. I vividly recall the formidable interview panel in Kensington Terrace, presided over by a larger than life Vice-Chancellor Bosanquet. From all the disciplines represented, it is historians Norman McCord and future Mastermind star Joan Taylor I remember, and I suspect my fascination with history may have helped me more than my Economics.

The top of the new Claremont Tower, with its unforgettable views over Newcastle, housed the 'business school' subjects of Economics and Accounting. It was formally opened in 1968 by Lord Chancellor Gardiner. An alumnus of that time and now Australia's Foreign Minister, Alexander Downer, made a nostalgic return to the Tower in May 2001, following the conferral of his honorary Doctor of Civil Laws. He recalled with pleasure his early days in the new Tower as a BA Economic Studies undergraduate. Switching to Honours registration had to be worked for in those days, and he later qualified for Honours Politics and Economics. His visit in 2001 just caught the end of an era, since Economics was soon to cede its favoured location to Computing Science and its departmental independence to a unified Business School.

In the late 1960s, the Department of Economics was headed by Stanley Dennison CBE, who had succeeded Sir Daniel Jack in the David Dale Chair. This commemoration of David Dale, an 18th-century reforming industrialist, aptly reflected the business orientation of post-war academic Economics. Both Jack's and Dennison's official honours recognized their contributions to planning for the industrial renewal of Britain and its regions. Sir Daniel had also promoted Accounting as a respectable academic pursuit. The Department had its own embryonic 'business school' – evening classes for local business leaders and an annual residential course at Lumley Castle. Business economist Gwyn Watkin and accountant Frank Nolan, newly recruited from industry, carefully cultivated these roots in the local economy.

Lecturers were supposed to wear a formal black gown for lecturing, but the 60s' informality soon won out, leaving only the highly respected Senior Lecturer, Krzysztof Zawadzki, to uphold tradition. Formality in

addressing students as Mr or Miss did not survive long either, although it was still an exceptional privilege to attend university. Classes were small, and it was possible to entertain one's few tutees privately on a departmental expense account.

Professor Dennison moved to Hull as Vice-Chancellor and was succeeded by Charles Rowley. His expansionist policy in the 1970s multiplied staff and student numbers for Accounting as well as Economics. BA Economics and Accounting attracted more of both sexes as the accountancy profession increasingly allowed women to preside over its mysteries. Accounting eventually outgrew its Economics parentage to become a sizeable independent department.

The 1980s were the decade of the third strand, management teaching. Distinguished alumnus Sir George Russell of Alcan (and later the Independent Television Authority and Camelot) secured his company's endowment of a Chair in Business Management. However, the Alcan Chair went to Mechanical Engineering rather than Economics, with Colin Gallagher its first holder. Aspiring engineers

Top left: A student, Jane Waller, with the project she did with Marks and Spencer

Top: Alexander Downer receiving his honorary doctorate

Above: Students in the foyer of the Newcastle School of Management

needed broader academic training to satisfy professional accreditation. Professor Gallagher and his expanding group introduced the first part-time Master's in Business Administration (MBA) programme for practising managers in north-east England, following soon with a full-time MBA and Master's programme in Human Resource Management. Strong links with local engineering also saw Tom McGovern, in Continuing Education, create an MBA course primarily for Northern Engineering Industries, later absorbed by Rolls-Royce. Meanwhile in Economics, Senior Lecturer and labour relations expert, Charles Hanson, introduced a BA in Economics and Business Management, drawing on the growing expertise in management studies and incorporating a sandwich year for practical business experience, something that has proved enormously rewarding for students. Local stockbroker Nigel Sherlock (an honorary alumnus) helped persuade local business managers to co-operate, adding to his many services to the University and the region.

The 1990s witnessed a merry dance with partners forming and re-forming. The management team moved from Engineering to Social Sciences. Accounting and Management were joined for a time under Professor Gallagher. New degrees in Business Management and

The Trade Globe on the Newcastle quayside celebrates Newcastle's trading links with Europe – links which are maintained through graduates of the Business School

International Business Management were created. Accounting, Management and Economics re-formed briefly under Ashley Wilton. The subjects separated once more, with Accounting led by Tony Appleyard and the Newcastle School of Management formed under its first Director, local industrialist (and alumnus) Roger Vaughan. This School cultivated multidisciplinary links across the University and outside, and collaboration in particular with a leading French business school, the École Supérieure de Commerce at Grenoble, would later give birth to a joint international Doctorate in Business Administration (DBA) programme.

The restless dance proved creative. Research activity flourished alongside teaching. Accounting investigated topical issues such as accounting rules during inflation and developments in finance, with market-based accounting research and accounting history added later. The Centre for the Analysis of Safety Policy and Attitudes to Risk gave Economics under Michael Jones-Lee a high research profile. Health economics research was added, with Cam Donaldson in a new Chair, created jointly with the Medical School and endowed by the Health Foundation. Management research has built on close connections to business, particularly in human resources and business organization, and on its multidisciplinary links. Business Innovation is now recognized by a chair, endowed in memory of David Goldman, local co-founder of Sage plc (Newcastle's world leader in accounting software, well known also for endowing The Sage Gateshead music centre), and occupied by David Charles.

The dance continued into the new millennium with University policy insisting on forming more inclusive schools. The traditional strands and some other threads were entwined to create the University of Newcastle upon Tyne Business School. Professor Ian McLoughlin, the existing Head of Management, became its Director. He has responsibility for balancing the interests of the different but complementary disciplines to ensure a promising future for a large and expanding group of undergraduates, postgraduates and academic staff. The School's stated mission emphasizes building on a strong research base, developing existing and new taught postgraduate courses and contributing to local and national enterprise culture. Plans are well advanced for a new Business School building, which will unify the disciplines in a more physical way.

Ivan Weir

ARCHAEOLOGY

Archaeology first developed in north-east England outside any formal university structure. Given the proximity of Hadrian's Wall and other Roman sites, it was not surprising that, in 1813, Newcastle acquired the first antiquarian society outside London and that its members soon became active in Wall studies and similar activities. However, it was not until well into the 20th century that the University of Durham became formally involved in archaeological teaching and research.

In 1933, Eric Birley was appointed to a lectureship, teaching in both Durham and Newcastle, before becoming fixed at Durham. Ian Richmond came to Newcastle as a lecturer in 1935 and, during the 21 years he remained there, King's College's archaeological interests continued to expand, achieving a distinction remarkable in view of the limited resources which the subject deployed in those early years. In his twenties, Richmond had already become a scholar of high repute, partly because of his major study *The City Wall of Imperial Rome*, still a standard work. To wide knowledge of Roman history, he added insight and technical ability in excavation. In both speaking and writing, he was a stylist of distinction; he was also a brilliant teacher. During his Newcastle years, he consolidated an international reputation as one of that generation's leading archaeologists, recognized by the conferment of a personal chair in 1950. When, in 1956, Oxford created a chair in the Archaeology of the Roman Empire, it was widely suspected that one motive was to entice Richmond from Newcastle. He became the first holder of that post, and was knighted in 1964.

In 1948, a Durham graduate, John Gillam, joined the Classics Department, where he eventually succeeded Richmond in the established readership in

Roman-British History and Archaeology. He carried out important excavations in the region, and his pioneer work on Romano-British pottery greatly widened the usefulness of dating evidence from this source. In the Extra-Mural Department, an ex-pupil in a local grammar school and another pre-war Durham graduate, George Jobey, after a distinguished war record with the Durham Light Infantry, complemented the Roman work of Richmond and Gillam by introducing for the first time a credible and systematic sequence into our knowledge of the early native societies of north-east England. This involved a prolonged and skilfully planned campaign of fieldwork coupled with selective excavation. Despite ludicrous underfunding, this was achieved by his success in welding together a team of volunteers, from many different origins, into an archaeological team with few, if any, equals in the Britain of those years.

During the post-war years, Durham and Newcastle archaeologists co-operated in running an annual summer course in Archaeology, based on the Roman site at Corbridge and providing practical training of a high order in excavation and the treatment of finds. This attracted many students from universities at home and abroad. Some of those who benefited from 'the circus', as it was affectionately called, went on to distinguished careers in archaeology.

In these early years, the nature of the College helped to facilitate progress in archaeology. It was a comparatively small institution, which made easier interdepartmental and even inter-faculty co-operation based on personal contacts among academic staff. This

Top: The Romano-British site at Burradon

Above: *George Jobey, who did important work on early native societies of the North East*

Left: *John Gillam excavating in Libya*

Ian Richmond outside the Erechtheion in Athens. He taught at Newcastle, 1935–56

practice, once established, continued in later years and allowed the fledgling discipline to work more effectively than its own small staff could have achieved alone. Examples of colleagues enlisted in this way included staff from Surveying (Commander Fryer), Metallurgy (Ronald Tylecote), Botany (Kathleen Blackburn), History (Norman McCord), Architecture (Barbara Harbottle) and Dentistry (Joan Weyman). Archaeology also managed to acquire a substantial number of the open research fellowships awarded by the University in these years; the holders of these temporary posts included a number of scholars who went on to successful careers in various fields of archaeology, including Michael Jarrett, Tim Potter, Paul Mellars and David Ridgway.

The number of professional archaeologists on the staff grew slowly. Colin Burgess joined Jobey in Extra-Mural Studies, extending prehistoric work, with a particular interest in Bronze Age metalwork. The creation of the Joint Museum of Antiquities in 1960, in

which the University housed the magnificent collection accumulated over two centuries by the Society of Antiquaries, provided additional team members during the following years (David Smith, Charles Daniels, Jock Tait, Lindsay Allason-Jones). David Smith, an authority on Roman mosaics, and Charles Daniels, who carried out research into Mithraism, apart from other interests, extended the University's archaeological activity by conducting excavations in Roman North Africa. Jock Tait produced a standard account of an important type of prehistoric pottery from Northumberland. Lindsay Allason-Jones, whose research interests include Roman glass and women in Roman Britain, is now in charge of the University's Archaeological Museums and much involved in the establishment of the Great North Museum. From the Department of Classics, Brian Shefton assembled from 1955 a remarkable collection of artefacts in the Greek Museum. From 1964, Martin Harrison, also in Classics, introduced Byzantine studies. Anglo-Saxon archaeology made a belated appearance with the appointment of Richard Bailey to the School of English in 1966.

By the early 1970s, the diverse archaeological activity that had developed within the University strengthened the case for a new structure. A Department of Archaeology was created, with Harrison, Gillam, Jobey, Smith and Daniels providing its initial staff. The new department could organize teaching and research in Archaeology more efficiently, but its creation did not involve the abandonment of the interdepartmental co-operation that had been so useful in the discipline's formative years. The Newcastle Department of Archaeology continued to teach increasing numbers of undergraduate and postgraduate students, while its research interests included a rich diversity of excavations and other activities. In the mid-1980s its staff were working not only in such staple fields as prehistoric Northumberland and Hadrian's Wall, but also in projects involving Italy, Yugoslavia, Hungary, Turkey, Sudan and Roman North Africa. In the University's recent major reorganization, the Department joined Classics and History in the new School of Historical Studies, a significant shift in organization implemented so smoothly as to offer an optimistic picture of Archaeology's future role within the University.

Norman McCord

91

04

Faculty of Medical Sciences

THE MEDICAL SCHOOL:
FROM THE SECOND WORLD WAR TO 1980

The University of Durham Act 1935 established King's College out of Armstrong College and the College of Medicine. The office of Dean of Medicine was created, with duties defined by statute, and R.B. Green, Professor of Anatomy, was appointed in 1937. In that year, the Dental School, housed within the grounds of the Royal Victoria Infirmary (RVI), became the dental division of the Medical School, led by Professor R.V. Bradlaw. The national Goodenough Committee on Medical and Dental Education noted that the Newcastle Medical School had an entry of 50 before the war, but recommended that it should aim at an intake of 100.

In 1942, with funding from the Nuffield Provincial Hospitals Trust, the first full-time Chair in Child Health in the UK was established in Newcastle, and J.C. Spence was appointed. In 1944, F.J. Nattrass, formerly physician to the RVI, became the first full-time Professor of Medicine. F.C. Pybus became Professor of Surgery, as did John Hamilton Barclay, but the first full-time Chair in Surgery was established in 1945; F.H. Bentley was appointed. The Professors of Obstetrics and Gynaecology, however, continued to practise part time; they were Farquhar Murray, 1935–51, and subsequently Harvey Evers. Full-time chairs were established in Psychological Medicine (Alexander Kennedy), in Anaesthetics (E.A. Pask) in 1949, and in Industrial Health (R.C. Browne) in 1945.

In the 1940s, the curriculum was traditional, with five terms of Anatomy and Physiology, including histology, culminating in the fearsome second MB examination, which had to be passed before one could proceed to three years of clinical training in the RVI.

In the Medical School in wartime, service in the Senior Training Corps was compulsory for all physically fit male medical students, who undertook firewatching duties in rotation, as well as military training, first for Infantry Certificate A, and later for Medical Certificate B in the Medical Unit. The latter was

Left: James Spence, who held the first Chair in Child Health in the UK at Newcastle

Above: Firewatching poster from World War II

Right: The Medical School showing the David Shaw Lecture theatre over the entrance

organized as a field ambulance, available to support, in the event of an invasion, the 51st Scottish Division, stationed in Northumberland. The Dean was Commanding Officer (Lt Col).

As no one then appreciated the health hazards of smoking, the anatomists, led by the Dean and Professor John Short, recommended that students smoke in the dissecting room to suppress the odours, and Professor David Burns and Dr Secker of Physiology also recommended smoking through their lectures and laboratory classes.

After passing the second MB, the students faced teaching in Pharmacology and *materia medica* and the Pathology teaching of Professor Arthur Frederick Bernard Shaw, who, when asked if he was any relation to *the* Bernard Shaw, would reply, 'I am *the* Bernard Shaw!' (In fact, George Bernard Shaw was his uncle). Microbiology was taught by Professor Ernest Dunlop and Alan Emslie-Smith, while lectures in clinical subjects and clinical teaching on the wards and in outpatients were provided by Professor Nattrass, whose teaching was a model of clarity; Dr C.N. (Natty) Armstrong, a world expert on intersex; Charles Ungley, a world expert on pernicious anaemia; Dr Alan Ogilvie; Dr Tom Boon, an expert on blood transfusion, and Dr R.B. Thompson, an international expert in haematology. Alan Ogilvie was a charming, if eccentric and forgetful physician, whose fierce percussion of the chest was unforgettable. The teaching of Professor Spence (later Sir James) was compelling, sometimes electrifying, and his colleagues, such as Freddy Miller and Donald Court also enlivened Paediatrics. In Obstetrics and Gynaecology, the dogmatic Farquhar Murray was succeeded by the flamboyant Harvey Evers, whose elegance of dress and behaviour was matched by the beautifully organized content of his lectures.

In clinical training, each student was required to deliver 20 babies prior to qualification; some were undertaken at the Princess Mary Maternity Hospital, where, because of the lack of qualified medical staff, all anaesthetics for forceps deliveries, and even for caesarean sections, were given by students. Some obstetric experience was gained by students at the Newcastle General Hospital under Linton Snaith and Dorothea Kerslake. Because of the shortage of qualified medical staff in the RVI, many students undertook House Officer appointments before graduating in a shortened wartime course in 1945.

PROFESSOR JOHN ROBSON MBBS

FIREWATCHING AT NEWCASTLE / 1939–45

I am hastening to report that I was one of the fearless who firewatched at the Medical School. I wish I could expand at length on our boldness under enemy fire, but I must confess that my group took their 3/6d and squandered it in carousing in the 'Twigs' (aka the Crows Nest) and the Dun Cow. I believe that neither of these exists any longer so it will not be possible to document our contributions as recorded on the Gents Room walls.

The new College of Medicine (now the King George VI Building) was opened by King George VI and Queen Elizabeth in 1939. It was not designed to include accommodation for clinical subjects, as it was then believed that all clinical activities and related research should be conducted in hospital. Subsequently, as academic departments developed, laboratory accommodation, often ad hoc and sometimes newly built, was created in the Newcastle hospitals so as to accommodate the research needs of the burgeoning departments. The number of medical students admitted annually was soon 100, and it became clear to leaders, such as Drs George Smart and Henry Miller, and Professor Donald Court (who followed James Spence) that the undergraduate curriculum was in need of change.

Harvey Evers, who lectured on Gynaecology

The Medical Faculty therefore established a Curriculum Review Committee which, in 1962, introduced an integrated curriculum with early clinical exposure for new medical students during their study of the basic medical sciences. Teaching was organized on a system and topic basis, with vertical integration between, for example, the structure and function of individual bodily organs and systems along with the pathological changes resulting from disease and the resultant clinical manifestations. This type of curriculum, pioneered in Case Western Reserve University in the US, gradually spread to other UK medical schools, but Newcastle was in the forefront, and yet further integration took place some ten years later.

Funding for medical education from the University Grants Committee (UGC) was then earmarked in the annual University grant and was distributed to individual Medical School departments according to a well-recognized formula, with some flexibility to take account of research and teaching achievement. On becoming Dean in 1971, John Walton found that the statutes of the University relating to the deanship had remained unchanged from the Durham original, even though Newcastle had become a free-standing independent university in 1963. These statutes stated: 'The spending authority for the Faculty of Medicine shall be the Dean and the planning committee for the Faculty of Medicine shall be the Dean.' These massive responsibilities were such that John Walton decided to establish a Dean's Advisory Committee to assist in disbursing funds to the Medical School Departments.

Soon, new specialties began to emerge in addition to general medicine, surgery, obstetrics and gynaecology, child health and psychiatry, which were among the earliest to be recognized by the University. An increasing clamour grew to recognize sub-specialties such as cardiology, gastroenterology, neurology, endocrinology and others. As UGC funds would not be increased unless student numbers rose, in 1972 the student intake was increased from 100 to 108, despite objections from Ray Scothorne, Professor of Anatomy, who claimed that there would be insufficient tables in his dissecting room. That increase gave additional funds, which enabled the establishment of lectureships in some sub-specialties. Later still, when the intake was increased to 132, yet more UGC funds became available.

At first the NHS refused to fund academic posts, but later that barrier was lifted. However, in order to appoint a Professor of Medicine (Geriatrics), a Joint Appointments Committee between the NHS and the University was established so that the appointee, if appointed as a consultant geriatrician, could be considered by the University members for the award of a personal chair. This device worked superbly in the appointment of Professor John Grimley Evans (subsequently Sir John, who became Professor of Medical Gerontology in Oxford).

The University Development Trust and several local benefactors, such as Mr Lionel Jacobson and Sir William Leech, through their generous support, enabled the University not only to provide accommodation, facilities and equipment for research, but also gave substantial benefactions, allowing the University to endow chairs, readerships and lectureships. Later still, Dame Catherine Cookson was another major benefactor; two wings of the new Medical School are called the Leech and Cookson Buildings respectively.

Developments in the Sub-Faculty of Dentistry, leading to the opening of the new Dental School in 1978, are described by Professor John Murray. In the meantime, in collaboration with the regional and area health authorities, plans proceeded for the building of a new medical school and, alongside it, a new ward block for the RVI. Negotiations proceeded at tortoise pace, not least because of major disagreements between the Department of Health and the UGC. One authority measured the floor space of buildings from the middle of the retaining walls, while the other measured it from the interior of each wall; hence major disputes arose relating to the square footage of the new buildings. On his appointment as Dean in 1971, John Walton was promised a medical school in five years; in fact, while he took part in a topping-out ceremony (when the roof was complete) for the new school in 1981, the new building did not open until 1984, and the new ward block was completed some years later. Such planning delays meant that much reconstruction was necessary in the new Medical School, as the popular 1960s concept of having multidisciplinary laboratories (much favoured by George Smart), in which each student had a reader place and laboratory bench with storage space, became outmoded by rising student

Top: John Walton, Dean of Medicine 1971–81

Above: Catherine Cookson, a generous benefactor to the University, with (from left to right) Dr Christopher Record; Laurence Martin (VC) and Hugo Marshall

numbers and by restrictions on teaching staff numbers; these laboratories had to be modified to meet the new needs of the School and its departments.

This account would be incomplete without mention of some notable figures of the post-war era. R.B. Green retired in 1960, to be followed by Professor A.G.R. Lowdon, the brilliant Professor of Surgery, who sadly died in office in September 1965. He was succeeded by the charismatic Henry Miller, who resigned the deanship in October 1968 on being appointed Vice-Chancellor of the University; he, too, died prematurely in 1976. George Smart, Professor of Medicine, followed him as Dean in October 1968 and was much involved in designing the new Medical School; however, in 1971, he became the distinguished Director of the British Postgraduate Medical Federation in London and eventually received a knighthood in 1978. Many other Medical School figures were leaders in their professional disciplines, locally, nationally and even internationally. Professor Ivan Johnston was an outstanding Professor of Surgery, Professor J.K. Russell led the Department of Obstetrics and Gynaecology with energy and authority, Professor David Kerr, an expert on kidney disease, had a distinguished Newcastle career before becoming Dean of the Postgraduate Medical School in Hammersmith, and Professor Reginald Hall, an expert on thyroid disease, became Head of Medicine in the Welsh National School in Cardiff. Alexander Kennedy in Psychiatry was succeeded by Professor Martin Roth, who was elected President of the Royal College of Psychiatrists (as Sir Martin), and later became founding Professor of Psychiatry in Cambridge. Many other notable individuals in the 1960s and 1970s helped to make the Newcastle Medical School a major centre of excellence, now justly recognized as a leader in UK medical education.

John Walton

The Medical School: 1980–2005

By the 1980s, the Faculty of Medicine was expanding further to encompass the emerging disciplines related to Medicine, Dentistry and Biomedicine. This 25-year period was to see the consolidation of innovative curricular changes of subject integration and early clinical experience in undergraduate medical teaching originally introduced during the deanship of Andrew Lowdon in 1962, and carried forward by his

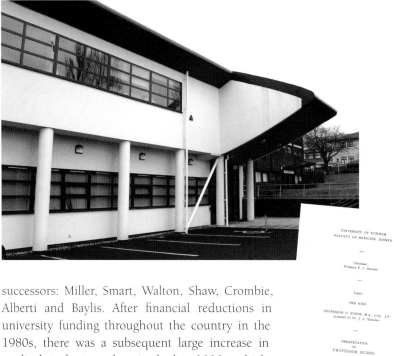

successors: Miller, Smart, Walton, Shaw, Crombie, Alberti and Baylis. After financial reductions in university funding throughout the country in the 1980s, there was a subsequent large increase in medical student numbers in the late 1990s, which not only stabilized University and Faculty finances, but also established Newcastle as one of the largest medical schools in England.

With such substantial changes came the need to restructure the Faculty, a process that started in the early 1990s, only to be finalized after a major initiative introduced by the new Vice-Chancellor, Christopher Edwards, in 2000–1. For the Faculty of Medical Sciences this meant a reduction from 36 departments to eight schools plus five research institutes, reorganization of academic and administrative structures, and streamlining processes to gain efficiency.

Top: The Biogerontology Research Unit at Newcastle General Hospital

Above: *Front of menu for University of Durham Faculty of Medicine dinner, 1949*

Below: *Students attending a lecture in the David Shaw Lecture Theatre*

TANYA PANKHURST

MEDICINE / 1990–5

The Medical School is now overhauled, so on returning for the reunion after ten years, it was unrecognizable, with a huge new lecture theatre protruding out at the front. We sat watching a video of younger versions of ourselves in the third-year 'revue' – a series of sketches that were far too long and that lost their comic value several hours before the predictable punch lines. It was hugely amusing to watch it all again.

Everyone at the reunion looked surprisingly similar to their former selves, although some had a little less hair and more breadth. There was an absence of that edge of insecurity that teenagers have, which had persisted through much of university – there was not so much to prove now, and the successful, more chilled versions of their younger selves were now beginning to relax into jobs and families. We are, as a group, one less: Lucy, blond, beautiful, died in 2005 from breast cancer.

The Purple Hooded Love Monks, complete with purple hooded cassocks, enjoyed a brief revival of their former glory. This funk band, who in their prime had so many members that they occasionally outnumbered their audience, had won great fame and following in their university years (apparently even complete with groupies), and were only a little rusty after their ten-year interlude.

As the wine flowed so did the memories, those afternoons of dissection with the strange smell of formaldehyde and all those pickled people. One poor chap in our group had turned green and fainted, and I made a mental note not to stand too close when feeling faint, as you never knew which way you might fall.

After the memories, we started to put the world to rights, and then it was late. Waking up the next day, with a surprisingly mild hangover, I walked along the sweep of sand at Tynemouth, barefoot in the blazing sun, discussing the events of the night before and the last ten years. It was good fun at Newcastle, and for me the choice of Medicine was right.

In 1984, the Medical School moved from the King George VI Building to a purpose-built, expansive facility on the Royal Victoria Infirmary (RVI) campus, just across Queen Victoria Road from the main University campus. The new site allowed close working potential between the Faculty, the RVI and the Dental Hospital. The academic or National Health Service (NHS) clinician could now walk readily from ward or outpatients to research laboratory or lecture theatre – a unique opportunity. Faculty satellites were established around Newcastle, the International Centre for Life (housing the Institute for Human Genetics, NHS clinical genetics and infertility services) near the Central Station; the Institute for Health and the Elderly (Wolfson Unit, Biogerontology Building and the Medical Research Council Unit) at Newcastle General Hospital and academic oncology in the Paul O'Gorman Building, situated adjacent to the Medical School. In addition, with the 85 per cent expansion in undergraduate medical students and increased bioscience and dental students, enlarged and improved teaching facilities were required. The medical library and teaching and learning services were expanded, and a large 405-seater lecture theatre was built overhanging and transforming the appearance of the Medical School entrance.

The 1990s was an era of partnership, a concept embraced by the Faculty. An essential and hugely important partner for the Faculty was the NHS, in particular the Newcastle Hospitals NHS Trust, newly formed in 1998, encompassing the Freeman Hospital, the RVI and Newcastle General Hospital. They were crucially interdependent. In the late 1990s, a strong partnership was established with Durham University to develop undergraduate medical teaching and the concept of a 'regional' medical school. The latter required close working of the two universities with virtually all NHS hospital trusts and very many GPs in an area stretching from the east to the west coasts and from Teesside north to Berwick.

For many decades, Newcastle has influenced British medicine and continues to do so even now. Lord Walton remains extremely active in the world of medical politics in the House of Lords. Successor as Dean to John Walton was Professor David Shaw, who on retirement chaired the General Medical Council's (GMC) Education Committee that produced 'Tomorrow's Doctors' – an innovative blueprint for teaching medical students, taken up by all medical schools. During the last years of the 1990s and the early 2000s, Newcastle provided three Royal Medical College presidents: Professor Sir George Alberti, President of the Royal College of Physicians; Professor William Dunlop, President of the Royal College of Obstetricians and Gynaecologists; and Professor Sir Alan Craft, President of the Royal College of Child Health and Paediatrics. Professor Sir Michael Rawlins became the first Chairman of the National Institute for Clinical Excellence, an extraordinarily influential body.

TEACHING AND LEARNING

Newcastle Medical School has a long history of innovative teaching. Wresting control of curricular development from the heads of department was a major achievement, and by the early 1980s a number of new organizational groupings – the Systems and Topics Committees – controlled the medical curriculum that consolidated integration of the student learning experience and extended early clinical contact with patients. The direction of medical pedagogy in England was set by the publication of 'Tomorrow's Doctors' and then by the Kings Fund's review on medical education, 'Critical Thinking'. Following the guidelines set out in these two documents, there was further fundamental development in Newcastle led by Reg Jordan and Peter Baylis to produce a medical graduate who understood more deeply concepts involving medicine and its specialities, as well as the underlying basic sciences, and had not just learned lists of facts.

In 1996, George Alberti asked the two sub-deans, Reg and Peter, how many more medical undergraduates Newcastle could admit annually. After a quick exchange of glances, the two responded, 'About ten'. 'No, that was not the right answer; think more in terms of 100 to 150', chuckled George. This heralded a large expansion of medical students. In response to the two bidding exercises issued by the Joint Implementation Group of the Higher Education Funding Council for England (HEFCE) and Department of Health, Newcastle's bids in partnership with Durham University were both successful. In the coming years, the annual intake for Medicine would rise from 185 to 340, an 85 per cent increase, with 95 students admitted for a two-year course to the Stockton Campus of Durham University, the remainder starting in Newcastle. All students would come together for third and subsequent years of the course, with clinical teaching delivered at one of four

Above left: Alan Craft, President of the Royal College of Child Health and Paediatrics

Above: George Alberti, President of the Royal College of Physicians

Left: William Dunlop, President of the Royal College of Obstetricians and Gynaecologists

clinical base units centred on Newcastle, Teesside, North Tyneside or Sunderland. A small cohort of about 25 students entered a four-year accelerated medical degree programme annually. The concept of a truly regional medical school had been realised.

In more recent years, the need for national expansion in dental student numbers was accepted; Newcastle was successful in attracting a further 25 annually, pushing the dental intake numbers up from 70 to 95 each year. Monies were secured to enlarge and update clinical dental teaching facilities. In addition, there was a modest rise in undergraduate and postgraduate bioscience students.

The delivery of high-quality teaching has always been at the heart of Faculty philosophy. Reviews of teaching by the GMC Education Committee Team were in general satisfactory, but not until 1998, with the first formal assessment of teaching and learning by the Quality Assurance Agency, did Newcastle Medical School secure real evidence of excellence in teaching. Along with three other medical schools, Newcastle gained maximum scores in the quality assessment of teaching. Furthermore, teaching evaluation of other Faculty areas in Physiology, Psychology, Pharmacology and Biomedical Sciences achieved equally impressive

Michael Rawlins, the first chairman of the National Institute for Clinical Excellence

The Centre for Life where the University is involved in important stem cell research

research funding of universities was related to the volume and quality of research. The increasing cost of research, the RAE, and the intense competition for grant money, drove universities to focus on and develop specific areas of research strength. In recent years, Newcastles medical research excellence has been concentrated in research institutes; the three strongest in the Faculty are: Human Genetics; Ageing and Health; and Oncology, with two new institutes in neuroscience and bioscience emerging. Pockets of research excellence also rest outside the institutes, for example liver disease, diabetes, and musculo-skeletal diseases.

The Faculty's RAE results in the 1980s and 1992 were good, but not exceptional. The 1996 RAE result was distinctly mediocre except for Biological Sciences, which immediately initiated a very robust review of Faculty research. Only research excellence was supported by the Faculty. As a consequence of this selective approach, the RAE result of 2001 was exceptionally good in all eight subject domains assessed. Three domains (Clinical Laboratory Sciences, Psychology and Biological Sciences) secured the maximum quality award of 5*, with the remaining five domains (Hospital-based Clinical Subjects, Community-based Clinical Subjects, Clinical Dentistry, Physiology and Nursing) scoring 5. Seen in a national context, these scores ranked amongst the best in the country alongside Oxford, Cambridge, Imperial College and University College London.

STEM CELL RESEARCH AT THE CENTRE FOR LIFE

A major research development has been established at the Centre for Life, about one mile from the Medical School, just next to the railway station. In the mid-1990s, there emerged the ambition to create an integrated facility that spanned fundamental genetic research, clinical practice and bioscience companies, and that fostered public understanding of genetics. The concept was driven by Professors John Burn and Tom Strachan (Institute of Human Genetics at the University of Newcastle), Mr Matt Ridley, Mr Alastair Balls and Ms Linda Conlan (Chairman, Chief Executive and Director of the Centre for Life) and Professor Alison Murdoch (Newcastle NHS Hospitals Trust), with major funding from the Millennium National Lottery, the Regional Development Agency and the Wellcome Trust.

From the original research interest in genes regulating development, there has been rapid progress over the past 10 years in research into the human

scores, with Dentistry dropping just one mark out of a total of 24. This unprecedented result was the basis on which the University secured the *Sunday Times* 'Best University of the Year' award in 2000. In due course, these successes led to further achievements: the UK Learning and Teaching Support Network Subject Centre for Medicine, Dentistry and Veterinary Medicine in 2000, the award of the Department of Health 'leading edge site' for interprofessional learning in 2002, and the award of the HEFCE Centre for Excellence in Teaching and Learning to Newcastle and the four other universities of the North East in 2005.

RESEARCH

For a number of decades Newcastle has enjoyed a reputation for good clinical research. Traditional research strengths have been in neurology, muscle diseases, endocrinology, diabetes, renal disease including kidney transplantation, cardiology and dermatology. Newcastle was regarded as one of the strongest provincial schools for research. Over the past few years its research reputation has been enhanced in both clinical and non-clinical areas.

In the 1980s the Research Assessment Exercise (RAE) was introduced to evaluate all university research, assessment occurring at regular intervals of about four years. A crucial aspect of the RAE was that

embryo, development of genetic mouse models (supported by the William Leech Charity), establishment of the Life Knowledge Park to study the ageing genome led by Professor Tom Kirkwood, and the emergence of embryonic stem cell research.

The stem cell work has fostered strong links between Newcastle and Durham Universities as well as a crucial link with the NHS Fertility Clinic, which is also situated at the Centre for Life. Significant advances include the establishment of a number of unique embryonic stem cells, including primitive blood stem cells, which marks a step closer to developing therapeutic cell lines. Further advances in the technique of nuclear transfer between cells have been made. In addition, a Centre for Policy, Ethics and Life Sciences Research (PEALS) has been established to consider the difficult emerging ethical issues.

Over the past 25 years, the Faculty has continued to conduct research and deliver teaching and learning at the highest level. Medicine, Dentistry and Bioscience flourish. The pace of change accelerates and a strong platform for further advancement has been firmly established.

Peter Baylis

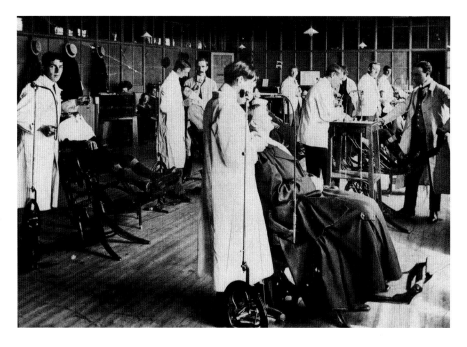

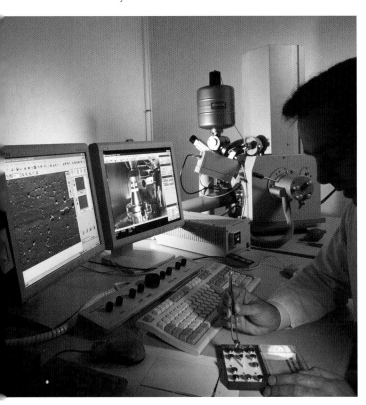

Stem cell research in the laboratory

THE NEWCASTLE DENTAL SCHOOL AND HOSPITAL

The first dental hospital in Newcastle was opened on 22 April 1895, the seventh dental hospital to be established in Great Britain. One year later, it moved to larger premises in the Handyside Arcade, Percy Street, and in 1911, the University of Durham instituted a Licence in Dental Surgery. Pressure on the Dental School and Hospital increased markedly at the start of the First World War. Many potential recruits to the Army, who had been turned down on the grounds of 'dental inefficiency', applied to the Hospital to be rendered 'dentally fit' (which required the extraction of large numbers of decayed teeth). The passing of the Dentists Act in 1921, which restricted the practice of dentistry to registered dentists and registered medical practitioners, resulted in an increased demand for student places, putting further pressure on the resources available in the Handyside Arcade.

Application was made to the Royal Victoria Infirmary (RVI) to provide a dental hospital on their site. This was granted by the Governors of the RVI in December 1930 and had the support of the newly constituted Dental Board of the United Kingdom. Sir Arthur Munro Sutherland came forward with a gift of £12,000 to pay for the cost of the buildings, which were officially opened on 28 January 1932 by the Chancellor of Durham University, the Marquis of Londonderry, who paid tribute to Sir Arthur's 'magnificent gift'.

Top: Interior of the Dental School and Hospital in the Handysiade Arcade, 1910

Above: *Sutherland Dental School and Hospital, RVI, 1931*

Sir Arthur expressed his thanks in a breezy speech. 'Sir Robert Bolam has told you what I did', he said, 'but he has not said what he did in this matter … In London, [he] took me to see the dental hospital built by Mr Eastman, of Kodak fame. Then he asked me to go to Percy Street to see the best we had in the shape of a dental hospital here … He rubbed it in that there were no proper dental hospital facilities between Leeds and Edinburgh. So what else could I do? As you all know, I am proud of Newcastle, and we are not going to let London, Edinburgh or Leeds beat us. I think you will be convinced after looking around, that Newcastle can now hold its own with any dental school in the country.'

THE BRADLAW ERA (1936–59)

For the first 30 years of its existence, the Dental School and Hospital was staffed mainly by honorary dental surgeons, who gave 'gratuitous service to the necessitous poor', on a part-time basis, whilst working mainly in their own practices. With the opening of the new building, the time had come to appoint a full-time Principal, a post that would also include the duties of Director of Dental Studies and Sub-Dean within the Faculty of Medicine. The Dental Board of the United Kingdom made a definite offer of £1,000 towards the salary of a full-time Director of Dental Studies. On 4 June 1936, Mr Robert V. Bradlaw MRCS, LDS Eng, LRCP London, was appointed Professor of Dental Surgery and Director of Dental Studies, and Honorary Dental Surgeon and Director of the Dental Hospital. The Dental School became the Dental Department of the Medical School, King's College. In spite of the difficulties caused by the start of the war, Professor Bradlaw continued to drive the Dental School and Hospital forward. The number of students admitted increased, so that in 1942, 105 dental students were registered, the third highest in the country. The building was proving unable to cope with the increase in patients and students, so extensions and alterations were planned. By the end of the war in 1945, 167 students had been enrolled.

Above: The Dental School in Northumberland Road, 1948

Above, right: Professor Bradlaw, Aneurin Bevan MP, Sir Arthur Sutherland and the Lord Mayor at the opening of the Northumberland Road Dental School in 1948

In 1946, it was decided that, rather than extending the present building on the RVI site, the Dental School and Hospital should be moved into the former College of Medicine building, Northumberland Road and College Street, which had stood empty since 1941. The official opening of the new premises took place on 29 May 1948 and was performed by the Minister of Health, Aneurin Bevan, especially significant because the new Dental School and Hospital was the first hospital to be opened following the announcement of the National Health Service Act. Mr Bevan thanked Sir Arthur Sutherland for his gift of £50,000 for the provision of additional equipment. The Dental Hospital continued to grow during the 1950s. Expertise in oral surgery, restorative dentistry and orthodontics increased, but the expansion in student numbers, encouraged by Professor Bradlaw, resulted in clinical resources being stretched to the limit.

Mr Bettenson, a former Registrar of the University, referred to Professor Bradlaw's contribution in his *History of the University, 1934–71*: 'Perhaps the most dramatic of all events in the first flush of post-war activity was the way in which Dental Surgery, under the daemonic (dynamic is an inadequate word) impetus of R.V. Bradlaw, was re-housed in the old Medical School and became the largest Dental School in England.'

THE NEW DENTAL SCHOOL

The possibility of rebuilding the Dental Hospital and School at the northern end of the RVI site was first mentioned in 1957. When Professor Bradlaw left in 1959 to become Dean and Director of the Eastman Dental Hospital in London, it was left to his successors, Professor Maurice Hallett, the new Dean of the Dental School, and Professor Lovel, Sub-Dean and Director of the Dental Hospital, to plan for a new dental hospital and school. The Rector of King's College, Dr C.I.C. Bosanquet, reported that a new dental school and hospital was to be constructed, in close association with the new Medical School, on the RVI site. 'The new Medical School, Dental School and hospital complex will be developed in such a way as to form with King's College, a single large educational and hospital precinct.'

The next 15 years were dominated by the need to negotiate, plan, design and build the new Dental Hospital and School. Professor Hallett cut the first turf on 29 May 1974 to initiate the building programme. The building was officially opened by the Chancellor of the University, his Grace the Duke of Northumberland, on 15 September 1978, accompanied by Professor Roy Storer, who had succeeded Maurice Hallett as Dean in October 1977.

Professor Roy Storer graduated from Liverpool University Dental School in 1950, and after a two-year tour of duty with the Royal Army Dental Corps returned to Liverpool as Lecturer in Dental Prosthetics. He was then appointed Professor of Prosthodontics in Newcastle in 1968. Over the next 15 years, he played a prominent role, locally and nationally, in the development of dental education. He was ably supported by Professor Howard Tonge, Professor of Oral Anatomy and first Dental Postgraduate Sub-Dean, a post he held from 1970 to 1983. Professor Tonge was President of the British Society for Dental Research from 1968 to 1971 and President of the British Dental Association (BDA) in 1981–2, when the annual conference of the BDA was held in Newcastle.

Neil Jenkins was appointed to King's College, Newcastle, as the Nuffield Lecturer in Physiology to dental students in 1946. After graduating from Liverpool in Chemistry, Physiology and Biochemistry in 1936, he completed an MSc in Biochemistry before moving to Cambridge to carry out research leading to a PhD. The first edition of his book, *The Physiology of the Mouth*, was

Left: The official opening of the Dental School and Hospital on the Royal Victoria Infirmary site in 1978

Below: A dental student practising on a phantom head

ROBIN VARMA

DENTISTRY / 1968–73

Finals results used to be read out by the Dean from the staircase in the foyer of the old Dental School down Northumberland Road. Only successful students' names were announced, in alphabetical order, so you can imagine the effect on those whose names were missed out. In 1973, the Dean only read out three names, the 'Honours' graduates, since every student had passed! Tradition dictated that he wore a pair of white gloves on such occasions.

published in 1954 and became a standard text for generations of dental students. He was promoted to the Chair of Oral Physiology in 1963.

Andrew Rugg-Gunn and John Murray, appointed in the 1970s, continued the School's interest in nutrition, diet and fluorides and were involved in the national survey of child and adult dental health organized by the Office of Populations, Censuses and Surveys. Research in dental material science blossomed under the ability and enthusiasm of John F. McCabe and attracted research students from many parts of the world. Robin Seymour developed his interest in dental pharmacology with Mr J. G. Walton and Professor Thompson, so that Newcastle became a centre for dental pharmacology research. With the arrival of Professor Roy Russell in 1991, the focus of oral biology research was directed to microbiology and molecular biology.

Roy Storer retired on 30 September 1992. His Christmas letter of 1991 included a picture of three deans: Hallett, Bradlaw and Storer, at Sir Robert Bradlaw's house in Stoke Goldington, Buckinghamshire. A few months later, on 12 February 1992, Sir Robert died, so bringing to an end a life of immense influence on the dental profession in Great Britain and overseas. Between them, Bradlaw, Hallett and Storer served for 55 years as deans of Dentistry in Newcastle.

Professor John Murray succeeded Roy Storer as Dean. The School celebrated its centenary in 1995. During his tenure, Doctors Seymour, McCabe, Watts and Heasman were promoted to professorships and Professor Peter Thomson was appointed to the Chair of Oral and Maxillofacial Surgery. John Murray strengthened the research ethos of the Dental School, resulting in the award of a grade 5 for research in the last Research Assessment Exercise in 2002. He retired in September 2002 and was succeeded by Professor Robin Seymour as Dean of Dentistry.

The building, planned in the 1960s and built in the 1970s, has proved to be an excellent resource for the treatment of patients and the teaching of students. During the last 25 years, parts of the building have been re-equipped to ensure that patients are treated in the best environment and that students have the benefit of using up-to-date dental equipment. Oral surgery facilities on the ground floor of the Hospital were upgraded in 1998. A Dental Emergency Clinic was developed in 2001 to improve access to dental care. In 2003, a Restorative Dentistry Clinic was re-equipped, comprising 20 dental chairs of the latest design, together with eight operating microscopes, which enable many restorative procedures, particularly endodontic (root canal) treatment to be carried out to a higher degree of accuracy than ever before. A comparison of the first and most recent clinics show some of the changes in dentistry that have occurred over the last 100 years.

John Murray

Above: Celebrating the centenary of the Dental School in 1995

Below: The three Deans (from left to right): Hallett, Bradlaw and Storer

Right: The refurbished Restorative Dentistry Clinic

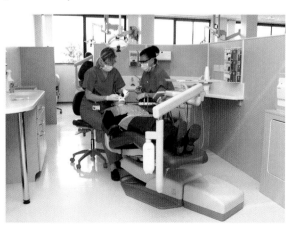

MEDICINE

An institution depends much more upon the character of those who are responsible for its activities than upon its localisation or its buildings.

– George Grey Turner and W.D. Arnison,
The Newcastle upon Tyne School of Medicine 1834–1934

The Newcastle School of Medicine and Surgery was established in 1834. In 1870 the School became the University of Durham College of Medicine at Newcastle and, in the same year, Dr Dennis Embleton became the first Professor of Medicine. Over the next 70 years, Embleton was followed in the chair by a series of distinguished physicians, notably Sir George Hare Philipson, Sir David Drummond, Sir Thomas Oliver and Sir William Hume.

Hume's departure in 1940 represented the loss of a well-loved teacher and talented physician, who pioneered the recognition of medical specialties in Newcastle. Hume was a cardiologist and his successor in the chair, Professor Fred Nattrass, a neurologist. In 1942, Dr (later Sir) James Spence (who during the 1930s had been Hume's assistant physician) was appointed to the Chair in Child Health – the first in the country. Both Nattrass and Spence were commemorated in a song presented in the RVI Christmas House Concert of 1947:

> *My name is Curly Nattrass, neurology I profess,*
> *And tickle ladies' stomachs with endearing tenderness.*
> *Now I'm Professor Spence JC life really is a bore*
> *I've lectured up and down the land on bottoms pink*
>   *and sore.*

On Nattrass's retirement in 1956, Dr (later Sir) George Smart succeeded to the chair. George Smart had originally intended a career in chemistry and his scientific approach, together with the biochemical and metabolic orientation of his work as a physician, bespeaks this early interest. He was referred to by students (and some colleagues) as 'Electrolyte George'. The Department of Medicine was richly endowed with characters at this time: there was C.N. (Nat) Armstrong, a noted endocrinologist with particular expertise in intersex – the House Concert song of 1947, referring to Nat, stated:

> *I've boys like girls and men with curls and 'this' instead*
>   *of 'that'*
> *There's nothing like the hormones for melting down*
>   *the fat.*

George Smart became Professor of Medicine in 1956

Dennis Embleton, first Professor of Medicine in 1870

In addition to his heavy clinical commitment, Nat served as Clinical Sub-Dean of the Medical School for many years. He died in 1998 in his 102nd year. Charles Ungley, a much respected haematologist, was a meticulous clinical observer who had been the outstanding clinical research worker in Newcastle during the 1930s. Alan Ogilvie ('the Og') was a fine respiratory physician. Other talented physicians at that time were Hewan Dewar, a cardiologist in the Hume mould, and Tom Boon, an enthusiastic gastroenterologist. One of the most loved characters in the Department was Henry G. ('Gorgeous') Miller; a distinguished neurologist who had been drawn into the specialty by Fred Nattrass's example. It was Henry who established a department that became so respected nationally and internationally that the city of Newcastle was, for a time, known in medical circles as 'Neurology-on-Tyne'.

George Smart was a man of immense energy and enthusiasm. However, his ability to pick a team and to provide a happy and productive environment for first-class work, both clinical and research, were the qualities that ensured a high measure of academic success for his department. Amongst Smart's team were David Kerr, who established nephrology as a leading specialty in Newcastle, Reg Hall, a brilliant endocrinologist whose work had an international reputation, and S.G. ('Griff') Owen, a talented cardiologist and medical educator. Metabolic medicine, endocrinology, haematology and neurology, strengthened by the appointments of John (later Lord) Walton and David Shaw, continued to flourish but, in addition, other specialties emerged and developed, amongst them dermatology, geriatric medicine, rheumatology and clinical genetics.

The expansion of Medicine and its specialties inevitably brought the physical and functional separation

of new departments from the Department of Medicine. Originally the Department occupied a small suite of rooms in the Old Medical School, which provided nothing like the capacity needed for the present work, let alone for continued expansion. Fortunately relief was at hand, and in 1967–8 the Department acquired new buildings as a result of the perseverance of George Smart and the help of the Wellcome Foundation. Ugly, but functional, Wellcome Research Laboratories, with accommodation for the Departments of Medicine and Clinical Biochemistry, were erected on the roof of the RVI, providing libraries and meeting rooms together with much needed office and laboratory space.

The next major development was in 1984, with the opening of the New Medical School adjacent to the RVI. Since then expansion has continued apace, and excellence in the provision of clinical service, research and teaching has been maintained.

The General Medical Council's 1957 'Recommendations on Medical Education', together with increasing criticism of the orthodox curriculum, triggered the genesis of the 'New Curriculum' in Newcastle, a truly multidisciplinary achievement. At the behest of the then Dean, Professor R.B. Green,

Queen Victoria Road Medical School, now the King George VI Building, viewed from St Thomas's Street

Andrew Lowden, the Professor of Surgery, called together a number of colleagues, most notably George Smart, to discuss curriculum reform in the light of the General Medical Council's recommendations. The group defined a number of guidelines for a new medical curriculum. Amongst the most important were the principles of: system-based teaching; horizontal and vertical integration; early clinical experience; a limitation on the amount of factual knowledge a student was required to assimilate; and a greater emphasis on care in the community and on primary care.

Student choices, study projects and the intercalated degree of Bachelor of Medical Science were established. From these guidelines curricular objectives evolved – Newcastle was the first medical school in this country to produce stated objectives.

With the New Curriculum came new methods of teaching and assessment; the former included various audio-visual aids and programmed learning. As to assessment, multiple-choice questions were introduced into the examinations, all of which (including clinical examinations) became multidisciplinary in structure and content. This led to (for example) orthopaedic surgeons examining alongside psychiatrists; alarming, perhaps, to the student, but a great delight to the examiners!

The New Curriculum was introduced in 1962 and was an acknowledged success, establishing Newcastle internationally as an innovative and liberal medical school. In the UK, many of Newcastle's curricular principles were adopted by the new medical schools at Southampton, Nottingham and Leicester.

'Curriculum review is an occupational disease of deans whereby the same subjects are taught in a different order' (Henry Miller). But a curriculum cannot be allowed to stagnate if enthusiasm and interest on the part of students and teachers are to be maintained. There was a further major review in 1971, and curricular review is now a continual process, with emphasis on critical thinking and computer-assisted, problem-based and self-directed learning.

In the sense that a culture represents the shared beliefs, customs, practices and social behaviour of a group of people, Medicine in Newcastle is a culture. A proud culture; aware of its achievements, conscious of its heritage and determined to aspire to and maintain the highest possible standards.

John Anderson

FAMILY AND COMMUNITY MEDICINE

In the early 1960s, Edinburgh was the only British medical school with General Practice as a significant component of its undergraduate curriculum, despite the fact that half of medical graduates were likely to become general practitioners (GPs). In Newcastle, Andrew Smith of Whickham, a Foundation Council member of the new College of General Practitioners, along with Roland Freedman and H.G. 'Bingy' Barnes, began to sensitize members of the Faculty of Medicine to the potential of General Practice education. A new curriculum in 1962 provided the opportunity and, supported particularly by Donald Court (Child Health) and Richard Pearson (Public Health), a four-week experimental course in Family and Community Medicine was introduced. The original teaching group consisted of 12 local GPs, several public health staff and six volunteer teaching hospital consultants. John Walker, Durham graduate and lately Lecturer in General Practice in Edinburgh, was appointed Lecturer in Public Health as co-ordinator.

The course comprised placements in general practice and the community, and concluded with case presentations at a multi-disciplinary seminar. Unique in its collaboration between general practice, public health and hospital medicine, the course attracted national and international interest and many visitors from the UK and overseas. Immediately popular with both students and staff, it became an integral part of the curriculum.

Meanwhile, the Department of Public Health continued to teach social and preventative medicine and the postgraduate course leading to the Diploma in Public Health, but in 1968 changed its name and ethos to Family and Community Medicine. The same year, it collaborated both with Medical Statistics to establish the Medical Care Research Unit (now Centre for Health Services Research), and the postgraduate organization to plan a vocational training programme for GPs. Based within the Department and co-ordinated by Andrew Smith, the programme started with seven teaching practices. Successfully evaluated, the programme rapidly expanded to become one of the largest and most successful in the country. This development coincided with the establishment of the examination for membership of the (by now) *Royal* College of General Practitioners, in which the Department also played a significant role.

Curriculum review in 1974 led to further innovation in the form of the groundbreaking Human Development, Behaviour and Ageing course. Notable

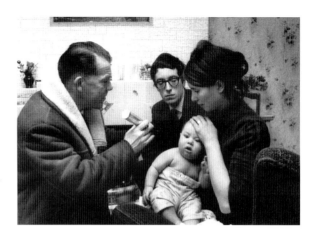

Dr Andrew Smith practising in the community in the 1960s, accompanied by a postgraduate medical student

features were the community-based Family Study in first year and Patient Study in second year. In the former, each student followed the progress of a pregnant mother, her baby and family; in the latter, the impact of long-term illness on a patient and their family. Popular and memorable, these projects remain part of the curriculum to the present day, and similar programmes are now found in most UK medical schools.

Departmental academic status was recognized in 1976, when John Walker received a personal chair. In 1977, Chris Drinkwater was appointed Senior Lecturer and joined Krish Kumar, a single-handed Benwell GP, to create the University Teaching Practice. Based originally in run-down premises, the practice moved to a shopping centre in 1984, and later to the purpose-built Adelaide Medical Centre. Although funded mainly from NHS income, all GPs in the practice had academic appointments; to date four have gained chairs themselves. Don Foster was appointed Senior Lecturer in Community Medicine the same year, with specific responsibility for postgraduate teaching and research. Increased staffing extended the Department's range of activities and, while education at both undergraduate and postgraduate levels remained a priority, important research was undertaken, for example in prescribing. The Department also established a major local and national profile in service development in areas as diverse as care of the elderly, clinical audit and teamwork. International projects included training GPs and nurse trainers in the Basque region of Spain, and GPs in Kuwait.

In 1988, John Walker retired, and the Department became two divisions, Primary Health Care, and Epidemiology and Public Health, marking the start of a series of titular and organizational changes in the University and Faculty.

GEOFF TAYLOR

OCCUPATIONAL HYGIENE / 1985-6

I am from Perth, Australia, and attended Newcastle University on a World Health Organization Fellowship to complete an MSc in Occupational Hygiene in the Faculty of Medicine. I had very good lecturers in John Steel and Bill Ellis and others, a well-equipped laboratory, and friendly and helpful people at Plus Products in Ryton, where I undertook my dissertation research. My fellow students were from Iran, Malaysia, Ireland and the UK. It was a very practical course so we also undertook group work in ten industrial enterprises in the area presenting different occupational hygiene problems.

The William Leech Chair of Primary Care was established in 1990, with Roger Jones its first incumbent. The first Chair in Epidemiology and Public Health was also established, and Raj Bhopal appointed. Both made significant contributions to developing research in their respective departments.

By the time of the 1994 curriculum review, Primary Health Care was again central to all aspects of the curriculum. Indeed, the Faculty turned to them for guidance and leadership in further developing curricular topics, such as communication skills and ethics, pioneered in the Human Development,

Medical students training at the Royal Victoria Infirmary

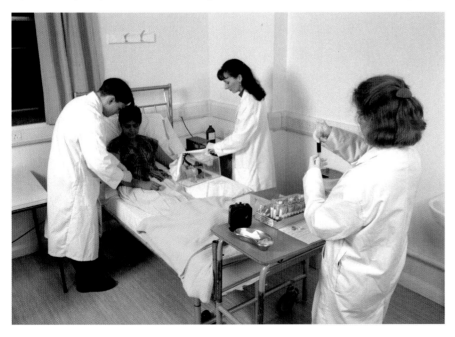

Behaviour and Ageing course. Over 130 practices in the region were by this time involved in teaching. A service-based clinical rotation in public health was also introduced, one of the first of its kind in the UK.

The most recent curriculum review (2001) saw further expansion of community-based teaching. Around 200 practices are currently involved in the teaching programme, with GP input to all years of the curriculum. Feedback from students remains consistently positive.

In 2002, major restructuring took place in the University, with the dissolution of departments and the reorganization of schools. Somewhat paradoxically, the University, having been one of the first English medical schools to establish a Department of General Practice, became the first to dissolve one! General Practice and Public Health teaching in the early years of the curriculum stayed within the School of Population and Health Sciences, as did primary care research (the latter based in the Centre for Health Services Research) and research in epidemiology and public health. However, *clinical* teaching in General Practice relocated to the School of Medical Education Development. Meanwhile, in the same year, Adelaide Medical Centre separated from University administration and reverted to being an 'ordinary' practice, although remaining involved in teaching.

All aspects of academic enterprise that started out under the heading 'Family and Community Medicine' remain alive and well, albeit operating in different contexts and locations within the Faculty, and lacking the visibility and identity they enjoyed when under one roof. However, Community-based Subjects achieved 5* ratings in the 2001 Research Assessment Exercise. The research 'portfolio' spans clinical effectiveness, the impact of dementia, clinical decision-making, environmental epidemiology, health inequalities and foetal and perinatal epidemiology, as well as major involvement in the Newcastle Clinical Trials Unit. Primary Health Care and Public Health have also consistently made significant contributions to the success of recent teaching quality audits. On these grounds it would seem that the uncontrolled experiment initiated over 40 years ago has been a resounding success!

John Spencer

John Walker

NEUROLOGY

While Byrom Bramwell, an Edinburgh neurologist, spent part of his early career on Tyneside, the practice of neurology, for practical purposes, began with Professor F.J. Nattrass, the first full-time Professor of Medicine in Newcastle, appointed in 1944. While he taught and practised general medicine, his major interest was in neurology, and his book, *The Commoner Nervous Diseases*, was deservedly popular in the 1930s. A paper he wrote on 'recurrent polyneuritis' resulted in the French calling this condition *Maladie de Nattrass*. And a 1954 paper on the muscular dystrophies, of which he was the second author (Walton, J.N. and Nattrass, F.J., *Brain*, vol. 77, p. 169) was perhaps the first step towards the establishment of one of the world's leading centres of research into muscle diseases.

In 1946, newly demobilized from the Royal Air Force, where he was a neuropsychiatry specialist, Dr Henry Miller was appointed Assistant Physician to the Royal Victoria Infirmary (RVI). He soon developed a large private practice in medicine, but specialized increasingly in neurology, and undertook, with colleagues, research into immunological disorders of the nervous system (conditions in which changes in the body's immune system, often mediated by a type of white blood cell or circulating antibodies, damage the brain, spinal cord, nerves or muscles); multiple sclerosis was his particular interest.

Nattrass and the health authorities were persuaded that Neurology should be developed as an independent discipline, but several years passed before this was achieved, even though there was for some years a Department of Neurosurgery at the Newcastle General Hospital (NGH). Three wards were available there, largely because of the heavy burden of head injuries on Tyneside. However, no physician in neurology practised there, and any patient seen by Nattrass or Miller at the RVI requiring neuroradiological investigation had to be transferred to the neurosurgeons.

In 1947, following the appointment of Alexander Kennedy as Professor of Psychiatry, a Department of Electroencephalography (EEG: electrical recording of the brain waves through the intact skull), under Sandy Osselton, was established in the RVI, and in 1950, after three months at the National Hospital, Queen Square, in London, John Walton undertook EEG interpretation and introduced electromyography (EMG: a technique of recording the electrical activity of muscles using needle electrodes) in a research laboratory on the top corridor of the RVI. Eventually, in 1956, a former surgical ward, Ward 6, was allocated to neurology and neurosurgery, and Henry Miller became the consultant neurologist. He continued in consulting practice and in research into multiple sclerosis and accident neurosis (he had a large medico-legal practice and infuriated psychiatric colleagues by calling psychiatry 'neurology without physical signs').

In 1956, following Henry Miller's appointment, Walton became his First Assistant. Planning was proceeding for the building of a Regional Neurological Centre (RNC) at the NGH, and a Department of Neuroradiology, under Dr Gordon Gryspeerdt, was opened in 1956. In 1958, Walton became the first 'regional' consultant neurologist, with responsibilities at the NGH and in outpatient clinics for consultant reference only, as far afield as Middlesborough and Durham. He persuaded the Regional Hospital Board, through its research funds, to expand plans for the Centre by adding two floors of research laboratories for neuropathology, neurochemistry and neurophysiology. The building opened in 1962, by

Left: Fred Nattrass, the first full-time Professor of Medicine

Below: Henry Miller, Consultant Neurologist at the RVI and later Professor of Neurology

Medical School,
30th May, 1966.

I strongly deny that the Stage III Examination Papers were compiled by a random selection of idiots from St Nicholas.
It was not a random selection.
I hand-picked the idiots myself.

H. Miller

which time Dr J.B. Foster had joined as a consultant neurologist, assuming some of the regional responsibilities.

The Director of the Pathological Institute at the NGH, Dr (later Professor Sir) Bernard Tomlinson initiated neuropathological studies, while Dr E.J. Field was appointed as Professor of Experimental Pathology, later becoming Director of the MRC Demyelinating Diseases Research Unit, housed in a new laboratory building on the NGH site. (Demyelinating disorders are those in which the fatty sheaths surrounding nerve fibres in the nervous system are damaged by disease; one such disorder is multiple sclerosis.) The RNC was expanded through charitable funding by adding a block of muscular dystrophy research laboratories, including an animal house and experimental facilities in neurophysiology, neuropathology, neurochemistry and electron microscopy. (The muscular dystrophies are a group of progressive inherited diseases of the muscle; the most severe – the Duchenne type – causes progressive muscular weakness and is ultimately fatal.)

JOHN WALTON

MEDICINE / 1941–5

After completing my registrarship, Nattrass invited me to join him in research into neuromuscular diseases. A local man, whose son was dying of muscular dystrophy, had received letters alleging that five individuals diagnosed as suffering from dystrophy had recovered. These were seen by Dr (subsequently Dame) Albertine Winner at the Ministry of Health, who showed them to several distinguished London neurologists. They said that if the patients had recovered, the diagnosis of dystrophy must have been wrong. Undaunted, she brought the letters to Nattrass, who felt that the matter deserved further investigation; the diagnosis in one of the cases had been made by himself. He obtained funds from the Ministry to appoint me as Research Assistant, and my examination of the five 'recovered' patients showed that the diagnosis had indeed been wrong. I reviewed the clinical and genetic characteristics of patients and families with muscular dystrophy in the North East of England and introduced, with Nattrass, a classification that was accepted internationally.

Despite my manifold clinical, research and administrative duties, I did manage at weekends to play golf at Bamburgh, where, in 1978, I had my first hole in one and became captain of the club. In 1979, the Berwick upon Tweed Advertiser's lead story began, 'In her Majesty's New Year's Honours List, Mr George Crawford, a Tweedmouth trawler skipper, has received the OBE, and the Captain of Bamburgh Golf Club has been knighted.' Little was said about other things where I thought I might have made a mark!

David Barwick became consultant in clinical neurophysiology at the NGH and ran the service in EEG, EMG and nerve conduction velocity studies, being later joined by Peter Fawcett.

When Henry Miller retired, Dr David Shaw, trained in Edinburgh and at Queen Square and at the Mayo Clinic in the US, took over Neurology at the RVI as Senior Lecturer and subsequently as Professor. Because of the University's need for neurological teaching in disciplines such as speech studies and educational psychology, new neurological appointments were created, and Dr Niall Cartlidge and Dr David Bates were appointed joint senior lecturers and consultants, later to be awarded personal chairs. Research on many neurological topics, including cerebral vascular disease ('strokes') and multiple sclerosis, was enhanced in the RVI by the provision of laboratories and teaching space adjacent to Ward 6.

Many postgraduate trainees from across the world, including Australasia, Thailand, India, the Middle East, Europe, Canada, South Africa and the US came at different times to work in Newcastle Neurology, at the NGH or RVI, as did Dr Peter Hudgson of Melbourne, later consultant and Senior Lecturer at the NGH. Dr David Gardner-Medwin became consultant in paediatric neurology and, in 1974, in a national competition for funding by endowment of two research chairs by Action Research, Newcastle was awarded the first Chair of Experimental Neurology, to which Walter Bradley, formerly Senior Lecturer, was appointed; the capital sum available was enough to establish also a senior lectureship, held by Dr (later Professor) J.B. Harris. When David Shaw retired from the Chair of Neurology, Douglass Turnbull was appointed, and now works in collaboration with colleagues in genetics at the Centre for Life; he has become a world expert on mitochondrial disease. (Mitochondria are tiny energy-producing structures lying in the cytoplasm of cells, outside the nucleus; many diseases afflicting them are progressively disabling.) Recognition of Newcastle's place in the neurological firmament was marked by the author's election as President of the World Federation of Neurology. The Department of Neurology of the University was subsequently absorbed into the School of Neuroscience and, with much new blood, continues to develop its teaching, clinical and research roles.

John Walton

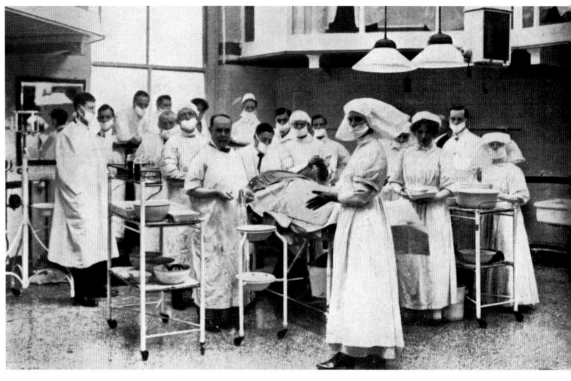

SURGERY

Newcastle has boasted many distinguished and famous surgeons both recently and in the past. It is worthwhile recalling some of the most celebrated who paved the way for the future of academic surgery in Newcastle's Medical School.

Rutherford Morison is arguably the best starting point. He was the son of a colliery doctor from Hutton Henry near Hartlepool and, after qualifying in Medicine, became first a general practitioner and then a physician in his local hospital. This is where he started his surgical practice, before moving to Newcastle as a surgeon. His Newcastle career began in the Infirmary at Forth Banks, but he transferred to the Royal Victoria Infirmary when it opened in 1906 at its present site on Queen Victoria Road, and there became Professor of Surgery. His name is still remembered today by all abdominal surgeons throughout the world: he described the recess behind the liver which could be the seat of an abscess in patients with intra-abdominal infection following on from diseases such as acute appendicitis – the hepato-renal pouch of Rutherford Morison.

Like many surgeons of his day, Morison was a critical and acute observer of clinical signs. His tale of missing jaundice in a patient simply because he had examined the patient in an inappropriate light is one well known

to surgeons. One of his protégés was Grey Turner, who had this same clinical skill. He became Professor of Surgery in 1927 and described the sign of skin discoloration occurring in the abdominal wall of sufferers of acute haemorrhagic pancreatitis. Such observations were of huge importance in those days when techniques of investigation were either rudimentary or non-existent.

Grey Turner was a highly skilled and practical surgeon. He felt that no surgeon could be regarded as being properly experienced until he had removed an appendix from a patient on a miner's kitchen table! Grey Turner completed his career as Professor of Surgery in the Hammersmith Postgraduate Hospital in London. Rutherford Morison and Grey Turner were at the very top of the clinical tree in surgery. It is a surprise that neither received an award such as a knighthood in recognition of their achievements.

Another surgical doyen of the first part of the 20th century was Frederick Pybus, who was in turn a protégé of Grey Turner. Another man of towering intellect and talent, Pybus was interested in the disease of lung cancer and in the clinical need for clean air. Also appointed Professor of Surgery – an honorary appointment as the University had not yet funded a Chair of Surgery – Pybus was an avid collector of early medical books. The Pybus Collection,

Above: Professor Page operating at the New Infirmary as a guest of Riutherford Morison

Top left: Case of 19th-century surgical instruments from the Barber-Surgeons' Company's Hall

110

*Frederick Charles Pybus,
1883–1975, who left his collection
of early medical books to the
University*

now housed within the University, is one of the foremost and most important anywhere in the world.

Pybus was a great clinical innovator. His attempt to cure diabetes by pancreatic transplantation – written up in *The Lancet* in 1924 – was defeated by immunology rather than anything else. He was also the effective founder of the North of England Surgical Society, which continues to go from strength to strength in the 21st century.

In a conversation with George Proud in 1974, Pybus showed him a book prepared by Grey Turner and which Pybus had illustrated: in it was a post-operative temperature chart in an uncomplicated case. A rise in temperature was noted in the first 48 hours, which Pybus attributed to the response to surgery. He bemoaned the fact that many patients would receive antibiotics at that stage – abusing their use – when all that was happening was the normal metabolic response to surgery. He was of course correct in his assertion, and it is tempting to think that some of the problems of antibiotic resistance could have been avoided if this lesson from Pybus had been in clinical use.

There is no doubt that Surgery in Durham University carried a very high reputation in medical circles, as did the Medical School in general. It was Grey Turner who said that '…an institution depends much more on the character of those who are responsible for its activities than upon its location or its buildings'. It is no wonder that the University's reputation was high!

Pybus taught until the time of the Second World War. Yet it was not until 1945 that the University of Durham funded for the first time a Professor of Surgery for whom honorary clinical status was accorded in the

Royal Victoria Infirmary. It was to this chair that Andrew Lowdon was appointed in 1954. Professor Lowdon knew his students: he knew their achievements and their various sporting interests. It was not long before he was elected Dean of Medicine, a responsibility he took on in 1960. Under his guidance the undergraduate medical curriculum was revised, and teaching became multidisciplinary and integrated at both clinical and pre-clinical stages. Structure and function of systems were taught at the same time. Clinical subjects would be taught on the same basis with contributions from physiologists, pathologists, radiologists, physicians, surgeons and others as appropriate. It was a curriculum destined to remain. It is tempting to think that the introduction of this type of teaching also had an influence on clinical patient management, for there is no disguising the fact that patient management is no longer the sole responsibility of one clinician. Specialists are now team members, with each member having well-defined responsibilities within the team.

Andrew Lowdon also had a firm belief in the importance of introducing the surgical trainees to the

DR PHILIP COWEN

MEDICINE / 1950–6
The Thursday ward-round

Despite its name, this was a tutorial held by the surgeon, Professor Norman Hodgson, after he had finished his outpatients' clinic. He would bring in two or three of his patients and one would sit on a chair on the dais. Hodgson would stand in front of the students and point to one of them at random and then to the patient behind. This indicated that the student was to take a history and examine the patient. While that went on, the remaining students were addressed by the surgeon on any topic from the morning newspaper. Hodgson would then turn to the chosen student and ask 'Well, what do you see?' The victim of the inquisition too often fell into the trap. He/she would answer, 'A parotid tumour' or whatever. The surgeon would glare through his monocle and ask, 'Do you see a tumour sitting on that chair? What's the patient's name, where does he live, what's he complaining of, past history?' Only after this information had been taken would a diagnosis be accepted.

techniques of research. Whilst he was Chairman of the Regional Hospital Board's research committee, he established the prizes that were to be awarded to registrars for their research work.

In 1965, Professor Lowdon died at a tragically early age whilst out hill-walking. Nevertheless, his impact on teaching and training has remained to this day. Much of what he started was continued by his successor Ivan Johnston. Within a relatively few years of his arrival, the standard surgical training path for young surgeons involved the University very closely. Young surgeons competed for teaching posts that had been established in the Department of Anatomy by Professor Short. They undertook one year as demonstrators of Anatomy to undergraduates in Medicine and Dentistry, whilst working for the primary FRCS (Fellowship of the Royal College of Surgeons) examination. Although the syllabus for the FRCS examination has now changed, trainees still want to teach Anatomy for a year, which helps them develop a deeper knowledge of a subject that is so important for the potential surgeon. The trainees invariably enjoyed this year, and lifelong friendships often ensued: there was also a near 100 per cent pass rate amongst them in the primary FRCS examination!

After the FRCS was obtained, the trainees would then seek to gain a year or two of full-time research experience in one or other of the surgical disciplines active in the 1960s, 70s and 80s. Ivan Johnston was a tower of strength to the research trainees and worked tirelessly to try and find money for them to attend meetings and visit units both within the UK and abroad – especially in the US. Most surgical trainees of that era owe a large debt of gratitude to Professor Johnston for seeing them through to their consultant or senior lecturer post. The Department of Surgery had a very considerable influence on this group of young surgeons.

Surgery was now increasingly specialized. In the days of Rutherford Morison, the surgeon would treat a large variety of clinical conditions. A list of Rutherford Morison's patients for a day in 1900 included those with a fractured clavicle and associated brachial plexus lesion, a case of popliteal necrosis, a gastrostomy, an abdominal hydatid, a fractured spine, an empyema, etc – conditions that would now be treated by spinal surgeons, gastrointestinal surgeons, vascular surgeons, gynaecologists, neurosurgeons and plastic surgeons.

Urology and orthopaedic surgery were two of the earliest major specialties to emerge before the Second

World War. It was not until the early 1970s, however, that the first Professor of Orthopaedic Surgery was appointed by the University. Jack Stevens was a bluff North-countryman and his clinical base was provided in the Infirmary. He expected total commitment – woe betide anyone who missed the Saturday morning teaching! It was also no surprise to the young on-call surgeons to find him in his office late at night catching up with the day's work – his levels of energy were almost legendary.

Some years later a Professor of Urology was appointed although John Swinney, a consultant urologist in the NHS, and the original founder of renal transplantation in Newcastle, had previously been awarded a personal chair. There have also been appointments to chairs, by personal promotion, in Neurosurgery and Cardiothoracic Surgery, and a Chair of Otorhinolaryngology was also created.

Postcard of the Royal Victoria Infirmary, early 20th century

Gradually, the trend towards specialization continued. The general surgeon of 1975, already a much changed person from the general surgeon in existence before the war, has now been replaced by even more specialists, such as the vascular surgeon, the endocrine surgeon, the transplant surgeon etc. Similar changes have been seen in the newer specialties, particularly orthopaedic surgery, urology and plastic surgery.

It is probably not appropriate for the University to reflect all of these changes in its appointments. Personal chairs recently awarded by the University to clinicians of academic distinction should help maintain links between the academic and the clinical facilities so important for good clinical research and for the teaching of students – and, at the same time, keep the University in touch with all of the changes occurring as specialization develops.

One way in which the University maintains links with the medical student population, which becomes so widely scattered in the clinical stages of training, is through the Clinical Sub-Dean's office. For much of the later part of the 20th century, a surgeon was the Clinical Sub-Dean. Brian Fleming seemed a natural choice for this post. He endeared himself to students but they remained in total respect – almost awe – of him. There would be great disappointment in Brian's office if the annual student concerts did not feature him. However, woe betide any individuals who overstepped the mark – the mark being a line drawn imperceptibly in the sand. Brian's impact on undergraduate medical training was immeasurable.

The Department of Surgery's impact on young surgeons has also changed. In the 1960s, 70s and 80s, it had a very profound influence – a role that seemed entirely appropriate at the time. However, universities have become increasingly judged by their research efforts, and by the quality of undergraduate teaching. Postgraduate teaching did not fit comfortably into this regime at a departmental level and, with the recommendations of Kenneth Calman (later to become Vice-Chancellor of Durham University), this became the responsibility of the Postgraduate Dean, who now liaised with the royal colleges and the specialist associations.

The huge influence the Department of Surgery had on postgraduate surgical training was systematically reduced. Furthermore, the strong link between the Department and surgical trainees did not seem to continue – at least for many of them – beyond their appointment to a senior post. They drifted away from the Department. For many consultants, the Department of Surgery was not a happy place to be in the 1980s. It was a surprise to many academic surgeons in the UK that there were no appointments to personal chairs in any of the disciplines of general surgery after Dennis Walder's appointment in the 1960s, until about the turn of the century. Dennis, an international authority on hyperbaric diseases – especially on their effect on the blood circulation of bone – and a renowned surgical physiologist, was the last such promotion. How could it be that a department of such high reputation and profile throughout the world was unable to produce anyone worthy of such recognition? A number were justified, but none appeared. The Department of Surgery gradually became isolated.

Bridges needed to be built once more, and ultimately this has happened. It is reassuring, and positive, now, to see the increasing integration between the University's Department of Surgery and the clinical departments of Surgery that has occurred in the last few years. This can only be to the benefit of each party, particularly if each can accept and nurture the role of the other.

Where will Surgery be in the next 50 years? The practice of surgery by then will probably have changed out of all recognition. Medical treatments will become available for many patients who presently require an operative intervention. Who, 30 years ago, could have imagined that one of the commonest of conditions for the surgeon to treat – peptic ulceration and its complications – would become such a rare surgical problem? Treatment, and prevention, is now the province of the physician!

Clinical departments such as Surgery are undergoing huge changes in our universities today, and Newcastle faces those changes. From having been a basic and fundamental part of any medical school, departments of Surgery are nowadays becoming much more specialized and perhaps more engaged in postgraduate activities, such as research, than in undergraduate. Will Surgery become a postgraduate specialty only? Yet we still have a Professor of Surgery in the University. Long may that continue!

George Proud

05

Faculty of Science, Agriculture and Engineering

AGRICULTURE AFTER THE WAR

A high profile for Agriculture was ensured by wartime near-starvation and the continuation of food rationing into the 1950s. The Government this time seemed to have learned the lesson of the need for Britain to provide its own food, but took the view that nanny knew best. The all-powerful Ministry of Agriculture, Fisheries and Food, bloated with the Stalinesque powers of the War Agriculture Committee, took over much of the farm demonstration and advisory role provided by the Agriculture Department. Northumberland County Council took the opportunity to save itself some money by terminating its contract with the Department. The 999-year lease on the farm at Cockle Park was taken over by the University, and the tenancy of the farm at Nafferton in the Tyne Valley added to our stock. This farm belonged to Lord Allendale, whose tenant had been dispossessed by the said War Agriculture Committee for not doing what he was told! The Farm Business Survey, paid for by the Ministry, remained at Newcastle, reportedly because the farmers, who were asked for details of their businesses, trusted the academics' discretion more than the men from the Ministry! The creation in the 1950s of a Department of Food Marketing, the first in Britain, provided new opportunities, not least for Bill Weeks, researcher, local councillor, TV personality and raconteur, who did much to bring the subject to the notice of the public.

Student numbers were inflated by the return of servicemen whose studies had been interrupted, as well as by the new-found fashion for agriculture and food. The women who had taken the place of the servicemen during the war altered the composition of the student body greatly; in the late 40s nearly half were female. All these students had to be taken on farm visits, and staff cars were used for transport. Professor Wheldon's Rolls was preferred. His creation of the Faculty of Agriculture had involved the transfer of all the chemists and biologists, who had formerly been in science departments, into the new organization. This also created the opportunity for new degree options in Agricultural Chemistry and Botany. The expansion in student and staff numbers meant that the teaching and practical classes overflowed into huts at the rear of the Clement Stephenson Building. Wheldon worked tirelessly on his creation and was to die at his desk in 1954.

Right: The Agriculture building

Left: Mac Cooper was Dean of the Faculty of Agriculture and Professor of Agriculture from 1954–72

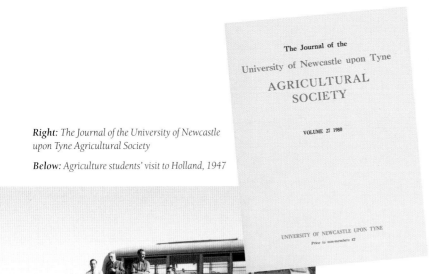

The Journal of the
University of Newcastle upon Tyne
AGRICULTURAL
SOCIETY

VOLUME 27 1980

UNIVERSITY OF NEWCASTLE UPON TYNE
Price to non-members £2

Right: The Journal of the University of Newcastle upon Tyne Agricultural Society

Below: Agriculture students' visit to Holland, 1947

The new faculty was in a strong position to attract good applicants for the vacant chair and the appointee was to be an antipodean Scot with a penchant for ruffling feathers; Mac Cooper's address to the 1954 British Association for the Advancement of Science was entitled 'British farming is going off at half-cock'. He was thereafter known as Half-Cock Cooper. He personally was anything but half-cock, more the brash colonial bull in the provincial china shop. Mac was a superb lecturer. He lectured without notes to students and had the ability to hold his audience's attention throughout. His books on farming, especially on grassland and animals, sold widely, including back in his native New Zealand, and his *Sheep Production* remained in print after his death. The local newspapers and media loved him because of his provocative approach, and he was without doubt the best publicist since Professor Gilchrist. Not all, though, was roses. Despite assurances to the contrary, all but Palace Leas of the original experiments were ploughed out; the story goes that Mac told the farm staff to do this, they refused, so he did it himself. Having served at Monte Cassino during the war, he was not easily put off.

One catastrophe of the period was that the record room was cleared and much of the Faculty's archive of results was lost. Mac embraced the 'new agriculture' of pesticides and fertilisers that the Ministry and its new advisory service were promoting and, as a result, work on what we now would call organic farming was lost for 50 years. However, Mac was highly successful in expanding the Faculty. He had brought with him staff from Wye College, who would do much to strengthen the scientific aspects of the faculty's work. In particular, Peter Askew was, in the late 1970s, to begin the move towards a wider view of the environment and away from out-and-out food production. These new faces brought not only new skills, but new ideas and new blood. They also increased the size of the Faculty so that a new building was needed and, in the spirit of the 1960s, a tower block was created at the far side of the campus from the Quadrangle. By the 1970s, even this was too small and space was taken in the Herschel and Bedson Buildings to provide more science labs, while some of the old Newcastle Brewery buildings became Agricultural Engineering.

The Agricultural Students' Association was refounded in 1944 and for 25 years Sandy Main, the Senior Tutor, was to be its able Secretary. Its constitution was amended to allow membership to include farmers who were not graduates, and it soon had a membership of 700. Its journal attracted papers from Sir Kenneth Blaxter of the Rowett Institute through to figures from the Ministry and the Common Market, as well as home-grown contributors. It generated substantial advertising revenue because of its links to the industry and reported each year on an overseas trip by members to examine agriculture in another country. These trips began in 1946, and students were able to see at first hand the reconstruction of farming in Europe. The journal continued to be published regularly until the 1970s, when publication became sporadic, petering out in 1983. Happily, it was restarted in 2005 by Eric Evans and Bill Bourne.

A regular contributor to the journal was Professor David Armstrong, unarguably the greatest of the Faculty's scientists. Like many other staff, he was a Newcastle graduate. He took over Brynmor Thomas's mantle,

'Nancy the Nationalized Cow' won the prize for best Rag float in 1947

As the 1970s wore on, concerns grew for the impact of the new agriculture on the environment; this was made worse as Common Market surpluses – grain mountains and wine lakes – grew uncontrollably. Pesticide residues and pollution of water became increasing concerns and later, as the threat from the Warsaw Pact countries diminished, the need for strategic food production decreased. Food from our own resources became a somewhat tarnished concept, and ecology and the environment became new watchwords. Peter Askew strove to set up a degree in Agricultural and Environmental Science, which was to attract large numbers of students, and Martin Whitby's Countryside Management degree brought a new approach to the social sciences in Agriculture. Both of these developments were to bear further fruit; Peter's degree became the name for the new department that brought together Soil Science, Agricultural Engineering and Agricultural Biology, while Martin's research would lead to the formation of the Countryside Change Unit, which itself evolved into the Centre for Rural Economy. These changes, and the need for a more unified location, led in the early 1980s to interest in the 'Old' Medical School. The medics were getting a new palace and their old one was a lot better than anything else on offer – it was a listed Art Deco building. Agriculture moved into the Animal House on the third floor after the medics let their dogs out!

Disputes now opened over the future of Biology in the Faculty of Science. This had been the former home of the Agricultural Botany and Zoology Departments, but now the suggestion was that the biologists come to Agriculture; this was not universally acclaimed. Also the 'pure' biologists were in the Ridley Building at the diametrically opposite side of campus from the Agriculture Building and the King George VI Building. The biologists drifted forwards and backwards between the three buildings. This unhappy situation persisted until the new millennium when the latest reorganization demoted the Faculty of Agriculture and Biological Sciences to being a school within the new super Faculty of Science, Agriculture and Engineering. Some of the biologists, soil scientists and biochemists went off to pastures new, leaving a structure remarkably similar to the School of Agriculture of the 1960s! With the declining popularity of sciences, a drift back into the tower-block Agriculture Building of the Mac Cooper era began.

Agricultural Chemistry now split into Soil Science (under the leadership of Peter Arnold, the first British professor of the subject), and Agricultural Biochemistry. By the time that David retired, more was known about the digestion and diet of ruminants than that of humans; there is no doubt that the diet of animals was getting healthier while that of *Homo sapiens* was deteriorating! In fact, David's department latterly evolved into human nutrition, though the new human subjects are somewhat more argumentative than were the cows!

The Heslop Harrisons, who dominated Biology for two generations, provided the University with its greatest controversy. John's identification of Mediterranean plants growing on R(h)um off the west coast of Scotland led to a dispute popularized in *A Rum Affair*. His son George and daughter Helena (Dolly) lectured in Entomology and Botany respectively and Dolly researched the genetics of primitive cereals (and published her results in the *Journal of King's College Agriculture Society*) – work that still remains the basis of archaeobotany. With her sister-in-law running the Gilchrist Library, the Heslop Harrisons were ubiquitous.

Social life for the Agriculture degree has tended to centre upon the junior branch of the Agricultural Society referred to earlier. This group, after attending the evening talks, usually repaired to the Bun Room or other watering hole for a robust evening of entertainment. Feats, such as the attempt to drink a pub dry (they were beaten by the spirits, having finished the beer) led to the cap for overindulgence, a title disputed regularly with the medics, dentals and engineers on the rugby pitch, in formal debate or, often, in a less well-structured environment.

Rugby has always been the sport of choice, with grudge matches against some of the formerly mentioned groups; several students have represented their country, most notable being John 'the Great White Shark' Jeffreys who played for Scotland and the British Lions. Of all the cohorts in the University, the agrics have always been one of the most coherent and conspicuous. As well as enjoying themselves, they have also been leaders in fundraising and have contributed much to Rag Week. The agrics' float – they never had problems getting a tractor, trailer and straw bales – has always had a message and often a squirt of water for the unwary. 'Nancy the Nationalized Cow' of 1947 sold a message appropriate today that the most productive animal imaginable would be fed on a diet of government forms – it produced tins of Klim, rationed powdered milk.

Robert Shiel

CHEMICAL ENGINEERING

On the morning of 5 December 2001, the results of the 2001 Research Assessment Exercise (RAE) were announced. The Department of Chemical and Process Engineering had succeeded in doing what no other Chemical Engineering department had managed by increasing its performance by two grades from 3 to 5. This was public recognition that its research activities had achieved international standing. A year earlier, the Department had been awarded £1.7m from the Joint Infrastructure Fund to renew and expand all its experimental research laboratories and provide new upgraded study space for all the postgraduate students and research associates working therein. With the building work almost completed by the date of the RAE announcement, some 48 years had passed since the Chemical Engineering Department was founded in a small corner of the Stephenson Building, under the auspices of the Mechanical Engineering Department, headed at that time by Professor Aubrey Burstall.

In the early 1950s, Mechanical Engineering had offered a final-year option in the then new subject of Chemical Engineering before appointing John Metcalfe Coulson from Imperial College as Professor and Head of Department in 1954. JM, as he was affectionately known, started an MSc course that year and admitted the first undergraduate students to a three-year BSc Hons (Dunelm) in Chemical Engineering in 1955. He gathered a small team of colleagues to teach the fledgling course, including Frank Goodridge from Constantine College in Middlesbrough, Dr Patterson from Sunderland Technical College, who brought Charlie Curry with him to be chief technician, and Jim Forsyth who came from Leeds along with Ray Plimley as a postgraduate student. In 1958, John Desmond Thornton, known as JD, joined the Department from Harwell and later took the chair endowed by Procter & Gamble, and in 1961, Ian Fells was appointed Reader in Fuel Technology on the retirement of Dr Patterson. The lecturing staff was completed by 1962 with the appointments of Hugh Murray, Ken Peet, John Harker and John Porter. JM's philosophy was to prepare his students for a life in industry where, as chemical engineers, they would have to work alongside chemists, mathematicians, metallurgists, and mechanical and electrical engineers. His strategy was to ensure that students attended lectures in these disciplines, whether or not the subject of the lecture was relevant to chemical engineers.

The staff and the growing number of students were soon making demands for space that the Stephenson Building could not meet and, in 1964, the Department was moved into a new building, Merz Court, opened by the Prime Minister, Harold Wilson. The facilities were excellent for that time, and much credit must go to JM

Group photo of first Chemical Engineering graduates and staff, June 1958

for his outstanding ability to persuade industrialists to donate money, equipment and expertise so willingly to his department. He established an advisory board to formalize some of his requests and started the annual dinner to offer thanks to all those who had helped in the previous year. In the early years, the dinner was a formal and worthy occasion and it has continued every February, becoming more relaxed, considerably noisier and much more enjoyable as the years pass. Staff, students, former graduates and guests from industry still gather to hear of the work and achievements of the Department and to keep in touch with each other.

Heads of Department (left to right): John Backhurst (1994–2002), John Coulson (1954–68), Ken Peet (1984–89)

By the early 1970s, the staff had increased with John Backhurst, Colin Howarth, Julian Morris and Peter Norman joining colleagues who had been in post from the earlier days. It was a remarkable attribute of the Department that, once appointed, members of staff stayed. This reflected the family-like atmosphere within the Department, which was so noticeable and appealing to its students. Sadly, John Porter died suddenly in post in 1988, after pioneering heart surgery several years earlier. Sandy Mearns had the same operation at the same time, but fortunately was able to enjoy life into his retirement.

The success of the Department took JM on leave of absence to help found the Chemical Engineering Department at Heriot-Watt University, Edinburgh, passing the headship to John Thornton. On his return to Newcastle and nearing retirement, JM devoted his final years in the Department to the revision of the remarkable textbook *Chemical Engineering*, which he and Jack Richardson produced while at Imperial College, the first volume of which was published in 1954. He enlisted the help of John Backhurst and John Harker on a textbook project that would continue beyond both their retirements and that, as a bestseller for nearly 50 years, must represent a record for a specialist text. JM had a long and happy retirement, returning to give a lecture on the Department's 30th anniversary. He died in 1990.

Under John Thornton, research in the Department assumed greater prominence. Frank Goodridge, since establishing Electrochemical Engineering as a discipline with a huge grant of £250,000 in 1964, had become a world authority in the subject. Gas phase electrochemical work never achieved quite the same success, although Ian Fells and John Harker popularized and pushed the boundaries of fuel and energy through

television and the printed word respectively. Julian Morris started to establish Newcastle as a leader in process control, and the reputation of the Department as a centre for research grew, complementing the success of its undergraduate activities.

As fixed headship terms were introduced in departments, Frank Goodridge, Ken Peet, Julian Morris and John Backhurst were eventually to assume that role, but life and times in universities were changing. Early retirements were implemented to bring in younger staff and raise research profiles; teaching was being assessed as never before; and research assessment, which began as an internal university procedure, became a national activity of great importance. Budgets were devolved to departmental levels and student numbers became a vital resource implication. Whereas in earlier years, the annual undergraduate intake could vary considerably, the quota now became an unmissable target, coupled with specified A-level grades. The four-year MEng was intended for the highest-qualified entrants, but the three-year BEng, which succeeded the earlier BSc, also had to attract excellent students who genuinely wanted to take that degree. Degree courses became programmes, and the introduction of new postgraduate degrees was demanded. Documentation, being readily assessed, proliferated and there was a danger of changing from a department where personal contact between staff and students had been the outstanding attribute of departmental life to one where the production of paper became the measure of success. Ken Peet confronted these early challenges, but left plenty for his successors to face.

The students have always been the lifeblood of the Department. From small beginnings, the annual undergraduate entry averaged 40 for many years. It was not until 1970 that the first woman was admitted, and she

Chemical Engineering students at work in the laboratory

was duly awarded a First. Female entrants increased rapidly and, for many years, of any UK university Newcastle had the highest proportion of women entering its doors. They averaged 25 per cent of the intake from the late 1970s onwards and changed for ever, and for the better, the social life of the Department. Over the years, at least ten couples have married after graduation, and five offspring have followed their fathers into the Department.

Increasing numbers of overseas students enhanced the atmosphere in the Department, and the 'buzz' was often noted by visitors. Academic standards have always been maintained at a high level, and the Department has been recognized by the quality of the jobs that its graduates have succeeded in obtaining since 1958. JM set out to produce chemical engineers for a career in industry, and the Department can take pride that industry has been the main destination of its graduates. Many have made successful careers in the process industries, others have founded their own companies within the sector. Colin Ramshaw, one of the graduates of 1958, returned to the Department in 1992 as Professor of Chemical Engineering. Some have chosen

different paths – a career in deep-sea diving, television, journalism, the financial world, football management, bookmaking, and charity and missionary work in Africa to name a few. Staff have always tried to help their tutees and that support has always been acknowledged and appreciated.

At one of the most recent annual dinners, an industrialist speaker said that over 25 years he had asked graduates 'Why did you come to Newcastle?', and always received the same answer: 'Because of the warmth of the initial welcome to the Department'. That warmth of welcome has always been there and all alumni will testify to it.

With a change of Vice-Chancellor in 2001 came restructuring of the University and, on 1 August 2002, the Department joined with parts of Mechanical Engineering and Physics to become the School of Chemical Engineering and Advanced Materials under the headship of Julian Morris. The days of the Department were over and a new era was beginning.

John Backhurst

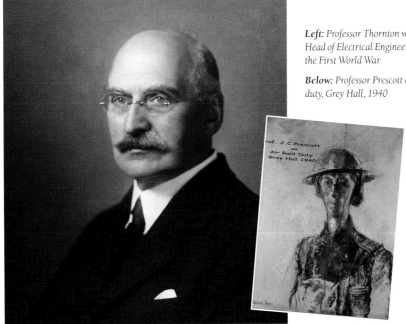

Left: Professor Thornton who was Head of Electrical Engineering after the First World War

Below: Professor Prescott on air-raid duty, Grey Hall, 1940

ELECTRICAL AND ELECTRONIC ENGINEERING

As the Industrial Revolution of the Victorian era gathered pace, the College of Physical Science at Newcastle proved woefully inadequate for the advanced teaching of Electrical Engineering. All around the North East great strides were being made: Joseph Swan with his electric light; Charles Parsons about to produce his turbo alternators; J.H. Holmes with his electrical machines. All these needed a place of higher education where their fundamental principles could be taught.

Armstrong College provided that facility when it inaugurated its Electrical Engineering Department. In 1871, deep in the basement in cramped conditions, laboratories were installed and teaching began. Staff and students had a difficult beginning. Large electrical machines were difficult to locate in the restricted spaces. However, cometh the hour, cometh the man – or men, as it proved, for the College was fortunate to appoint to its teaching staff many men of outstanding ability to fulfil the ever-growing needs of the hungry, industrial North East.

Foremost among them was Professor W.M. Thornton, who headed the Electrical Engineering Department after the Great War and who was brought back from retirement to help out during the Second World War. He brought honour to the department by being elected President of the Institution of Electrical Engineers. He was followed by the delightful and charming Professor J.C. Prescott, who was not only renowned for his work on electrical machines, but was also a man of great integrity and kindness. On being sought by his secretary one day to fulfil an engagement, she smiled benignly on being told that he had gone shopping to buy a present for the sick daughter of his youngest lecturer – he regarded that as more important! His portrait, painted in oils and showing him in wartime garb as a University 'firewatcher', complete with steel helmet and stirrup pump, still causes much amusement.

The Electrical Engineering world between the wars was changing, however, as radio communication developed. The Department kept pace with its teaching – one of its staff, Dr Emrhys Williams, produced an undergraduate textbook that became a much consulted work. Ever present, however, was the problem of space for the large machines and, later, space for the huge transformer necessary for the study of high-voltage engineering. Hence, in 1947, the Department was moved from the old Armstrong Building to the empty Presbyterian church opposite the Students' Union building. 'A transformer in the transept and a power factory in the pulpit', as some wit remarked.

It was not very satisfactory accommodation in the post-war university world, because a new and exciting technology had been unleashed by wartime developments: Electronic Engineering. The subject was new and few textbooks existed, but the Department was moved rapidly into the new field by the appointment of Mr F.J.U. Ritson. Fresh from his outstanding wartime work on radar, he was one of the few men well versed in the latest developments. Within the space of a year, he established lecture courses, teaching laboratories and research programmes in both electronics and automatic control. Undergraduates vied for places and the Department blossomed as never before. During this

121

Electrical Engineering was housed in Grey Hall, an old Presbyterian church, from the end of the Second World War until 1964

time, lecture courses were also established in Digital Electronics and joint courses were operated with the Department of Digital Computing.

All these developments were accomplished within the framework of a new building – Merz Court, named after C.H. Merz, the electrical chemical engineer who had done so much to foster the teaching of advanced technology in Newcastle. Opened by Prime Minister Harold Wilson in 1965, it finally provided the space that had been so woefully lacking until then. The new building enabled an expansion of research and development and saw the appointment in 1969 of Professor Hans Hartnagel, an expert in the field of semi-conductor devices. A clean room was built and Professor Hartnagel attracted to the Department large numbers of foreign researchers. Postgraduate and post-doctoral research flourished, and the Department became known for its publications on new types of semi-conductors throughout Europe. Through his efforts the Electrical Department was renamed the Department of Electronic and Electrical Engineering and its name became and remains synonymous with advanced research and teaching throughout the world.

Terry Kennair

CIVIL ENGINEERING

Civil engineering involves the development of sustainable infrastructure that maintains and improves people's quality of life. The first engineering students at Durham University were admitted in 1838. They were awarded the academic rank of Civil Engineer, the equivalent of a degree. The courses had high mathematics content, a strong practical emphasis and regular scientific laboratory classes, but employers refused to recognize university training because going

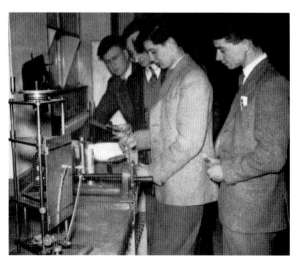

Students testing clay samples, in 1956

HUGH NEFFENDORF

CIVIL ENGINEERING / 1967–70

I was in the class of 1970. What is unusual about our class is that we have frequent reunions in Newcastle, certainly the only CivEng class to do so. We also set up the Civil Engineering Society, developed its logo and tie, and talked the establishment into giving us a social room to use as a bar and games centre. We include a blacksmith, a pig farmer, policeman, museum chief (with CBE), accountants, professors, even some civil engineers! We meet at least once every five years and had our last reunion, with over 30 present, in June 2005.

Above: The Cassie Building which houses Civil Engineering

Above right: Civil Engineering students using concrete in a practical exercise

to university cost less than the premiums demanded of apprentices in engineers' offices, and by 1851 no further students registered.

The Department of Civil Engineering at Newcastle was established in 1945, although Professor William Fisher Cassie was appointed to the Chair in Civil Engineering in 1943. Employment was plentiful in the post-war years and most undergraduates read for the three-year pass degree rather than the four-year Honours degree. After 1957, the Honours degree became the norm.

From 1957 to 1981, three-year courses in Civil Engineering evolved as a BSc Honours degree, with students following two years of common study and a final year specialization in one of eight options: computer-aided design, geotechnical engineering, hydrology and hydraulic engineering, public health engineering, structural engineering, transport engineering, project and investigation and a general option. The degrees produced graduates who met the broad-based needs of practice, including the managerial aspects of Civil Engineering.

In 1973, a three-year Honours degree in Natural Environmental Engineering was introduced which included a blend of Civil Engineering and Environmental Control Engineering. The degree was changed, in 1977, to Civil and Environmental Engineering.

By 1980, it was clear that increased time at university was required for higher-level engineers. Consequently, a four-year BSc/BEng Honours degree in Civil Engineering, and in Civil Engineering and Environmental Engineering, was introduced, later becoming the MEng. The first two years established the technical and scientific background for the later, more professional studies. In the third year, core subjects such as geotechnical engineering, hydraulic engineering and structural engineering, with optional subjects computer-aided design, geotechnical engineering, public health engineering, structural engineering and transport engineering were available. In the fourth year, courses were professionally orientated and included economics, civil engineering practice and management. Advanced analysis and design were assigned a high priority, with an industrially based project allowing the student to apply acquired knowledge to the solution of a real-world problem.

Following changes in the Institution of Civil Engineers recognition of degrees, the three- and four-year degrees became, in 1987, BEng and MEng respectively. In 1994, major changes to the structure of the degrees were made. The far-sighted introduction of BEng and MEng degrees in Structural Engineering provided a broad curriculum, which included architecture, building and applications of structural engineering in naval architecture, offshore engineering and mechanical engineering. These high-quality degrees allowed the Department to attract a diverse range of nationalities within the student body.

Originally, the Department was housed in the Armstrong Building, with the laboratories being in Haymarket Lane. The three-floor Cassie Building was formally opened in 1955 by Sir Ben Lockspeiser, previously the Government's chief scientific advisor, who inadvertently referred to the Cassie Building as being part of the University of Bristol! In 1974, an additional floor was added. Further space for Transport Engineering was taken over in the Claremont Tower and following the amalgamation, in 1988, of Geotechnical Engineering into Civil Engineering, the Drummond Building also became departmental space. The Cassie Building and the Drummond Building now house the School of Civil Engineering and Geosciences.

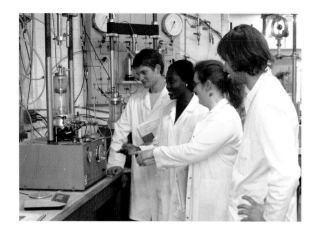

Students preparing to test clay samples in 2005

William Fisher Cassie was Head of Department from 1945 to 1970. He was dour, even severe, despite his Morris dancing! Yet he was modern in much of his thinking and believed in the education of the whole person. The undergraduates, initially men only, were usually in their mid- to late twenties. Many had completed national service and already had a Higher National Diploma. They were expected to comply with a professional dress code, wear a gown to lectures and be able to draw to a high standard.

Professor Peter Isaac was Head of Department between 1970 and 1981, having been appointed to the Chair of Public Health Engineering in 1964 on All Fools' Day! Peter was known not only for being a prominent expert in the history of printing, but also for his ability to clear a room of staff and students in seconds just by looking at his wristwatch and coughing! Other heads of department were Paul Novak, 1981–3, Warren Pescod 1983–98, Barry Clarke 1998–2002 and the present Head of School, Professor David Parker.

A major reorganization took place in 2002, when the School of Civil Engineering and Geosciences was created to address the needs of research, teaching and professional development in a 21st-century society concerned with human interaction and influence on the natural environment. This new school included Civil Engineering, Geomatics, the Fossil Fuels and Environmental Geochemistry Institute, and staff with an interest in soil in Agriculture and Environmental Science. Bringing together 60 leading researchers and teachers from across the University, together with more than 30 support staff and state-of-the-art facilities, the school has consolidated activity in geophysics, geochemistry, geographic information science, environmental engineering and civil engineering into a distinctive focus in which new research, outreach and teaching synergies can be developed, and existing ones renewed.

The School offers to its 300 undergraduates, 11 MEng, BEng and BSc degrees together with, if needed, a Foundation Year to help widening participation for those who have the ability but not the necessary qualifications to enter directly onto the degree courses. There are 15 Master's courses offering postgraduate advanced courses and research programmes which are taken by 165 postgraduates. Recognizing that it has the potential to address major interdisciplinary research issues of global importance, the School has developed research that integrates earth systems science, engineering, technology, policy-making and governance to develop sustainable solutions to global problems.

The Department was assessed in the 1989, 1992, 1996 and 2001 Research Assessment Exercises and attained the highest rating of 5 in the latter three. The quality of teaching in Civil Engineering was recognized by very high gradings in the latest 1997 Higher Education Funding Council for England teaching quality assessment exercise.

The School has developed diverse opportunities for commercialization. Experience gained through both research and teaching is used to inform the professional development programme that can be delivered in the in-house Continuing Professional Development training suite. Similarly, the School's skills and facilities allow it to offer a comprehensive range of analytical, testing and consulting services.

The School acknowledges the rapid pace of change where the time lag between research, development and production is getting shorter and information rapidly becomes out of date. Consequently, constant updating is necessary to ensure students adapt to changing circumstances. Employers expect graduates to be prepared for the realities of the job markets where, for example, civil engineering design is carried out on computers, with Civil Engineering graduates being expected to manage and control large infrastructure projects.

A common theme of the School in the future will be the developing of engineering solutions for a sustainable society across all areas of civil engineering in the context of earth systems engineering.

John Bull

The Duke of Edinburgh addresses the assembly in the Heat Engines Laboratory

MECHANICAL ENGINEERING

In his excellent book on the University, E.M. Bettenson tells a lively story. In the early days of the College of Physical Science, Engineering began as an undivided whole. A concession to a related interest was marked in the style of the first Professor, the formidable R.I. Weighton (1891–1920), Professor of Engineering and Naval Architecture, but some years were to pass before independence was declared. His successor, Professor Hawkes, a veteran of the Royal Navy, acquired Mechanical, Marine and Civil Engineering with the title of his chair, thus launching a tradition of academic parturition that prevailed for some time.

The modern history of the Department began on a gala occasion in 1951, when HRH Prince Philip opened the Stephenson Building. Its planning had begun soon after the appointment of Professor Aubrey Burstall in 1945 and, with the powerful support of the Rector, Lord Eustace Percy, and the architectural skills of Professor W.B. Edwards, the building soon took shape on a site generously provided by the Freemen and the City of Newcastle upon Tyne. It was the first post-war engineering building in the universities of this country.

Engineering had previously occupied cramped quarters in the Armstrong Building where, after the privations of the war years, teaching facilities were sparse and research equipment minimal. As ex-servicemen returned in large numbers, the new building offered accommodation for more than 600 students, ample space for modern engineering laboratories, an excellent library and a well-endowed workshop. Impressive portraits of the Stephensons, father and son, soon adorned the walls, followed by a thoughtful Sir Charles Parsons. The new building attracted national attention.

The arrival of HRH The Duke of Edinburgh at the Stephenson Building, accompanied by the Rector, Lord Eustace Percy

The Stephenson Engineering Society was born one year later. Its aims were to promote staff–student relationships, to encourage alumni to maintain contact and to bring professional engineers into the life of the Department. At its inaugural dinner, the 145 diners included such VIPs as Lord Eustace Percy, the Deputy Lord Mayor of Newcastle, the current and the past President of the Institution of Mechanical Engineers, the managing director of Sir Charles Parsons Co. Ltd and many other luminaries. The Society's journal published papers of the highest quality, the first Stephenson Lecture having been delivered by Sir Ben Lockspeiser of the Privy Council for Scientific and Industrial Research. Open days for schoolchildren and occasional teas for hungry students added a spirit of conviviality.

Academic changes gathered pace. New structures for degrees broadened the General Degree (in which the final year was spent in another Engineering Department) and offered a wider range of options for the Honours degree. Young people without A levels, but with Higher National Certificates and Higher National Diplomas, were encouraged to apply, many of whom achieved high academic results and went forward to distinguished careers.

The following decades saw major advances in research activity and in postgraduate courses. National and international conferences were held in the Department, the largest being the Fourth World Congress of the International Federation for the Theory of Machines and Mechanisms attended in 1975 by several hundred delegates from 29 countries. The pioneering introductions of Production Engineering and of Industrial Management into undergraduate teaching were followed by new chairs in Chemical Engineering and Agricultural Engineering

125

Students from Mechanical Engineering at work in the lab

(1940–50s), and later in a sustained burst of creativity by new chairs in Energy Studies, Manufacturing Engineering, Industrial Management, a readership in Biomedical Engineering and, in support of Materials interests, chairs in Engineering Materials and in Composite Materials Engineering (1970–80s), all established with funds raised from friends and supporters outside the University.

Occasionally, the rapid changes generated a slight frisson. A sizeable hut, built in the courtyard of the Stephenson Building to offer space to Chemical Engineering, led to some sharp exchanges from the 'mechanicals' when the 'chemicals', having moved to new affluence in Merz Court, attempted to take it with them. At a lower level, research students in Chemical Engineering realized that their large old laboratory, now completely empty and newly painted, made an ideal football stadium in the dead of night. Unfortunately for them, the imprint of footballs on the otherwise immaculate walls led to their undoing. The next day, the mechanicals' chief technician, an ex-chief petty officer, returned to his naval traditions by offering very clear advice to the clean-up detail conscripted from Merz Court.

The Design Unit, launched in 1969, was funded by a modest grant from the University Grants Committee. Its aims were to strengthen academic–industrial connections, to assist the transfer of research results into engineering practice and to undertake original design and development on commission. The team of six had to earn their keep after the grant ran out, a task easier in concept than in execution. After some bumpy rides, it found its forte and went from strength to strength. By 1990, the Unit had earned impressive annual incomes, had acquired the national Gear Metrology Laboratory and, by the sweat of its brow, had established itself as a world leader in the field of gear research and development.

PROFESSOR DEREK GELDART

MECHANICAL ENGINEERING / 1950–4

I left school at 15 in order to take up an apprenticeship with a steel manufacturing firm, situated on Teesside. I was given day release to study Mechanical Engineering at technical college and, in 1949, I gained a scholarship to study Engineering at King's.

Many of the other Engineering students had similar backgrounds to mine. Almost all were the first generation in their families to attend university. The lecturers, too, had spent time in industry and/or the armed services. Few had doctorates, perhaps with the exception of the Head of Department, Professor Aubrey Burstall, and a marvellous and inspiring teacher, Dr W.S. Patterson, Reader in Fuel Technology, who gave many of us a love of experimental work.

All through my course the engineers had to attend lectures on Saturday mornings, the most memorable of which was Chemistry, enlivened sometimes by pyrotechnic demonstrations, impossible to be shown these days, with Health and Safety regulations to consider.

Each lab session was followed by report writing, an activity in which engineers were considered to be deficient. The Head of Department had the inspired idea of employing the recently retired headmaster of Newcastle Grammar School, Dr Ebenezer Rhys Thomas, to correct our written reports. This silver-haired gentleman was given an office in the new building and patiently worked through our turgid reports, explaining to us better ways of expressing ourselves.

Throughout my very happy four years at King's, there was immense good-natured rivalry between faculties. We engineers considered the agrics and the medics to be beer-swilling, rugby-playing thickies, only at university because their fathers were well-off farmers or GPs respectively. Anyone studying arts subjects was regarded as having an easy life with few lectures and plenty of time to spend in the Union Building, drinking and endlessly talking. I think that they regarded us as over-serious, dull swots, although sometimes we skipped lectures to visit the news cinema close to the Union Building. Oh! Happy days!

126

PETER VALE

MECHANICAL ENGINEERING / 1965–8
Engineering Drawing provided a wonderful opportunity to go ten-pin bowling on a Friday afternoon. This came home to roost in the last week of term, with frantic – albeit ultimately successful – efforts to design a car window-winding mechanism in time for the deadline. That was education in self-management, as well as engineering!

The large number of visitors from all parts of the world was matched only by the number of visits made by staff and students in opposite directions. Groups of Honours students in successive years who entered and won first place in the national Shell Supermileage Competition (in which you designed and made your car) achieved performances exceeding 800 miles per gallon, which could have taken them to, say, Provence on a gallon of petrol.

In 1987, when the Faculty of Engineering was restructured, the Departments of Mechanical Engineering and of Metallurgy and Engineering Materials were merged. This led, *inter alia*, to a new degree course in Materials Design and Engineering, exchanges of laboratories and increasing levels of co-operation in teaching and research. The national trend to four-year MEng degrees formed the background to an extended range of courses offered by the combined Department, including a ground-breaking degree course 'Mechanical Engineering (Europe)' in which groups of students from Continental countries exchanged with our own students for a year's study. The newly formed Foundation Year, which enabled applicants who had high promise but lacked full entry qualifications to be accepted, proved to be a marked success.

In the early 1990s, both the undergraduate entry to Mechanical Engineering and research funding reached their highest totals on record. The period also saw the rapid growth of internal academic audits on teaching and research by the University, and demands for detailed information on everything under the sun from research councils, professional institutions, university finance committees and others. The age of accountancy had arrived.

Leonard Maunder

MARINE TECHNOLOGY

Given the importance of the North East of England in the marine industries, it is no surprise that the teaching of Marine Technology has featured strongly at the University of Newcastle upon Tyne. In the 1890s, the North East was the leading shipbuilding centre in the world. With the support of the North East Coast Institution of Engineers and Shipbuilders, a Chair of Engineering and Naval Architecture was established in 1891, at what was then the Durham College of Physical Science. The first post holder was Robert Weighton, from Tyneside shipbuilders Hawthorn Leslie. In 1902, a lecturer in Naval Architecture, Francis Alexander, was appointed, and this led to the establishment of the Department of Naval Architecture in 1904. A Chair of Naval Architecture was established in 1906 and Joseph Welch appointed.

Full-time teaching attracted around 15–20 students, but evening classes had up to 100 part-time students, usually those working in local shipyards. From the start, there was flexibility in the approach to teaching, including the use of local shipyard technical staff to assist in evening teaching. However, even in 1909, one in three students was from overseas. An Honours degree was introduced in 1913, and the first postgraduate degrees were awarded by 1920.

Sir Westcott Abell was the second Professor to be appointed, in 1929, at a time when the depressed state of the industry in the UK resulted in low British student numbers. The growing reputation of the Department ensured that the degree in Naval Architecture remained popular for overseas students. Abell had been Chief Ship Surveyor at Lloyd's Register of Shipping (LRS), the premier ship classification society, which continues to employ many Newcastle alumni. Abell also worked commercially, including on the design of train ferries for the Southern Railway, emphasizing the close connection with industry that has been a hallmark from the start.

After 1945, the shipbuilding industry expanded and the Department followed the trend, with student numbers increasing from 18 in 1944 to 100 in 1960. During this period two major research facilities, the ship model towing tank and the propeller cavitation tunnel, were installed in the Armstrong Building. The cavitation tunnel was rebuilt from a German marine testing facility, acquired after 1945. When the rebuilt tunnel opened in 1949, one of the first sets of experiments was to test a systematic series of propellers, resulting in design charts that are still in regular use around the world. The model tank is primarily for teaching, but the cavitation tunnel, extensively modernized in 2000, has national commercial importance as the only such equipment operational in the UK in 2006.

Professor Burrill, the third Professor of Naval Architecture, increased staff numbers by bringing in lecturers in ship design and production. Greater flexibility in the degree programme was introduced, preparing students for employment in a variety of marine jobs. Burrill died suddenly in 1965, and Professor Muckle became acting Head of Department. He had been instrumental in introducing lightweight aluminium superstructures in passenger liners, notably *Oriana and Canberra*, allowing an increased capacity. In 1966, John Caldwell, from the Royal Naval Scientific Service, was appointed to the chair; he was able to make use of the generous funding to universities available after the Robbins Report. After John Caldwell's retirement, the Chair was briefly held by John Marshall, and then by Pratyush Sen who is in post at the time of writing.

Marine engineering developed separately from Naval Architecture, and was initially taught within Mechanical Engineering. A Chair in Marine Engineering was established in 1956 and George Chambers, a

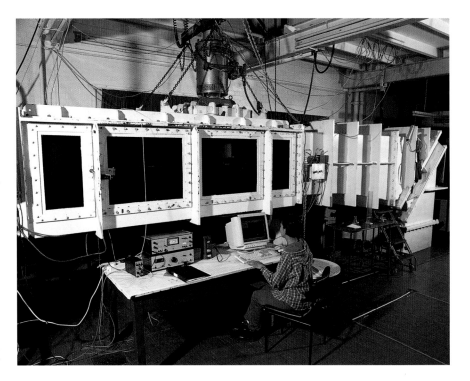

former Royal Navy engineering officer, was appointed. He was followed by Ray Thompson in 1975 and Tony Roskilly in 1999. Impressive experimental and teaching facilities included an engine laboratory with large marine diesel engines.

In 1966, a separate Department of Marine Engineering was created, based in the Stephenson Building. There was close collaboration between this new department and Naval Architecture, with many common lecture courses, and a formal federal arrangement was set up in 1975. This was followed by a 1989 merger to form the Department of Marine Technology, which saw the introduction of degrees in Offshore Engineering and Small Craft Technology, supporting new developments in the marine industry. A further merger in 2002 brought together Marine Technology and the Department of Marine Sciences and Coastal Management in a specialized school focusing on the whole range of marine research and teaching, with an increasing emphasis on environmental sustainability.

In 1970, Marine Transport was recognized as a new subject, and a readership was established in 1974. This was raised to a Chair in Marine Transport and Management in 2002. In parallel with increased offshore activity in the UK sector, a Chair in Offshore Engineering was established in 1975. This is currently held by the Head of School, Atilla Incecik, appointed in 1996.

The University houses two major research facilities: the propellor cavitation tunnel (above) – the only one in the UK in 2006 – and the ship model towing tank (left)

MINOS KOMNINOS

NAVAL ARCHITECTURE / 1965–9

Being a student in Geordie-land in the 60s was full of fun. I had a number of Greek friends who did much to prevent me becoming homesick, simply by speaking Greek. Often we gathered in one of our small flats for a dinner party with Greek food, prepared by ourselves, and a background of rather loud bouzouki music. On the odd occasion, we would invite non-Greeks, usually women, to these parties but on the whole they were all-male affairs, with the conversation centring on the University, Greece and the day we would return to a warmer climate!

Each of the three summer breaks I spent two months in shipyards and research centres, receiving a small salary while obtaining industrial experience. In 1965, the two months were spent in Swan Hunter's design room and Wigham Richardson Shipyard at Wallsend. In 1966, I worked at the British Ship Research Association in the same town. The highlight of my work experience came in 1968, when I travelled to Gothenburg in Sweden and worked in the Gotaverken yard, which was building container ships and tankers using the recently developed 'block-by-block' method. I was seeking experience in design and could hardly have been in a better place.

The fourfold increase in oil prices in the 1970s not only stimulated oil exploration, but also the work of the Ship Performance Group, led by Dr Bob Townsin. Collaboration with shipowners and paint companies to reduce hull friction has continued to the present day. Local industrial links are maintained with the world's leading marine coating supplier, International Paints, which is based at Felling on the Tyne.

From a total of 120 students (Naval Architecture and Marine Engineering) in 1970, the number of Marine Technology undergraduates had doubled by 2005. Growth in postgraduate numbers has been more spectacular. The first taught MSc, set up in 1968, had typically 10 students graduating annually. In 2000 there were 30 Masters graduates, but by 2006 over 200 MSc students are registered, including a large cohort on distance learning programmes. PhD numbers have also increased, and in both cases, many are from overseas.

Overseas students have always featured at Newcastle, indeed not just fathers and sons, but in one case three generations of a Greek family. In 1970, 26 Naval Architecture and 10 Marine Engineering Honours

John Caldwell became Head of Marine Technology in 1966

graduates came from the UK, Canada, Greece, Hong Kong, Norway, Sri Lanka and Singapore. Of the 36, 17 were from outside the UK. In 2005, the School had students from 48 different countries.

Although the building of ships in the UK, with the important exception of the Navy, has declined, the world fleet of ocean-going ships has reached 100,000 and the importance of the marine sector to the UK is still huge. The design content of ships has increased and with expanding regulations creates a demand for more qualified engineers. Newcastle graduates are increasingly moving into shipping services, offshore energy and marine leisure, as well as shipbuilding and marine engineering.

Alumni from Newcastle have gone on to leading positions in the marine world, for example in Singapore, from where students first arrived in the mid-1960s. By the turn of the century, they had risen to head the major shipyard groups and one is a cabinet minister. In 2005, Nigel Gee, a 1969 graduate, became President of the Royal Institution of Naval Architects (RINA). John Caldwell was the first academic to be President of RINA in 1984, and Ray Thompson was President of the Institute of Marine Engineers in 1995. Academic staff continue to make a major contribution to professional engineering institutions, regionally and nationally, and also sit on industry and government bodies, valued for their independent expertise.

The international nature of the marine business encourages alumni to keep in touch and also to maintain contact with the School. Many alumni visit, as part of reunions, as customers for research, recruiters of new graduates and as friends. Staff always find a ready welcome in the marine community when they travel overseas.

Marine Technology has remained in the Armstrong Building for over 100 years, anchored by its extensive research facilities, and benefiting from the impressive ambience. Over the century, Marine Technology at Newcastle has passed through difficult times as the industry it supports has ebbed and flowed. Particularly since 1945, there has been steady growth as the subject has adapted to changing needs in the international marine industries. As long as the sea remains a major element for international trade, resources and leisure, Marine Technology at Newcastle will provide the research and teaching to support the industry.

George Bruce

Above left: The Dove in 1908

Left: Commemorative plaque outside the main door

Above: The joint coat of arms of the Hudleston and Dove families with the motto 'Soli deo honour et Gloria' on the west gable of the Lab

MARINE SCIENCE AT THE DOVE MARINE LABORATORY

Newcastle is a city with a proud marine natural history heritage dating back to the pioneering naturalists of the 19th century. During this period, the emergence of naturalist societies throughout the region, including The Natural History Society of Northumberland, Durham and Newcastle upon Tyne, founded in 1829, provided a real stimulus to the pursuit of marine natural history. Naturalists including George Johnston (1797–1855), Joshua Alder (1792–1867), Albany Hancock (1806–73), Alfred Norman (1831–1918) and George Brady (1832–1921), were prominent in the field. Brady became Professor of Natural History at Newcastle's College of Physical Science and thus had an association with the embryonic university.

The establishment of a marine laboratory, in 1897, in a 'small unpretentious wooden building' next to the Saltwater Baths in Cullercoats Bay, was greatly influenced by Brady. It was built under the direction of Professor Alexander Meek, the first Professor of Zoology at Newcastle. Its purpose was to pursue fisheries science to address the issue of dwindling fish stocks. Fisheries research was seen as a means of furthering the prosperity of the region. Unfortunately, however, the wooden laboratory was gutted by fire in 1904.

The fire was ultimately of long-term benefit: a private benefactor and outstanding scientist, Mr W.H. Hudleston, provided funds to construct a new, more substantial building, which was opened in 1908. It was named the Dove Laboratory after his ancestor, Eleanor Dove. This was a significant turning point in local marine biology: professional scientists were to carry on from the firm base set by the 19th century pioneers in a purpose-built marine laboratory.

The marine research vessel,
Bernicia *on the Tyne*

The Laboratory became a department of Armstrong College. Considerable scientific progress was made and researchers from the Dove became known nationally. In 1911, the Laboratory procured its own first research boat, the *Evadne*. Professor Meek produced much research of note and, in 1916, he published a highly regarded volume *The Migrations of Fish*. The Dove's journal, *Report of the Dove Marine Laboratory*, acquired an international reputation.

Following the retirement of Meek, the Laboratory suffered a difficult period and *Evadne* had to be sold. Alfred Hobson became Director in 1933 and Herbert Bull joined the Laboratory. Bull was an exceptional marine naturalist, although his major work lay in fish physiology. During the 1939–45 war just one scientist, Bernard Storrow, a former schoolmaster, held fort at the Laboratory.

It was not until the early 1950s that the Dove began to recover. Another boat, the *Pandalus*, was acquired, although this was soon replaced by the *Alexander Meek*. In 1959, a substantial extension to the Laboratory was built. Research output, now including high-quality ecological and fundamental marine biological investigations, rose markedly.

In 1967, Newcastle University took over responsibility for the Dove, and the Laboratory became a facility of the University's Department of Zoology. In 1969, though, the Dove's public aquarium, which had been so valued by the local community, was closed due to high running costs.

During the 1970s, use of the Dove for undergraduate teaching substantially increased. A specialized Final Honours course in Marine Zoology was offered as an option for the BSc programme in Zoology. Students opting for this were based at the Laboratory for the final year of their studies. In 1978, this was replaced by a highly successful degree in Marine Biology, again with students being taught at the Laboratory for much of their time.

The Dove played a vital role in the understanding of the biology of the North Sea under the direction of Professor Bob Clark and Dr John Allen, supported by good numbers of postgraduate students. In 1973, a purpose-built research vessel *Bernicia* replaced the *Alexander Meek*, enabling the Laboratory to continue its offshore research. The classic monitoring work of Dr Frank Evans and Dr Jack Buchanan paved the way for our understanding of the dynamics of seabed and plankton communities and, ultimately, their coupling to commercial fisheries. In 1992, an international conference was held to mark the double retirement of these two staff. The presentations formed a special edition (vol. 172) of the *Journal of Experimental Marine Biology and Ecology*, published the following year.

During the 1980s, Dr David Golding's research on nervous systems led to the important discovery of a second major form of secretory release from nerve fibre endings in a wide range of organisms. Other Dove scientists developed the technology to farm ragworms. Seabait Ltd, established by Dr (subsequently Professor) Peter Olive in 1985, pioneered the commercial production of ragworms. This has reduced the environmentally damaging effects of traditional bait-digging, earning the company the Queen's Awards for Environmental Achievement in 1994, and for Sustainable Development in 2003. Seabait Ltd obtained another Queen's Award in 2003 for Enterprise in International Trade, and is currently expanding rapidly with new facilities in the US.

Under the directorship of Dr (subsequently Professor) Stewart Evans, during the 1990s, the Dove extended its activities to include research into the effects of anti-fouling paints and estuarine pollutants, and the training of postgraduates from Ghana and Indonesia through its overseas links programme. Dr Evans also established a community education programme:

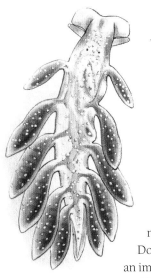

The nudibranch mollusc, Embletonia pulchra, *first described by Alder and Hancock and illustrated in their 'Monograph of the British Nudibranchiate Mollusca' published by the Ray Society*

'The North Sea: Our Joint Responsibility', engaging community groups in scientific projects. This outreach activity continues to be recognized nationally as a key strength of the Dove. In addition, the Dove remains an important base for student fieldwork. In 1997, the Laboratory marked 100 years of marine science at Cullercoats. An array of around 150 scientific alumni, many occupying influential positions, including those from Iceland, the US, Canada, Ghana, Singapore and Indonesia, attended a celebration dinner held in the University ballroom.

In 2000, *The Marine Fauna and Flora of the Cullercoats District* was published in two volumes. Edited by Dr Judy Foster-Smith, and with contributions from 17 national taxonomic experts (mainly emanating from the Dove), this forms one of the most comprehensive accounts of regional marine biodiversity.

Other substantial work undertaken at the Laboratory includes *The North Sea Fisheries Ecosystem Plan* produced under the direction of Professor Chris Frid, in collaboration with European partners. Based on an ecosystem approach to fisheries, this provides an important framework for the sustainable management of fish stocks. Also, the search for the molecular basis for tidal clocks in marine organisms, spearheaded by Professor Peter Olive, has kept the Dove abreast of developing technologies.

The Dove Marine Laboratory remains an essential University facility within the School of Marine Science and Technology, and with a new Director, marine biotechnologist Professor Grant Burgess, appointed in October 2005, it has considerable scope for developing innovative biotechnological approaches to medical, industrial and environmental problems that currently face the world. The words written in stone on the front of the building in 1908 remain equally relevant today: 'For the Furtherance of Marine Biology'.

Judy Foster-Smith

MATHEMATICS AND STATISTICS

The teaching and study of Mathematics (and in the last half century, also Statistics) emerged from the meagre seeds that were sown in the earliest days of the College of Physical Science in 1871. From its foundation there was a Chair of Mathematics, but this was the only appointment in the Department until 1888; then one assistant lecturer was added to the staff complement – and this remained the situation until 1896. Furthermore, three of the early holders of the chair (Aldis, Garnett and Gurney) had each been Principal of the College, so they must have had only limited time to devote to the teaching of Mathematics which, at this stage, meant a mix of pure and applied mathematics. The teaching, over this period, was essentially service teaching to the students of Medicine and other sciences. The level attained by the third year was not dissimilar to the A-level syllabuses of the late 1950s and early 60s: elementary calculus, the last books of Euclid and the dynamics of rigid bodies.

The Department grew slowly but steadily, in line with the growth of the College. In 1897, there was a professor, one lecturer and two assistant lecturers (one of these being G.W. Caunt, who is remembered for his influential text *An Introduction to the Infinitesimal Calculus*, written in 1914 and still in use into the 1960s). By 1921, there were six members of staff; this complement remained unchanged until 1942, when it rose to seven, then to ten in 1948, 21 in 1957, reaching 32 in 1966. Thereafter, until the present day, staff numbers have varied between about 26 and 34 and included, at various times, an administrator, demonstrators, research officers and a computer officer; the number of secretarial staff also increased. The Department was originally housed in dark, cramped accommodation in the Armstrong Building, then it moved to the Stephenson Building in 1958, and then, in 1965, to its present site within Merz Court which was designed specifically for the Department.

Mathematics, in the sense of a dedicated degree programme, was taught only at Durham until 1909; thereafter, with the coming of age of Armstrong College, proper departments were instituted at Newcastle, and the Department of Mathematics began to take a recognizable shape, although progress was slow. In 1893, the Professor of Mathematics reported that 'apart from exercise classes, five day lecture classes were attended by 96 students, and four evening classes by 72 students'. The Honours school in Mathematics had small numbers graduating until about 1961. For example, in 1927, there were four students in the final year: a Second, a Third and two fails; there were eight students in the second year. During the wartime years, 1940–5, the number of students graduating each year was small. Until 1961, the maximum number of students in the final year was 17, although the records show that the total number of students being taught in 1952 was about 500 – mainly service teaching.

From the late 60s, the Department expanded considerably, but it lost some service teaching and, in 1965, the Department of Engineering Mathematics was formed, to cover all the teaching to engineers. Now both three- and four-year degree programmes in Mathematics and Statistics exist, and a significant contribution is also made to the Joint Honours degrees in the Faculty of Science, Agriculture and Engineering. The service teaching currently encompasses statistics and mathematical methods for Biology, Medicine, Agriculture and some Engineering courses. In 2004–5, the numbers of students on programmes offered by the School (previously 'Department'), both Single and Joint Honours, were 186 at Stage 1; 102 at Stage 2; 131 at the Final Stage (third or fourth year); and about 1,250 students were taught in service courses.

The quality of the mathematics produced at Newcastle can be measured, first, by the increase in the number of chairs: one until 1914, then two from 1944, one assigned to Pure Mathematics and one to Applied Mathematics. In 1962, second chairs in each of Pure and Applied were founded. In this same year, a Chair of Statistics was also established, believed to be the fifth such chair in the UK. The first appointment in Statistics had been made in 1951, and by 1973 there was a group of four statisticians; Statistics, both at undergraduate and postgraduate level, now plays a significant role within the School, comprising one third of the staff membership in 2004–5. A second measure is the number of staff who were elected to fellowships of the Royal Society while at Newcastle. Starting with T.H. Havelock, who was appointed to the first lecturership in Applied Mathematics at Newcastle in 1906, and was elected in 1914 – the first such at Newcastle – at the age of 37, seven other mathematicians

Right: Thomas Henry Havelock FRS, the first lecturer in Applied Mathematics and a member of the Department, 1906–45

Below: The Klein Bottle: this is a special topological object which has no inside and no outside

A Soliton wave: a graphical representation of an exact solution for the interaction of waves, based on modern theories of nonlinear wave propagation

have been elected Fellows since then. Many others, having moved on from Newcastle, were similarly elected later in their careers.

Over the years, the Department has contributed to important developments in many branches of Pure and Applied Mathematics, and in Statistics. We may cite: geophysical/astrophysical magnetic dynamo theory, eg the properties of the Earth's magnetic field; operator algebras, an abstract pure mathematical topic with applications to quantum mechanics and some geometries; wave theories, from Havelock (wave drag on ships) to modern theories of non-linear waves; contributions to the theory of inference, multivariate analysis, experimental design and early work on computer-intensive methods; continuum mechanics; Bose-Einstein condensate. Much of this is still on-going, together with work, for example, on galaxy formation and structure, and in biostatistics and stochastic analysis. This excellence in Mathematics and Statistics continues to this day, resulting in a strong research environment that attracts research and postdoctoral students, and visitors.

Robin Johnson

NATURAL SCIENCES

JOHN SAUNDERS / CHEMISTRY / 1921–4
by ROSEMARY (DAUGHTER) / FINE ART / 1954–8
My father, John Saunders, started studying Chemistry at
Armstrong College in 1921. He graduated in 1924 and gained
an MSc in Chemical Bacteriology in 1929. He was subsequently
appointed as 'Full time Demonstrator in the Physiological
Department of the College' at a salary of £300 per annum.

My first memories of the College are of Saturday morning visits
to the 'new' Medical School in Queen Victoria Road, when my
father took me up to the animal house on the roof to see the
white mice, guinea pigs, rabbits and rats which all looked
contented in their hutches, but even as a three-year-old, I was
aware that there were some doors that were closed to me. My
father used to offer financial inducements to the neighbouring
small boys to supply him with healthy frogs. These ended up in
a large tank in the Lab, destined to be used by students to
discover the muscular reflex mechanism of jumping.

NIGEL HEPPER / BOTANY / 1947–50
King's College Naturalists' Society
Popularly known at 'The Nats', the Society was very active, having
73 members in my time as a Botany undergraduate. As part of
our course, we had excellent ecology trips to glaciated Teesdale,
Kielder raised bogs and elsewhere in the glorious North East, but
we added our own through the Nats. As Honorary Secretary and
later Chairman, I organized visits to the Farne Islands as well as
Arran in 1948, and a fortnight hostelling in Wester Ross, climbing
some hair-raising peaks, in 1949. The 1950 trip was based at a
Benedictine monastery on Caldey Island, Pembrokeshire. In our
party was John Cannon (later Keeper of Botany at the Natural
History Museum, London) and William Bradbeer (later Professor
of Botany at Imperial College). This was so interesting that I
returned two years later and published a flora of Caldey. These
trips formed a good basis for my subsequent tropical African
expeditions for the Royal Botanic Gardens, Kew.

SIR JAMES BADDILEY / CHEMISTRY PROFESSOR / 1954–83
One essential requirement for the growth of bacterial
cultures was a constant-temperature room. I suggested to
the Clerk of Works that he find out how best to adapt a
laboratory by discussing with Medical School technicians
how they had done this. He returned with a big grin on his
face and explained that there was such a room in the
Medical School. It was an ordinary room with an electric
radiator. If during the daytime the room temperature rose
too high, they opened a window!

Occasionally, I met University colleagues on the flight between
Newcastle and London. The Dean of the Dental School,
Professor Hallett, was a keen pilot and when I sat with him on
several occasions returning to Newcastle, I noticed he always
had a map on his lap. He would point out that the aircraft was
going the wrong way over London and we were in some
danger. We always returned safely.

I recall a number of occasions when about a dozen professors
would be invited to west Cumberland to visit Marchon Ltd, a
firm that made sulphuric acid, phosphoric acid and cement,
and which had good relations with the University. Henry
Daysh, Professor of Geography, had advised the firm that their
factory was sitting on a very large mineral deposit that could
be mined economically. The head of the firm was most
grateful and donated a substantial sum to the University.

A much-appreciated organization, started by Mrs Bosanquet,
wife of the Vice-Chancellor, was the University Wives
International Group (UWIG). My wife (Lady Hazel) was a
founder member and strong supporter. It was the first
organization in a British university that assisted and promoted
friendly contact with wives of senior visiting academics. It
holds regular coffee mornings for wives and helps in finding
accommodation, information on shopping, local affairs, etc.
Many other universities have now followed suit.

BERNARD DIXON / BACTERIOLOGY AND BOTANY / 1957–65

Meirion Thomas's distinction as a pioneer of plant physiology was coupled with endearing courtesy and reticence. However, one afternoon during my second year, it was another combination of personal thoughtfulness and sensitive criticism that set my heart aflutter. Professor Thomas had not only sought me out to make some nice comments about my writing style, but sat down to discuss at length a rather wild idea I had included in an essay. As I learned later, his colleagues in Newcastle and in the wider world of plant biochemistry warmed to Merion Thomas for similar reasons. While his intellectual thoroughness seemed to be reflected in his military bearing, he was also a person of subtle magnetism and gentle humour.

Thomas spent virtually his entire career in Newcastle. Yet he had a considerable international reputation for studies on topics ranging from crassulacean acid metabolism to respiration in apples. For me, the manner in which he described this work in undergraduate classes was thrilling. Dragging into the lecture theatre blackboards-on-wheels covered in tightly written notes, he would launch into a sequence of stories about precisely how the experiments had been done. This was the real stuff of research, not the somewhat idealised accounts found in journal papers, and it helped to cement my own lifelong attachment to science.

'Meirion's benign but complex personality made a deep impression on all who knew him', wrote Helen Porter and Stanley Ranson in their Royal Society obituary, 'and his influence for the general good of the university to which he devoted his many gifts will long be remembered.'

DR W. O'REILLY / PHYSICS / 1970s

I hope you will be able to include something about the Head of Physics, Keith Runcorn, who was among the most distinguished of the academics of the University. As a member of the Pontifical Academy of Sciences, Keith was on the committee that recommended to the Pope that the validity of the scientific work of Galileo should be recognised by the Roman Catholic Church.

Keith was an ideas man. He was always afraid that getting bogged down in the details of some activity could fatally distract him from his intellectual life. He regarded his work with his own students as 'the great experience of my life'. There are many of us whose lives were made much more interesting through working within the ambit of Keith Runcorn.

LEONARD SRNKA / PHYSICS / 1968–74

I had the good fortune to study at Newcastle as a Marshall Scholar from the US under Professor S. Keith Runcorn FRS in the Department of Geophysics and Planetary Physics. At the time, the Department was the second largest of its kind in the UK (after Cambridge). I had come from Purdue University, Indiana, to study lunar magnetism in the exciting years of NASA's Apollo Program. Professor Runcorn invited me to pursue PhD studies on the internal structure of the Moon. Miraculously, by the end of 1969, samples of moon rock arrived from Houston and began to appear in the Department's rock magnetism laboratories. Newcastle's lunar sample results soon became world-famous, showing that the Moon had been strongly magnetized in its early history by some (still unexplained) processes and fields.

Keith Runcorn: Chair of Physics in 1956 and retired in 1988

Newcastle drew a host of prominent space and other scientists to local conferences conceived by Professor Runcorn, including Nobel Laureates such as Hannes Alfven and Harold Urey. I remember tagging along with those august groups to the Barras Bridge SCR or the Student Union for a beer (or two), which I recall cost 2s 6p per pint. Those were exciting and heady days, indeed, especially for students such as me.

GAVIN HARDY / BOTANY / 1971–4

I remember a field meeting, in the second year, at Crag Lough, near the Roman Wall, when it had been raining solidly for days beforehand – the terrain was a raging torrent. Dr William Clark, in charge of the meeting, told us, in his inimitable Scottish accent, to 'step on the tussocks' – he did so and went up to his waist in water. It was on that occasion that one student turned up in a fur coat with high-heeled shoes...

Far left: *Students on a Geography field trip in Ireland*

Left: *Dr Hal Lister from the Geography Department on Fuch's Trans-Antarctic Expedition 1955–8*

GEOGRAPHY

Geography as a university subject at Newcastle began with the establishment of a department in Armstrong College in 1928. For nearly two years, the whole teaching load was carried single-handedly by a lecturer-in-charge until January 1930, when G.H.J. Daysh arrived to become effectively the founder of a department that he would guide and develop until his retirement 36 years later.

Teaching in those early years was in a wooden hut alongside Queen Victoria Road – one of three left from the Great War when the College had been a military hospital. Stark, with bare boards for a floor and heated by a coke stove, the hut was meagrely furnished with a couple of map chests and a few tables and chairs. An annual departmental grant of £50 matched the poverty of the accommodation. In these surroundings, Daysh and his assistant had to teach a full range of courses for an Honours degree. This was indeed a challenging task, but he was later to remark, 'There were some things I knew nothing about … but we often said to the first Honours that we were learning together, and that was an enjoyable process.'

Through the 1930s, despite continuing financial constraints, the Department grew slowly in numbers of students and staff. In 1937, the University created a Readership in Geography, by which time Daysh had three lecturers to help him. With less pressure from teaching time, research got under way, particularly in local economic geography; while on the physical side, work on the geomorphology of the Tyne river system made a significant contribution to the interpretation of the physiographic evolution of north-east England.

After the lean years of the war, expansion was resumed at an accelerating rate. Staff members returning from war service, together with newly appointed lecturers, had to cope with a flood of ex-service undergraduates, and the Department moved into larger premises – two adjoining terrace houses overlooking what was then the Great North Road. Sub-departments of Surveying, of Anthropology and (later) of Polar Studies were established, each under a Reader. Daysh was elevated to the rank of Professor, as holder of the first Chair of Geography in the University. Research flourished, especially in the field of Applied Geography, while on the teaching side an increasing variety of systematic specializations, such as Surveying, supplemented a central core of regional studies.

Following the Robbins Report on higher education, the 1960s saw rapid growth in British universities. This was a time of great site expansion and new building and, in 1966, the Department of Geography moved into its first purpose-built home with space, equipment and facilities on a scale vastly greater than before. This is the Daysh Building, named in honour of the man who had introduced the subject in Newcastle and who had just retired as the University's first and only Deputy Vice-Chancellor.

Matching the increased opportunities presented by the new building, numbers of staff and of students at both undergraduate and postgraduate level grew steadily during the following years. An MA course in Applied Geography was instituted, and a newly created Centre for Urban and Regional Development Studies was attached to the Department. Meanwhile Surveying (while remaining an option within Geography) had become a full department. By the end of the 1970s, it had outgrown its space in the Daysh Building and moved into larger premises elsewhere.

In its 75th year the Geography Department was incorporated within the new School of Geography, Politics and Sociology. Although this title may seem to

Professor Daysh, holder of the first Chair of Geography

KATHLEEN FARDEY

GEOGRAPHY / 1933–6

Professor Daysh was a great chap – I liked him very much. He could come down to the students' level. When we went on expeditions – we went away for a week during the Easter vacation – he was great fun.

Geography field trip to Scotland in March 1935

place an emphasis on the human side of the subject – which indeed had been a major theme since it began to be taught in Newcastle – the physical aspects still play a prominent part in both teaching and research. Studies of the processes shaping the landscape, and their ecological impact on environmental systems and management, take their place alongside work in cultural, social and economic geography at all spatial scales within a variety of regional contexts.

Such a range of options, made possible only by the facilities of a large modern building and an academic staff of more than 20, would have been beyond the imagination of Henry Daysh in that army hut in 1930. Yet it would surely have pleased him, inspired as it is by the same fascination with the world in which we live.

John Sharp

SURVEYING

Among the responsibilities of the post-Second World War Colonial Office was the surveying and mapping of the lands and resources of British territories in Africa, Asia and the Caribbean. King's College undertook to contribute to such vital overseas work by educating engineers and geographers in the methods and philosophy of topographic surveying.

Commander Douglas Fryer, an eminent naval hydrographic surveyor, was appointed to lead the effort in 1947. Fryer's lack of academic background proved no barrier to his appointment to a readership (the College awarded him an honorary degree on his arrival), whilst his erstwhile colleague Chief Petty Officer Ernie Fripp (after whom an important navigational landmark in Port Stanley harbour is named) joined as departmental assistant. In 1954, John Sharp was appointed to a lectureship in Geography and Surveying, and together this enthusiastic team, from military and schoolteaching backgrounds, formed an effective 'sub-department' of Geography, located in Sydenham Terrace and undertaking service teaching of geographers, engineers, planners and archaeologists.

Fryer retired in 1962, and it was left to his successor to establish a fully independent Department of Surveying. Pat Carmody had also come from a military background, as a serving Royal Engineers officer and then Assistant Director, Geodetic Control, Ordnance Survey. An expansion in teaching activity followed, when Surveying became a 'half degree' in the science Joint Honours portfolio. The first distinctly Surveying graduates left the University in 1967, and numbers increased from two pioneers to 15 per year by the late 1970s. Staff numbers increased also, and Joe Olliver (in post 1964–6), Ian Newton (1967–2000) and David Parker (filling Fripp's position at upgraded lecturer level, 1974 to date) boosted the academic team. Research activity was also initiated in the 1960s, with Newton's arrival bringing increased interest in photogrammetry (measurement from images), a significant grant for advanced equipment on the move into the new Daysh Building in 1967, and the appointment of Martin Evans (1969–98) as experimental assistant. Novel collaboration in measurement science with Medical School colleagues was a highlight of this period.

Increasing interest from school-leavers and the success of Newcastle graduates in commercial employment (notably in the North Sea oil industry) led Carmody to persuade the University to invest in a Single Honours degree in Surveying, unique in an English university. The professional recognition of the Joint Honours course by the Royal Institution of Chartered Surveyors was extended to this new programme. Further staff appointments followed – Martin Robertson (1977 to date), David Fairbairn (1978 to date), Robin Fursdon (1979–92) and John Knipe (who transferred from Geography in 1983), along with a succession of junior demonstrators.

Such expansion in student and staff numbers, teaching and research could not be contained within a small number of rooms spread across three floors of the Daysh Building. In 1979, the Department moved again, to specially modified space in the Old Haymarket Brewery Building. Carmody retired in 1985, after a fruitful and effective period of leadership, which saw Surveying transformed from a small sub-unit of three staff with no fully attached students to a nine-strong team (with administrative support), offering professionally recognised degree courses with over 20 graduates annually. A Chair in Surveying Science was established to accommodate his replacement, Paul Cross, who was charged with improving the Department's research profile. Alternating periods of headship with Newton, Cross succeeded in establishing a high reputation in three main areas of research – his own specialism, satellite geodesy (high-precision measurements of the size and shape of the Earth, and surveying of precise locations on the Earth's surface, using satellite systems), land information systems, and image handling. When Cross left in 1997, the Department was a vibrant, internationally respected centre of excellence in the whole field of 'geomatics', the

modern term applied to geospatial data handling and the name of the Department from 1996. It had moved its location once again in 1992, occupying grand facilities vacated by the old Departments of Mining Engineering and Geology in the Bedson Building.

Parker was appointed to the vacant chair, and further staff appointments, including Professors Blewitt (1994–9) and Moore (1999 to date), followed. The 2002 merger of Geomatics with Civil Engineering led to a further move, to the Cassie Building. Research in all aspects of geomatics maintains its high profile, and the undergraduate degree portfolio includes BSc Surveying and Mapping Science (with a measurement science emphasis), BSc Geographic Information Science (with a computing science bias), and (maintaining links with Geography and replacing the original Joint Honours programme) BSc Physical Geography.

David Fairbairn

Left: 1980s fieldwork: levelling on the shore of Derwentwater

Below: *Students using theodolites on a surveying excercise*

GEOLOGY

The Department of Geology came into being in 1871, when the College of Physical Science at Newcastle was founded. Professors were appointed in Mathematics, Chemistry, Physics and Geology, and Bettenson says that 'they and their students were housed in squalid discomfort in a number of rooms rented from the Coal Trade Chambers Company' and other organizations. From the late 1880s, the Department lay in the Armstrong Building but after 1958, because of developments and enlargement, the Department was never again to be a totally integrated group.

The first students came to the College intending to follow the mining profession. But it was not until 1875 that the first Professor of Mining was appointed to lead a department that would have close and mainly cordial relationships with Geology, until both departments were 'extinguished' towards the end of the 20th century.

Over the period of the Department's existence from 1871 into the early 1990s, there were nine heads of department, but three (Lebour, Hickling and Westoll) amassed between them just short of 100 years in this position: both Hickling and Westoll were Fellows of the Royal Society, and the Department became increasingly distinguished under their leadership.

Crystallography and Mineralogy were not taught within Geology, and a separate department was devoted to these two subjects in Newcastle for almost 70 years. Staffing was far from extravagant, and there was also a feature not uncommon among geologists: often they were ordained! The Reverend Mark Fletcher was virtually the entire staff of this tiny Newcastle department for more than 40 years, until it sensibly merged with Geology in 1940.

Significant expansions of geological staff at Newcastle took place in the years after both world wars. Very small until 1920, the staff had almost trebled in numbers by 1930 bringing, in particular, the igneous petrologist/geochemist Serge Tomkieff, a delightful Russian *émigré* (who demonstrated the spiral structure of the periodic table at the 1951 Festival of Britain), and Arthur Raistrick, a geologist and industrial archaeologist, who, through his research on peats and the differentiation of the microspore floras of coalfields in Lancashire and the North East, virtually became the founder of palynology. With Hickling, a palaeobotanist deeply interested in the nature and use of coal, and an excellent economic geologist, particularly in coalfield structure and hydrogeology, the Department became suitably broad-based for the times.

Expansion after the Second World War was greater. The appointment of Stanley Westoll in 1948 brought back a former brilliant student of the Department, who immediately set about expansion, both in staff and necessary material assets. Westoll, an eminent vertebrate palaeontologist, had a broad geological view and could see clearly the ways in which the subject was likely to develop. A University promise of a more spacious domain was fulfilled when the Department moved to the new Bedson Building in 1958. The move brought Geology and Mining physically closer together, but produced a contretemps between the departments: Geology was using increasingly sensitive equipment for research, while many mining research projects at the time were robust and disturbing. Eventually, there was settlement and the two departments then continued to rub along together amicably over the years.

Geology was particularly well known through the work of Hickling and his student C.A. Marshall (later Professor of Geology in Sydney, Australia) for their work on coal and oil shale. Building on this base, the Department moved into the petroleum field. By 1964, the Organic Geochemistry Unit was established, which expanded rapidly and was well supported by the University, the research councils and industry, particularly British Petroleum. Because of increasing size, this group again had to move, appropriately into a warehouse that had belonged to Scottish and Newcastle Breweries! In parallel, Engineering Geology, with strong symbiotic relationships with Mining and Civil

Engineering, expanded, and in 1972, Bill Dearman was appointed Professor. The industrial demand for appropriately trained students in this interdisciplinary field led to the formation of the Department of Geotechnical Engineering some ten years later. Establishment of taught Master's courses, supported by the research councils, in all these new areas of development provided a further source of well-trained students for industry.

In 1989, central government decided that there were too many 'pure science' courses throughout the country: rationalization in the interests of economy was essential! Geology, as compared with Physics and Chemistry, was relatively slight and would thus be ideal (and cheapest!) to review. But even this review proved too costly for central government funding and the exercise was abandoned, but not before Geology had suffered internecine destruction countrywide

A successful undergraduate Geology course at Newcastle was disbanded and a number of staff transferred to the University of Durham and to other universities. The Organic Geochemistry Unit, the only such group then in UK departments of Geology, was spared and transformed into a 'Research Group in Fossil Fuels and Environmental Geochemistry', accorded top-rank national status, fortunately still with several members of staff of the original department in post. Eventually the research group became a large and influential institute, under the leadership of Professor Steve Larter (now departed to Calgary), who was a former research student of the Department. Sadly, the Institute is no more, again a casualty of recent restructuring within the University. Mining went some ten years earlier. The Funding Council had told Leeds and Newcastle that there could only be one Mining department in northern England: Newcastle, the smaller and more narrowly based department, was the loser.

Geology and Mining as undergraduate subjects at Newcastle have vanished, although a number of geologists still work in different earth-science areas in the University. Over its existence of approximately 120 years, the Newcastle Department of Geology was always a successful contributor to the earth sciences in both teaching and research. Most of all, the Department was an effective and enjoyable place in which to be trained and in which to work as a geologist.

Duncan Murchison

MINING ENGINEERING

It is axiomatic that one should not carry coals to Newcastle. Not only was the region built on the wealth generated by coal mining: the very roots of the University are to be found in a minuted debate at the North of England Institute of Mining Engineers (NEIME), which led directly to the founding of the College of Physical Science in 1871, and to the offer of premises in their own building, which still exists in the Victorian splendour of the Mining Institute on Westgate Road, home of NEIME. The ensuing 120 years of Mining Engineering teaching and research at the University have left their mark globally: the reputation of the late Professor Potts and his colleagues still resonates worldwide, and it is rare to find a coalfield or orefield in which no Newcastle graduate has made their mark.

By the time the last students left the course in June 1991, Professor John Tunnicliffe, Dr Bob Fowell and Dr Lindsay Wade had spent a year commuting to and from Leeds University, where they maintained the Newcastle traditions in teaching and research. Two other colleagues had previously joined the short-lived Department of Geotechnical Engineering, whence Dr Ian Farmer went on to establish one of Tyneside's most respected geotechnical consultancies, and Dr Evan Passaris went on to teach Geotechnics in the Department of Civil Engineering, before finally entering private practice. Dr Jan Ketelaar, meanwhile, has long been heading up the UK government's aid programme in the mining sector, and is currently helping to relaunch diamond mining in Sierra Leone. The legacy of Mining Engineering at Newcastle remains strong: only in February 2006, the University won its first-ever Queen's Anniversary Prize for 'remedies to mine water pollution worldwide' (a programme led by Professor Paul Younger in the Institute for Research on the Environment and Sustainability, himself a chartered mining engineer and past President of NEIME). Largely thanks to the efforts of Dr Bob Fowell, 15 years after the last convocation, the spirit of the Department of Mining Engineering remains very much alive, as more than 30 graduates meet annually for a reunion dinner in Newcastle each November.

Paul Younger

Design for the proposed Mining College in 1870

The new Mining College in 1928

Right: Dr Ewan Page, the founder and first Director of the Laboratory, seen here in 1967. This photograph was taken shortly before the opening of Claremont Tower, where computing in its various guises has been housed ever since.

Below: (left to right): Rod Walker, Ella Barrett, Ian Scoines, Ewan Page, Jim Eve, Elizabeth Baraclough and Paul Samet

COMPUTING SCIENCE

In 1957, when the University Computing Laboratory in Newcastle – forerunner of today's School of Computing Science and of Information Systems and Services (ISS) – was established, hardly anyone in the University, much less in the wider population, had used a computer at all. The Laboratory, under its first Director, Dr Ewan Page, played a key role in developing computing, not only within the University and the region, but nationally and internationally – a focus its successors still retain.

Its first computer, a Ferranti Pegasus nicknamed 'Ferdinand', much less powerful than a current laptop, supported a growing community of users with a wide range of interests, including: simulating the evolution of primrose colonies along roadside verges; major scientific calculations for local industry (eg marine engineering calculations for C.A. Parsons & Co., electrical engineering for Joyce-Loebl); and administrative tasks for the University, including computerized timetabling and student registration. In the early 1960s, Ferdinand was replaced by KDF9 and, in 1967, by an IBM 360/67, the very first multi-access system anywhere in the UK. This, in part a collaboration with Durham University in Northumbrian Universities Multi-Access Computer, supporting users in both universities, also led to a partnership with several major North American universities in developing and exploiting the Michigan Terminal System, which initially supported 20 simultaneous users. Today, a campus-wide network supports more than 10,000 personal workstations; ISS has played a leading national and regional role in developing access to worldwide networks.

The Laboratory rapidly outgrew the various houses in Kensington Terrace that it initially occupied and, in 1967, moved into the then newly opened Claremont Tower 2, where its successor remains. Originally planned to occupy only the two floors below ground, the School now occupies nine floors, as well as floors in the adjoining Daysh and Bridge Buildings.

The Laboratory was a pioneer in Computing education, introducing a postgraduate course in 1959; its first undergraduate course – the second in the country – produced its first graduates in 1969; the first Master's course in the country was launched in 1972. Today, around 100 undergraduates are admitted to Computing degree programmes annually; more than 120 students are undertaking postgraduate study.

During the early 1960s, the Laboratory undertook pioneering research in computer typesetting and medical information retrieval, as well as more usual aspects of scientific computing. In 1969, there was a change of emphasis, particularly a specialization in dependable computing that has been a primary motivation for our research ever since. The School's research has twice won the British Computer Society technical achievement award, and achieved RAE 5 ratings in every national research review. Dependability, distributed systems, data-intensive computing and theoretical computing now provide the basis of continuing research success. The University has also established an Informatics Research Institute to pursue the interdisciplinary aspects of computing research, and hosts the Engineering and Physical Science Research Council's North-East Regional e-Science Centre, developing the software tools that will be required for scientific advance in the 21st century.

A major characteristic of the Laboratory was the close interaction between service and academic functions. Though the University chose, in 1991, to separate the two into the School of Computing Science and Information Systems and Services, the links, best exemplified by our shared common room, have been maintained to the present day; they shall jointly celebrate the 50th Anniversary of Computing in Newcastle with a series of events in 2007.

John Lloyd

141

06

Transition and Evolution

THE SECOND WORLD WAR AND BEYOND

The University's contingency plans for war, including the transfer of Medical School staff into hospitals and the evacuation of much of King's College to Durham, were never implemented. A war involving unprecedented demands for intellectual, inventive and technical skills saw staff drafted into the armed forces and other war work. A Joint Recruiting Board appeared in the Students' Union. King's College kept going, but this involved many expedients. In History, Lord Eustace Percy dusted off his expertise to contribute to teaching and, in 1943, Joan

Long was recruited from Roedean as a lecturer. (Later, as Mrs Taylor, she was to be the first female and first non-professorial faculty Dean and, in another sphere, the television 'Brain of Britain' of 1978.) Staff took to firewatching and other civil defence activities. Teaching continued despite shortages and having to resort to shortened and intensified degree schedules.

As victory approached, King's College planned ambitious post-war expansion. After 1945, many ex-service students took two-year degrees. There were 1,250 students at King's in 1937, which doubled by 1947. When the ex-service flood receded, student numbers grew, but on a relatively modest scale. For some, the quarter century or so after 1945 were halcyon years. In all except the largest departments, students knew most of the teachers, and there was close contact between students and staff. Academic tenure seemed secure and salaries reasonably satisfactory. Treasury grants, mediated through the University Grants Committee, grew – meeting 53 per cent of expenditure in 1946, but 78 per cent in 1956 – but universities were treated as independent institutions, making their own plans, aided by the general observance of a five-year planning cycle.

On several earlier occasions there had been talk of creating an independent university at Newcastle. An enquiry in 1952 decided in favour of the status quo, but pressures for change increased. In early post-war years, King's College was administered by a handful of officers; as staff and student numbers grew, the inconvenience of a University administration superimposed on College administration became clearer, especially for departments which had no Durham equivalent. When separation came in 1963, it was amicable, seen generally as inevitable and necessary. There were some regrets –

Right: Lord Eustace Percy: Rector of King's College 1937–52

Left: Vice-Chancellor Charles Bosanquet oversaw the separation of the University from Durham in 1963

The first meeting of the Senate of the University of Newcastle upon Tyne, 1 August 1963

MR PHILIP BOLAM

BSC AGRICULTURE / 1943

Standing precariously amongst bits of timber high up in the Armstrong Building amid an initial briefing, I vividly recollect the instruction, 'There are no medals for bravery, alive or posthumous, so if a fire gets a hold, get out and let it burn!' As an Agriculture student, that building held some interest, especially when we discovered our tutor's reports on our second-year progress.

most medical graduates chose to take Durham degrees as long as they were allowed to – but the divorce was largely painless. One argument involved Newcastle City Council, dissatisfied with its representation in the new university's government, but this was soon overcome and the city's co-operation became an invaluable feature of the University's future, crucial in planning and acquisition of sites for development.

Expansion accelerated after the Robbins Report of 1963. By 1969, Newcastle had nearly 6,000 students. Throughout the 1970s and 1980s, government interference increased, accompanied by the failure of successive governments to establish consistent policies; repeated demands for student increases alternated with unforeseen cuts in state funding. In 1981, the Vice-Chancellor complained that 'the record of the past few years has been one of promises repeatedly broken'. Eighteen years later, his successor acidly commented on the waste of scholarly resources induced by the 'self-serving meta-industry of reviewers, auditors, monitors, inspectors and consultants, all in the sacred name of accountability'.

However, the progress made in this difficult climate was considerable. Among the highlights were the new library in 1984 and the opening of the new Medical School by the Queen Mother in 1985. In earlier and easier years, the University had been able to distribute increasing resources across the board, but this was no longer possible and financial crises brought unwelcome losses. The Faculty of Arts saw its Departments of Philosophy and Scandinavian Studies disappear. A fierce rearguard campaign saved the threatened Music Department; timely reforms saw Classics embark upon significant growth. Donations from such benefactors as Sir William Leech and Catherine Cookson continued to

be important in giving the University flexibility in its operations. The University's own Development Fund, created in 1977, in ten years financed 12 new chairs and seven new readerships. Newcastle has a fine record in attracting outside research contracts and similar funds: £45m in 2000–1. In human affairs too, the University's record was good. Despite repeated cuts in funding, compulsory redundancies were avoided; this meant enforced savings in buildings maintenance and the acceptance of programmes of voluntary early retirement. Newcastle maintained a substantial Student Hardship Fund, for instance adding £120,000 to it in 1976–7; this attracted additional significance when the Government enforced increased student fees.

Between 1978 and 1990, student numbers rose from about 7,000 to about 9,000, while state-funded staff increased from 948 to 987. In 2000, the University's annual budget was approaching £200m and it had 13,000 students; in September 2000, Newcastle was selected by the *Sunday Times* as 'University of the Year'. In the half-century since the end of the war, the dramatic increases in scale resulted in an institution that was different in kind from the King's College of the immediately post-war years. In the early 21st century, the stage was set for another phase of change, development and expansion.

Norman McCord

PETER ELPHICK

DIP ARCH / 1948

I joined firewatching at the outbreak of war and shared duty with Lord Eustace Percy. Our first tour of duty started at the old tramsheds on the west side of Percy Street. On the first evening of duty, we had to collect greatcoats and these were issued by a storeman from an office in the tramsheds. Lord Eustace noticed a rather superior-looking greatcoat hanging on a row of hooks and grabbed it immediately. The storeman rebuked him and said, 'Hey! you can't take that – it's for some ruddy Lord or other!' Lord Eustace immediately replaced the greatcoat and took another one, telling me that he would get his coat later as he didn't want to embarrass the storeman in front of me!

Top: Bomb damage in Newcastle, Second World War

Above: *Goods Station damaged by bombing, Second World War*

Above right: *Victory tea party in 1945*

NEWCASTLE AFTER THE WAR

The coming of war in 1939 brought enhanced importance for the North East's heavy industries and encouraged concentration on them. The old Armstrong works at Elswick worked flat out during the war years, including a major contribution to tank manufacture. There was little in the way of innovation and re-equipment in local war industry, much more emphasis on working existing plant to maximum effect. Again, there was large-scale recruiting for the armed forces, and serious casualties, though not on the same scale of bloodletting as in 1914–18. Local war memorials are eloquent on the different death tolls of the two world wars. There was also much damage at home from German bombers, including the destruction of Newcastle's principal goods station in 1941. The U-boat war also brought heavy loss of life in local merchant shipping.

Victory in 1945 was followed by the re-emergence of economic problems that had earlier afflicted the region of which Newcastle was the centre. In 1961, the North East still had nearly 16% of total employment in the increasingly troubled coal, shipbuilding and marine engineering sectors, against a national average of only 4.4%. Government intervention to combat regional depression was now more intensive, but it was not possible to save some of the older interests. In 1947, coal shipments to overseas markets from the Tyne totalled only 216,000, the lowest figure since 1832. Ten

years later – probably for the first peace-time year in centuries – no coal left the Tyne for either France or Germany. By the early 1990s, almost all of the North East's collieries had closed.

In the 1920s, nearly 45% of Tyneside's work force was employed in manufacturing or mining. By the mid-1980s, manufacturing was down to 20% and mining 2%. The service sector was now providing well over half of total employment, a local demonstration of a wider national shift in employment patterns. In the late 1980s, the major state social services complex in east Newcastle was alone employing around 8,000. By the 1990s, the two universities – Newcastle and Northumbria – were among the city's most important employers. Early hopes that official initiatives could be relied upon to avoid the recurrence of unemployment proved over-optimistic, though there remained many local variations. Some local enterprises fostered by direct or indirect subsidies succeeded in establishing themselves, while others withered when this support faltered or ended. In the Newcastle of April 1987, unemployment in the old industrial suburb of Elswick was nearly 40%, but only 7% in the prosperous northern suburb of Gosforth. Newcastle saw some inward investment by foreign entrepreneurs, as, for example, in the establishment of Ikeda Technology, a contributor to the design of Nissan cars.

High technology enterprises played a significant part in providing a replacement for jobs lost in older heavy industries. Newcastle's new Armstrong Business Park was employing 4,000 within a short while after its establishment, including 1,200 in the Automobile Association's Insurance and Financial Services headquarters. Between 1988 and 1993, Newcastle Airport saw its turnover triple, its profits quadruple. The struggle to replace the old heavy industry and mining economy with new jobs in a variety of sectors has understandably been a principal focus of study of Newcastle and the North East in recent years.

Alongside this effort at economic regeneration has been a remarkable improvement in social conditions generally. In some cases, wartime medical advances paid later dividends. In 1938, there were 100 deaths from tuberculosis of children under 15 on Tyneside (in itself a remarkable improvement over earlier figures); there were 85 in 1947, 18 in 1951, 4 in 1954. The construction of large numbers of new houses was resumed after the war, although the building of large peripheral estates remote from central facilities, like Newcastle's Newbiggin Hall, could bring their own social problems. In ten years from 1951, Newcastle's housing stock increased by 34%. Infant mortality in Newcastle was 80 per 1,000 in 1933–5, 8.8 in 1983–5. In 1930, 67 Tyneside women died in childbirth, only one in 1986. In 1930, two-thirds of all Tyneside deaths were in the under-65 age bracket, in 1986 less than a quarter.

There were other social changes of note. Women provided 20% of the Tyneside work force in the 1920s (many of them domestic servants), but 45% in the 1980s. When filling in official forms in the late 1980s, 83% of Tynesiders claimed some form of religious affiliation, but less than 10% attended church or chapel. Political allegiances were far from uniform; if Labour dominated the local electoral scene, there were still substantial Conservative elements, including a large minority in Newcastle itself. It remained impossible to equate electoral allegiances with social status in any simple fashion.

Educational provision continued to improve at all levels, even if the North East still lagged behind some more prosperous regions in this respect. Newcastle's two universities have expanded hugely, and now make a major contribution both to the regional economy and to the city's social life. The scale of urban regeneration in Newcastle expanded markedly in the last years of the 20th century, with huge sums expended in the

Top: Eldon Square shopping precinct, 1970s

Above: Trolley Bus in 1950s

Right: Newcastle Quayside today, showing the Millennium Bridge, BALTIC and the Sage concert hall

rebuilding of the old quayside area that had been the original heart of the town, but which had experienced serious decay in the 19th and early 20th centuries. From a depressing slum area, this riverside district has been transformed into a lively and popular centre of social activity.

When Newcastle's Eldon Square shopping precinct opened in the 1970s, it was the largest of its kind in

A busy Newcastle airport is an indicator of regeneration in the area

of higher standards of recreation and opportunity. In the early 21st century, Newcastle has gained a wide reputation as a major centre of social activity in various forms, but the observer of some aspects of the city's nightlife may conclude that affluence does not necessarily end all social problems.

No doubt the immense changes in standard and mode of living that the 20th century wrought cannot simply be equated with an increase in happiness, a commodity notoriously difficult to measure, but in the period since the end of the war, Newcastle, like Britain more generally, has seen a marked and unprecedented increase in opportunities for happiness, in so far as these are governed by factors such as health, income, material comfort, leisure, recreation, tolerance, and availability of support by communal agencies.

Europe. Even now, most of those visiting this centre fail to appreciate what a historical miracle they are witnessing, in the enormous variety and ready availability of goods, and the astonishing sophistication and extent of the worldwide organization which is required to procure and distribute them. The extent of holidays, and holidays abroad, are additional indicators

Norman McCord

View from the Terraces: 1980–2000

This highly selective look back at the last 20 years of the 20th century has to be set in the context of the immense changes in higher education nationally during this period. Until the earlier 1980s, the University Grants Committee had, since its inception, operated as a buffer between universities and central government. It respected university autonomy and allocated funds within broad guidelines laid down by government policy, but with little intrusion from government. However, the increasing cost of the university system and other factors led to more direct government intervention. In 1981, government funding for the university sector was substantially reduced by 11% overall. The effects were differential. Some universities, like Newcastle, suffered relatively small reductions, while others had to cope with recurrent losses of 20%. Henceforth, successive higher-education funding bodies, influenced by worsening national economic problems, became increasingly intrusive in university

affairs, offering detailed and specific 'guidance' that had to be heeded if funding was not to be reduced.

It was against this backcloth that another significant event took place in 1992. The so-called binary line was abolished, and the polytechnics were awarded university status with the right to award their own degrees. The government was thus able to take a holistic view of higher education, exercising oversight and control over all elements of it.

Increased Accountability

Hand in hand with greater central intervention was the growing requirement for accountability from which, as recipients of public funding, universities could not expect to be exempt. This led to the start of an inevitable series of audits, inspections and reviews. National processes for assessing teaching and research quality were developed alongside quality assurance procedures. Based on peer review and held every four or five years, these exercises have had a major impact on the operation and reputation of all universities. The results are published and, in the case of research, are significant in the allocation of government funding.

Newcastle University has fared well in this national scrutiny, obtaining several outstanding ratings in both teaching and research. A remarkable set of teaching quality assessments in 1999–2000 contributed to its designation as 'University of the Year' by the *Sunday Times*. These assessment exercises have inevitably diverted an increased amount of staff time to dealing with external and internal enquiries. Other possible consequences that have had to be resisted are excessive prescription in the curriculum and an overemphasis on short-term research programmes leading to swifter publication of results to the detriment of longer-term research. Notwithstanding these challenges, there have

Above: *Medical students celebrate Newcastle winning Sunday Times' 'University of the Year' award in 1999–2000*

Left: *Kensington Terrace (top) and Park Terrace (bottom) are administrative buildings of the University*

	1980–1	1999–2000	% CHANGE
Total income (£ millions) including:	95.5*	170.2	+78
government funding: block grant plus UK fees (£ millions)	74.5*	77.0	+3
research grants and contracts (£ millions)	13.25*	42.1	+218
Student numbers (full-time equivalent)	8,100	12,650	+56
Student–staff ratio	9.0	16.0	+78

* Recalculated to 1999–2000 values using the British Retail Price Index, which enables the percentage changes to be presented in real terms

Top right: Students on the Assessed Summer School 2005, part of the PARTNERS programme

been some benefits. Newcastle is generally more systematic in the scrutiny of its teaching and curricula and in the overview of the students' learning experience, and is more strategic and focused in its pursuit of research excellence.

MAJOR CHANGES AT NEWCASTLE

Critical factors in the management of universities during a 20-year period of massive expansion were the significant variations in annual government allocations and the almost static level of core public funding in real terms over the whole of the period. The figures in the above table highlight the enormous changes that took place at Newcastle over the 20 years within the national environment described above.

There was considerable growth in all areas of the University's business. Total income, particularly external earnings in the form of research grants and contracts, rose steeply in real terms, contrasting sharply with the virtual lack of any increase in core government funding. Highly significant is the fact that the core used to be 75% of our income and at the end of the period was only 45%. The achievement of a huge increase in student numbers without additional core funding entailed a considerable fall in the amount of resource received by the University to educate each student. This is of course reflected in the substantial rise in the student–staff ratio over the 20 years.

This picture, far from being unique to Newcastle, largely mirrors the national picture. Newcastle has vigorously addressed the implications of this massive

change through the energy and sustained efforts of its teaching staff, the development of innovative teaching programmes, and the provision of high-quality learning support facilities for the students. All the figures in the table above undeniably point to an enormous increase in the University's output during this period. They reflect the high quality and huge commitment of the staff and confirm the institution's major contribution to the development of the UK university sector.

DEVELOPMENTS AND ACHIEVEMENTS

The growing strength of Newcastle's international research and teaching links confirmed its status as a truly global university. By the end of the 1990s, more than 100 nations were represented in the student population: 15% of Newcastle's students were from overseas, in roughly equal proportions from the European Union and other countries.

The University's high research standing led to its being a founder member of the informal Russell Group of major British research universities, which plays an important role in the discussion of research strategy at national level. The immense growth in external research grants and contracts reflects the consistently high regard that national and regional grant-awarding bodies have for the quality of the University's research. Success in securing funding from the EU's substantial research programme was particularly conspicuous. The University's ability to disseminate the benefits of its research is confirmed by its outstanding record in knowledge transfer and its management of strikingly successful commercial ventures. These include the development of flourishing companies such as those concerned with advanced medical and computer software applications.

Teaching and research collaboration between departments has long existed. However, during the

1980s and 1990s, recognition that an increasing amount of exciting and far-reaching research lay at the interface between subject areas led to the formal establishment of major cross-departmental and interdisciplinary research programmes such as those in biomedical and biomolecular sciences and in land use and water resources. By the end of the century, there was a great number of designated interdisciplinary research groups ranging from loose federations to closely integrated coalitions, underpinned by administrative structures.

The University's significant impact on the region became increasingly clear. There are many striking examples including the critical role its research reputation played in the decision of leading industrial companies, such as Samsung and Siemens in the mid-1990s, to invest in the region. The University's commitment to the economic health of the region led to ever stronger co-operation between the universities of the North East through the establishment of groups such as Higher Education Support for Industry. The University's input into the region's economic and cultural activities was significantly reinforced by its formation of the Regional Development Office in 1995–6.

Particularly gratifying was the successful pursuit of the University's strategy to broaden participation in higher education. By the late 1990s, the PARTNERS programme was providing hundreds of young people from areas of low participation in Tyneside and Northumberland with the opportunity to build their confidence and demonstrate their potential for success in higher education. With the same overall objective the Students into Schools programme was enabling many students from across the University to work with local children in the classroom.

One of the many positive features of working in the University during this period was the enjoyment of constructive and friendly relations with the student body. Although there were inevitably difficult issues from time to time, they were always openly and freely discussed by the Union Society and the University in an atmosphere of mutual respect and good humour, with a genuine desire among all parties to reconcile differences and agree the way forward. After graduation, the University makes a determined effort to foster close and lasting relations with its ex-students. By the turn of the century, an active Alumni Association was keeping 55,000 members in 211 countries in touch with the University.

During financially testing times and within a rapidly shifting landscape, the University continued to manage its affairs judiciously, remaining in charge of its own destiny and true to its core values. It successfully pursued its strong commitment to growth and quality in both teaching and research, to the personal and intellectual development of its students, to the widening of access, to the dissemination of its research, to the active support of the region, and to the sharing of its expertise with local business and industry. During the challenging years ahead, it will continue to be a beacon for the university system, remaining both distinguished and distinctive in all it does

Derek Nicholson

Selection of ARCHES magazines produced by the Alumni Association

THE INTERNATIONAL OFFICE

The tradition of establishing international academic links is a long one, but the history of the International Office is comparatively short. In their quest to work with those who are considered the best in their subject area, academics have ventured as far afield as many a ship's captain out of Newcastle in its heyday as a port and trading centre. Numerous informal links with institutions overseas, built mainly on individuals' interests and obsessions, made Newcastle an international establishment long before it considered itself to be one. As higher education systems and the supporting research culture evolved throughout the world, the staff of many overseas universities came to learn their trade at Newcastle. The picture of alumni from the Armstrong College Old Students Association, China, taken in 1931, shows just how long a history there is.

In the 1980s, the University took the first cautious steps towards formalizing and professionalizing its international presence, and towards providing support for the increasing numbers of students from overseas who were choosing Britain for their undergraduate or postgraduate education. A small 'Overseas Office' was established, consisting of two associate directors, who had somehow to find time for this around their day job as academics: Liz Anderson (currently Head of the School of Modern Languages) and Graham Armstrong,

who taught in the Department of Marine Engineering, and later left the University to work for a local shipyard. They were ably assisted by their secretary, Judith Reay, and Alf Heron of the Registrar's Office provided administrative support. Maternity leave obliged Liz to hand over after only a very short spell to Ilona Cheyne of the School of Law. A Pro-Vice-Chancellor, Professor John Cannon, took on the role of first Director.

Many will remember the early days when this small band worked hidden away in a corner of the third floor of the Old Library Building. In those days, the majority of overseas students on the campus came from Hong Kong, Malaysia, Norway and Singapore. The part-time associate directors and their staff worked very hard to establish a special induction programme at the beginning of the academic year for those not only new to

the University, but also unfamiliar with Britain, its culture and language – not forgetting beginners' Geordie! This programme continues today as 'International Welcome'. Other projects included a Junior Year Abroad programme to enable students from the United States to experience part of their studies in a different environment. Owing to a printer's error, the proof of the first brochure describing the scheme gave the impression that the North East of England had managed to annex Norway!

The part-time associate directors had to spend time travelling the world as ambassadors for the University to formalize the links that had previously been nurtured by lone academics and individual departments. This proved no mean feat alongside a normal workload back at home.

From this shoestring and sealing wax beginning, the Office gradually evolved. Dr Richard Long, who had a background in the British Council, was appointed first permanent Director of the International Office, and the number of associate directors was increased to share the load. The International Office moved into new accommodation near the rest of the University's administration offices at 10 Kensington Terrace. One of the associate directors, Terry McCarthy, was appointed in 1994 as the second full-time Director, and then the University invested in a number of other full-time, professional staff, one of whom is based permanently in Malaysia. This coincided with a significant increase in the number of overseas students registered at the University. The University had established a separate European Office to deal with the student and staff exchange schemes funded by the European Union, as well as other activity in Europe, but this was soon merged with the International Office.

The years have seen an enormous change in both the University and the international community it serves. Between 1986–7 and 2004–5, the numbers of students from outside the United Kingdom increased from 914 to 2,503, representing around 25 per cent of the total student population. There has also been a change in the source of students who come to the UK to study. The largest national groups represented in the current year are China, India, Nigeria, Taiwan and the Middle East, although there are still large constituencies from Malaysia, Singapore and Hong Kong, and well over 100 different nationalities are represented altogether. Some 20 staff now work in the International Office, but many more staff of the University as a whole are engaged in supporting the University's international work through exchange schemes, teaching and research projects, and their participation in educational counselling overseas. An indicator of how truly international the University is becoming is the fact that around 25 per cent of its research and teaching staff have origins outside the UK: 66 different nationalities are represented, from Albanian to Zimbabwean.

Today the University can take pride in the contribution of its alumni scattered throughout every continent. Its role as an international university is now articulated clearly and demonstrated in every aspect of its life. Exchange schemes with universities in countries across the globe provide opportunities for young minds to grasp the value of and learn from other cultures. Many staff, including some heads of schools, were educated in other cultures and bring that experience to play. Academic staff are encouraged to travel and develop links and to work in international research groups.

Global alliances are beginning to form. The first joint programme with an overseas institution, leading to the award of a joint MSc in Biodiversity, Conservation and Ecotourism, is underway in Thailand. Newcastle is also now working closely with the Australian university, Monash. Building on tradition, we are now well placed to provide a truly international education as part of a global community of educators and researchers.

Alison Tate

US Connections with Newcastle

On 22 September 1877, the former American President, Ulysses S Grant, visited Newcastle upon Tyne. It was estimated that 80–100,000 people turned out to honour Grant with a parade and to hear him speak. The victorious Civil War general visited the Armstrong factories to express his thanks for the armaments that had played a vital role in the Union victory. A hundred years later, President Jimmy Carter came to the North

Martin Luther King receiving his honorary degree in November 1967

East in May 1977. He was visiting London for the economic summit, and James Callaghan brought him to the North East as part of a number of measures designed to keep the region's disgruntled Labour MPs happy; they felt their support, unlike their Welsh and Scottish counterparts, was being taken for granted. (The go-ahead for the Tyneside Metro was another such measure of appeasement.) Carter planted a tree at George Washington's ancestral home in Washington, Tyne and Wear. Sadly, the tree was already dead when planted: it had not survived the flight in the cargo hold, and later had to be replaced surreptitiously. Carter received the freedom of the city in front of the Civic Centre before a huge crowd that spilled over in to the University car park. He endeared himself to the Geordie gathering by proclaiming 'Ha'way the lads'.

Grant's visit had not involved Armstrong College, but Carter took the occasion of his visit indirectly to reach out to the University. He announced the establishment of a Friendship Force link between Atlanta and Newcastle. The Friendship Force had been established by Carter when he was Governor of Georgia to develop exchanges between ordinary citizens of Atlanta and cities across the world. On the first exchange, in July 1977, the future President of Emory University, James Laney, came to stay with Professor of Latin and, later, Pro-Vice-Chancellor of the University, David West. Professor Laney went on to become US Ambassador to South Korea. Among the Newcastle visitors to Atlanta were John Grimley Evans, future Professor of Clinical Gerontology at Oxford, and Anthony Badger, future Paul Mellon Professor of American History at Cambridge and Master of Clare College. The Friendship Force included student exchanges, and several Newcastle students went to Iowa.

The Friendship Force connection merely exposed the tip of an iceberg of academic links with the United States. Many staff at the Medical School had spent time in US medical schools, most notably Vice-Chancellor Henry Miller. Similarly, Keith Runcorn, Professor of Physics, was intimately linked to the space programme and the analysis of moon rocks. So often was he in the United States that Henry Miller sometimes referred to him as the 'visiting Professor of Physics'. There is a story that Professor Runcorn popped out one morning for coffee, only to phone his secretary in mid-afternoon from Heathrow, having found a cheap transatlantic flight on the way back to the Department. It was Keith Runcorn's reputation that led Bruce Babbitt, future Governor of

Arizona and Clinton's first Secretary of the Interior, to take a Master's in Geophysics at Newcastle, when he was awarded a Marshall scholarship. Runcorn was responsible in 1980 for the nomination for an honorary degree of Carter's scientific adviser, Frank Press.

In the 1960s, T. Dan Smith was perhaps Britain's closest equivalent to an American city 'boss'. He attempted to make Newcastle the 'Brasilia of the North'. Smith had visited the Research Triangle Park in North Carolina, established by the state government to attract high-tech industries to an area surrounded by three research universities. Smith aimed to replicate that idea in the North East, exploiting the presence of Durham University, Newcastle University and the Polytechnic.

PETER DAVIES

ENGLISH LANGUAGE AND LITERATURE / 1975–8
Jimmy Carter's Visit

On a bright May morning in 1977, the University and the city ground to a halt for the visit of President Jimmy Carter, who addressed a crowd of thousands outside the Civic Centre. Suntanned and beaming, the millionaire peanut farmer from Atlanta charmed the Geordie throng. Flattered by his attention, entranced by the spectacle of the presidential entourage trailing the world's media in its wake, the Toon had never seen anything like it before or since. Rapture was complete when the President's first words were, 'Ha'way the lads!'

A colder welcome met the presidential chaperone, Prime Minister Jim Callaghan. He cut a more mundane figure in a grey suit and light blue cardigan. With unemployment rising on Tyneside, his government was unpopular and he drew jeers. He responded with a tetchy homily about being sure of a different greeting if only he'd been able to bring a new factory in his pocket and economic realities had been less harsh.

That afternoon – when the crowds had drifted off and Carter had departed for Washington – in County Durham, our tutorial on Elizabethan poetry metamorphosed into one on Geordie pride and passion and Newcastle's indestructible sense of identity.

153

Newcastle University's dramatic expansion in the 1960s in the city centre was closely linked to the ambitious goals of Smith and the City Council, and the political influence of Labour life peer, Professor of Chemistry, William Wynne Jones, and the Professor of Computing, Ewan Page. (Page, to his great credit, would be a character witness for Dan Smith when Smith was convicted of conspiracy and corruption in 1974.)

In November 1967, the University of Newcastle awarded an honorary degree to Martin Luther King Jr – the only honorary degree outside the United States that Dr King ever received. Two years earlier, Dr King had been fêted in American universities and northern US cities, but in 1967 he was a much more controversial figure. Black power radicals and young urban rioters challenged his non-violent protest tactics and faith in integration. His eloquent opposition to the Vietnam War alienated him from the White House, which had previously given him his greatest victories. Newcastle nevertheless awarded him a Doctor of Civil Laws as a 'Christian pastor and social revolutionary'. The award owed much to the Vice-Chancellor, Charles Bosanquet, who was committed to a sense of corporate responsibility beyond the University cloisters, and whose wife's American family had been closely involved with the noted black college in Alabama, Tuskegee.

At the time of King's award there was little or no study of the United States at Newcastle: there were no specialist Americanists in the Departments of History, Politics or English. In 1974, Judie Newman was appointed in the English Department, built up American and post-colonial literature and then went to the Chair of American Studies in Nottingham in 1999. In 1971, the History Department advertised for a modern British historian who could also teach American history. They were deluged with applications from historians of Britain, but the Department was keen to develop American history. Since Tony Badger was the only Americanist who applied, he got the job. He was an historian of Roosevelt's New Deal who happened to work on how the farm programme was implemented in the South. One of his achievements was to bring Alger Hiss to lecture to a packed Curtis Auditorium in 1976. The desire to explore and teach great pioneering histories of slavery, which were the most interesting books being published on American history in the 1970s, led Badger to teach a course on the American South. Student demand to find out about the civil rights movement led to the replacement of a special subject on the New Deal with one on Martin Luther King. By the time Professor Badger left for Cambridge at the end of 1991, the course on the South had become the most popular option in the Department and the course on King the most popular special subject.

His successor, Brian Ward, not only built up a graduate programme in American history but also followed up Newcastle's remarkable decision to award King an honorary degree. He inaugurated two scholarly conferences on the civil rights movement in 1993 and 1998, which led to two important edited books: *The Making of Martin Luther King and the Civil Rights Movement*, and *Media, Culture, and the Modern African American Freedom Struggle*. Apart from leading academics from both sides of the Atlantic, veteran civil rights leader Julian Bond spoke at both conferences and Harry Belafonte, singer and friend of Dr King's, was awarded an honorary degree on the occasion of the 1998 conference. As a result, Newcastle University can claim to have made a major contribution to the remarkable strength of scholarship in Britain on the history of black protest in the modern South and to have honoured leading members of the civil rights movement in the process.

Anthony Badger

Harry Belafonte receiving his honorary degree with Mo Mowlam in May 1998

Students experimenting with an ice drill on the first ever Student Expedition in Iceland in 1948

STUDENT EXPEDITIONS

Today, Newcastle stands as one of the leading universities in the UK for conducting independent expeditions to destinations all over the world for research objectives, but also in the pursuit of adventure. The founding father was Hal Lister, Reader in Geography and a noted Arctic and Antarctic explorer and glaciologist.

Starting with Iceland in 1948, student teams were guided and part-funded by the University to take part in 15 expeditions over the following decade. Destinations included northern Norway, Newfoundland and the Alps. Geographical research into geology, hydrology and botany were the core activities of these trips, and reports detailing the results can be consulted in the Special Collections section of the Robinson Library.

The basic pattern of these ground-breaking expeditions has been reflected in virtually all our subsequent exploits. Small teams of two to eight students hatch a plan in the form of a goal and a destination. They then set to work organizing and fundraising during the academic year, so that everything possible is arranged before departure, usually in the long summer vacation. Planning the research thoroughly by identifying objectives, specifying study sites, training and equipping the team in appropriate methods, developing a time line and fundraising, all consume huge amounts of time, with tasks meted out to team members by an emerging leader.

This is all an early test of the team's fitness for the tasks ahead and involves much consultation with experts in various fields in the University and elsewhere. Some expedition ideas, and even some teams, come apart at the seams during this phase, but it is a filter through which all successful teams must pass to achieve their aim. Expeditioning, after all, is an activity reserved for a very few of our most exceptional students.

The success of many expeditions in the field has depended on the development of good relations with host country contacts, such as university staff and government officials, successively by letter, phone, telex, fax and e-mail as the years have gone by! Our students are often joined by counterparts from local universities when in the field, and these team members have proved themselves time and time again to be crucial in acting as interpreters, organizing logistics, identifying physical features, species and cultural artefacts. Increasingly, we are benefiting from the presence of alumni all over the world, who offer their time, influence and expertise in assisting students who are following them through Newcastle to realize their plans.

Fundraising has become the key activity in the preparation phase, as student incomes have progressively declined and expedition plans have become ever more ambitious! Our expedition teams have benefited greatly from approval and financial support from the Royal Geographical Society (with the Institute of British Geographers), which can be said to set the 'gold standard' for expeditioning activity by young people in the UK. A glance though past reports reveals that literally hundreds of other charities, professional bodies and commercial concerns have offered funds or help in kind to our teams over the years.

Fortunately, the University and a succession of recent vice-chancellors has seen the good publicity for Newcastle that student expeditions can foster overseas, and have offered funds accordingly. Hal Lister established the Exploration Council, a committee of staff charged with screening proposals, offering approval and funds, receiving reports and, in the early

years, helping returning expeditionists to produce an annual issue of the *Journal of the Exploration Society*, now lodged in the Robinson Library's Special Collections. In 1992, the Chancellor, Viscount Ridley, led a fundraising campaign that yielded over £50,000. This is invested by the University Development Trust, and the annual interest helps to fund expeditions via the Expeditions Committee. And, since 1999, returning teams have contributed to an annual November presentation entitled 'Tales from the Bush' in the University's 'Insights' public lecture series, accompanied by eye-catching coverage in the local press and broadcast media. Some expeditions give students the opportunity to undertake work towards their dissertations that could not be dreamt of within our own shores, and some have published their work in academic journals. Since the early days, both the destinations and purposes of the expeditions have diversified spectacularly. Islands featured early (Madeira 1953, 1954; Skiathos 1965, Azores 1970), and botany and zoology became important areas of study (Canaries 1963). An early epic was a five-week overland trip to northern Afghanistan (1968) to study meteorology, hydrology and the teeth of different tribal inhabitants of the area. Tropical Marine

Above (clockwise from top left):
Student expeditions to Kenya, researching the Samburu; biodiversity research in Papua New Guinea; in search of the snow leopard in Kazakhstan; looking for red hartebeest in Namibia

Biology soon came into the picture (Kenya 1972, 1974; Java 1977) and has continued as a strong theme ever since (Curaçao 1984; Israel 1987; Honduras 1995, 1996; Eritrea 1997; Indonesia, 2001; Kenya, Belize 2002; Tobago 2003, 2004; Turkey and Caicos 2003; Thailand, Tanzania 2005).

Soil science and sustainable land management have also been core disciplines over a long period (Senegal 1972, 1973; Morocco 1978; Nigeria 1991, 1992; Tanzania 2000; Vietnam 2001). Social science was launched through an investigation of the impact of the construction of the Karakorum Highway (Pakistan 1982) and the aftermath of earthquake damage in the Andes (Peru 1984), with several expeditions since (India 1992; Israel 1997; Nepal, Indonesia 2002). Anthropology and archaeology emerged more recently with a study of the yak-herding, horse-riding Golok indigenous people of the Tibetan plateau (China 1993), followed by a study of carved artefacts on Tanimbar Island (Indonesia 1994) and two studies of rock art (Mongolia 2004; Kenya 2005).

Humanity's impacts on the natural world have included studies of marine pollution (Indonesia 1993; Sri Lanka 2003), human–wildlife conflict (Ghana 1999; Papua New Guinea 2003; Khazakstan 2004), and threatened birds and mammals (India 1985; Philippines 1987; Malawi 1997, 1998; Greenland 1998; Ghana, Zimbabwe 1999; Ecuador 2001; Tanzania 2002; Namibia 2003; Seychelles 2005). An epic in this series was an expedition to study the threatened manatee (sea cow) in brackish creeks through mangrove forest (Venezuela 1992): but this first required the construction of a Kon Tiki-like platform and its navigation over an 80km stretch of ocean!

Medicine was rather more recently pioneered through an investigation of provision for AIDS patients (Zimbabwe 1993), and followed by surveys of bilharzia (Indonesia 1996; Tanzania 2005) and leprosy treatment in Dafur (Sudan 2003). Lastly, Newcastle's Geomatics students have completed detailed surveys of a desert area (Jordan 1998) and the lagoon of the Rodrigues coral atoll (Mauritius 2000).

In 2006, we still await first expeditions focused on disciplines such as architecture and music, and look forward to more activity in South America, which remains something of a forgotten continent as far as Newcastle student expeditioners are concerned.

Peter Garson

Turtle photographed during the 1995 Project Utila trip

Left: The library in the Armstrong Building, 1929

Below: Kate Greenaway, Almanack, 1890, in Special Collections

THE UNIVERSITY LIBRARY

The idea of any kind of library did not loom large in the early days of either the College of Medicine or the College of Physical Science. In 1871, the entire book collection of the College of Physical Science was housed in a single bookcase. It moved through various locations in the College and, subsequently, in the Armstrong Building over the next 45 years. Its funding was similarly patchy, and indeed from 1910 to 1921, it was provided not by the University, but by the City of Newcastle.

The theme of building provides a common strand running through the Library's history. It was during Frederick Bradshaw's term as Librarian (1921–36) that the first library building was constructed at the west end of the Quadrangle. As was the fashion, this was built on the principle of separate reading rooms and stacks, housing 200 users and 200,000 volumes. The libraries of the Royal Victoria Infirmary and the Durham College of

Medicine had been merged with the existing library shortly before. Planning soon began for a major extension, but the Second World War and financial stringency delayed the opening until 1960.

The extension comprised a U-shaped building wrapped round three sides of the 1926 library. While retaining the principle of separation of functions, it was a light, airy building with a semicircular north flank facing on to Claremont Road. Quality of materials was a feature, with Portland stone copings and San Stefano marble linings to the windows. The extension was four times the size of its parent, and the whole housed 450,000 volumes and 780 users. It was named the University Library, Newcastle upon Tyne, perhaps looking forwards to the separation from Durham three years later. The building is now occupied by the Research Beehive and other academic schools.

Even before the new library was opened, work was beginning on plans

Above: The Arts Reading Room, King's Library

From Special Collections in the Library

Above right: Woodcut by Joseph Crawhall

Below:

Top: Evelyn Everett-Green, Little Ruth's Lady: a story for children. *London: Shaw (1890s)*
Centre: The Little Old Women. *London: Dean & Son*
Bottom: Robert Record, *Record's Arithmetick*

for further development to provide space for 750,000 volumes, taking the University up to 2000. Library services, however, were changing radically. More user- and service-oriented approaches, the developing use of information technology, and awareness of change as a permanent feature of information development had to be reflected in any future building. The Library, which eventually opened in 1982, reflected all these features: it was highly flexible, brought users and stock together, had provision for the teaching of information skills, and was designed for the use of computers in library management. Its architect was Harry Faulkner-Brown, a pioneering designer of modern library buildings in the UK and a graduate of the University. The original square building reflected the character of a Northumbrian castle, and could house 700,000 volumes. In the short time between the opening of this building – now named the Robinson Library in tribute to Philip Robinson, a distinguished bookseller and generous benefactor to the Library – and an extension being added in 1996, thinking had developed further. This provided major computer clusters, better provision for staff–user interaction and more teaching space, as well as conventional space for stock and users.

The pace of change accelerates. The Library's role has moved from that of a storehouse, through the service phase to one where its support of teaching, learning and

research is more integral to these activities. The emphasis on stock size as a measure of quality has been replaced by the extent to which these core functions of the University are enhanced by the Library's activities. The explosion in digital resources has also meant that instant access to resources held elsewhere is available. The Library licenses

William Blake, Illustrations of the Book of Job. *London (1825)*

159

some 10,000 journals in 2006, where in 1999 it provided access to 5,000. By 2000, its stock was already 900,000, but the measure has different significance from 1982, let alone 1960. Liaison librarians work closely with the various schools and carry out information literacy teaching. Special Collections are more intensively used and exploited. Services are delivered over the web, providing continuous access to many services and resources. The Library is gradually helping to improve the impact of university research through its repositories of University research output.

Tom Graham

SPECIAL COLLECTIONS AND ARCHIVES

The Special Collections department contains rare books and other printed works, manuscript material, photographs, museum objects and ephemera. It counts amongst its holdings more than 100 collections that are of institutional (University Archives), local (Burman-Alnwick), national (Runciman Papers) and even of international significance (Gertrude Bell Archive). Material spans from the 15th century to the present and has been built up through bequests, gifts, long-term deposits and acquisitions. Although access to the collections is not restricted to students and academic staff, collection strengths reflect teaching and research interests within the University, such as the history of medicine, children's literature and political history. Also noteworthy are the Robert White chapbooks, English Civil War tracts (a number of which have resonance for Newcastle), the chapbooks, woodblocks and correspondence of 19th-century Tyneside engraver, Joseph Crawhall, and the Pattinson daguerreotypes which include the first-known photographic images of the Niagara Falls.

Despite the growth of electronic resources, Special Collections has seen its usage increase dramatically in the last two years: requests to consult items rose by 55 per cent in 2004–5 and, if recent usage can be sustained, figures look set to increase by a further 61 per cent in 2005–6.

Not only is the department responsible for collection management but it also deals with enquiries; both delivers and facilitates hands-on teaching sessions with primary materials; and pro-actively markets its services via posters, subject guides, exhibitions and an online 'treasure of the month' feature.

Melanie Wood

Above: Thomas Bewick, A General History of Quadrapeds, Newcastle upon Tyne: S. Hodgson (1790) in Special Collections

Right: The Robinson Library named for a local bookseller who was a generous benefactor to the Library

KATHLEEN WALKER

ENGLISH LANGUAGE AND LITERATURE / 1956–9
King's was a part of me from as long as I can remember. My parents met while both worked in Armstrong College, in the Library. My father, Harold Walker, was the photographer-technician there, based in the 'stacks' in the basement, and my mother, Evelyn Perkins (known as 'Peggy' for some now-forgotten reason!) was, from the age of 14, a library assistant on the desk, until their marriage in 1935, when she had to leave, due to rules at that time. Dr Bradshaw was the Librarian then.

I remember as a small child visiting my father in his 'dark cavern', as it seemed to me, in the stacks. Often he was developing film and the red light was on above the doorway, so we had to wait. The distinctive smell of the chemicals he used pervaded the tiny area. The bookbinder, Mr Bissett, worked nearby.

My father worked there from the early 20s until forced to retire in 1966, through ill health. His was a lifetime's service to the College over 44 years. A Professor of the University wrote: 'In his own field his work is beyond all comparison ... We have a keen respect and affection for him, and are very much in his debt.'

07

The University in the 21st Century

NEW BUILDINGS, NEW FOUNDATIONS FOR A NEW CENTURY

The appointment of Vice-Chancellor Professor Christopher Edwards in the first year of the new millennium fittingly heralded the renaissance of building development at the University. Increases in government capital development funding, since 1998, provided the catalyst for the restructuring of the University from seven faculties (and 76 departments!) down to three (with 26 associated schools), the engine for growth and focus viewed by Professor Edwards as key to success in an increasingly competitive environment.

Restructuring, undertaken in August 2002, was a prerequisite for achieving Edwards' objective of Newcastle becoming one of the top ten research-led universities in Britain. Combining departmental accommodation into schools necessitated relocation and reconfiguration of accommodation which, coupled with increasing focus on commercially relevant multidisciplinary research of 5 or 5* RAE (Research Assessment Exercise) status, brought about new approaches to teaching and research, and spawned an era of new building development. Increasing student numbers created a need for more student residences, more teaching rooms and the larger lecture theatres now being developed in shared teaching centres.

Whilst focusing on the functional needs of the University, its external environment has not been overlooked. Historical development of the campus as two distinctly separate colleges had resulted in entrances to buildings being in locations inappropriate to current needs, and the campus, over many years of increasing car ownership, had effectively become a large open car park between the buildings. To address these

issues and provide a physical framework for academic restructuring, it was decided in 2002 to develop a Campus Masterplan and, Sir Terry Farrell, a Newcastle graduate, was appointed as Masterplanner. His work established guidelines for the integration of spaces and places, both existing and new, whilst in parallel asserting the University's role as an active part of the city: the development of the 'Cultural Quarter' is intended to link town and gown in the north-east quadrant of the campus. Recognizing that landscaped public areas are needed to create an attractive environment for teaching, learning and research, as well as a sense of identity for the new schools and research institutes, Farrell's Masterplan provides a clear and flexible structure for future building developments.

Right: The Campus Masterplan designed by alumnus Sir Terry Farrell

Below: The award-winning Devonshire Building is home to the Institute for Research on Environment and Sustainability. It is an environmentally friendly building, using solar power and rainwater recycling

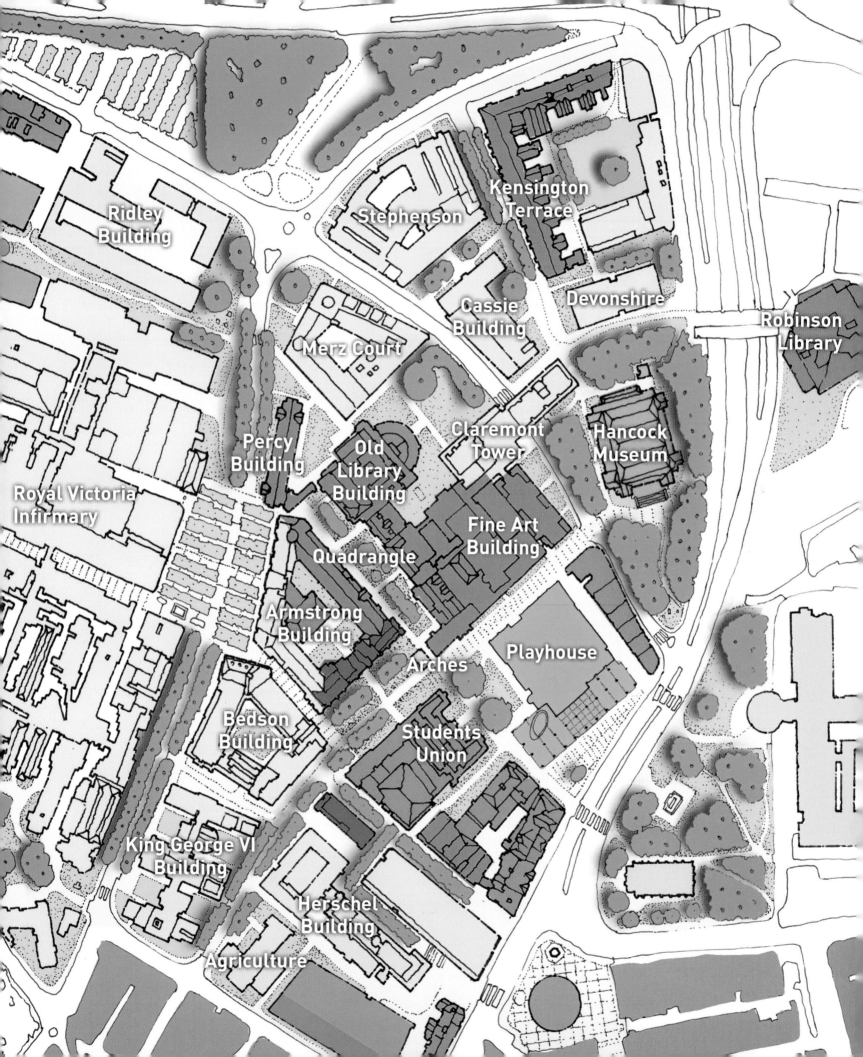

The existing quadrangle is at present the only public space of any quality giving the most historic part of the campus its collegiate identity and character. Farrell takes this as a model and proposes the creation of additional landscaped quadrangles elsewhere on campus, the most significant being Kings Quad, which will be a hard-paved, mixed-use area between the Armstrong Building and the Union Society Building on the main east–west pedestrian route through the University. It is made possible by the demolition, in 2003, of the Union's debating chamber and, upon the completion of the Great North Museum in 2008, of the Museum of Antiquities, a particularly undistinguished 1958 building at the heart of the University. The Kings Road Centre was completed in 2005 in what was the refectory, and is accessed directly from what will be the new Kings Quad. Its entrance area and interior have been innovatively reconfigured to create additional meeting rooms, a social learning centre and a large multi-use event space, doubling the size of what was the ballroom and now seating up to 500 in the largest flat floor space within the University. It is the first stage of a development that will include a covered atrium between it and the Union Society building.

More open internal environments characterize the University's recent new buildings and facilitate the emerging culture of interdisciplinary research and teaching. The Henry Wellcome Building, David Shaw Lecture Theatre and the Devonshire and Paul O'Gorman Buildings, both completed in 2004, are characteristic of a new generation of University buildings. These buildings and their designers have been the recipients of many awards for design, sustainability and construction management, and are considered exemplary in their fields.

The O'Gorman Building, designed by FaulknerBrowns, is home to the Northern Institute for Cancer Research and the first of the research buildings being developed for the Faculty of Medical Sciences to replace the original Newcastle Breweries Claremont Brewery buildings at the rear of Claremont Terrace. On three floors of an L-shaped building, it brings together the University's world-class scientific and clinical research into cancer treatment and related drug development under the direction of Professors Calvert and Newell, respectively its Clinical Director and first Scientific Research Director. Open-plan office accommodation on the south and east frontages faces an attractive paved courtyard and gives direct access at each level to adjoining laboratories and tissue culture areas. The building is ground-breaking in its open-plan accommodation and efficient use of space, which derive from studies commissioned from the University by the Higher Education Funding Council and which facilitate interdisciplinary working. Funding was in part from the Government's Science Research Investment Fund (SRIF), plus charitable donations, including a large donation from the O'Gorman family without which this important research facility could not have been developed.

The O'Gorman Building is the first of the medical research buildings, and is dedicated to the treatment of cancer

Above: Artist's sketch of part of the interior of the Great North Museum

Left: Open-plan offices in the Devonshire Building

The new University Sports Centre opened its doors for the first time on 25 July, 2005

The Devonshire Building accommodates the University's Institute for Research on Environment and Sustainability headed by Professor O'Donnell, the University's Informatics Research Institute (IRI) and the Regional Centre for Informatics. Also part-funded by the SRIF programme, it is another culture-changing development having, to the end of 2005, won nine awards, several in the field of environmental sustainability. It is a five-storey building designed by Dewjoc Architects with laboratories on its north side separated by a lofty atrium from open-plan offices to the south; it was developed to bring environmental research initiatives together, accommodating diverse disciplines from civil engineering to medicine. The building itself incorporates 'green' systems ranging from the recycling of rainwater into toilet flushing and partially heating or cooling of the building, to DTI-sponsored roof-mounted photo-voltaic panels generating a proportion of the electricity consumed within the building. It was the first laboratory building in Britain to reach an 'Excellent' rating under the Building Research Establishment's Environmental Assessment Methodology (BREEAM).

Teaching, learning and research activities are now undertaken by the University in ways more relevant to modern-day requirements. In parallel, cultural, sports and social facilities are being improved to attract the best students and staff in the increasingly competitive world of higher education. To this end it is developing further en-suite residences, and up to 2,000 additional study bedrooms will have been completed by 2010. Sports, social and cultural facilities are also being considerably improved: a new sports centre was completed in 2005, and the Great North Museum, an important part of the Cultural Quarter, is planned for completion by 2008.

Since its constitution in 1963, the University has had neither an appropriate front door to the city, nor a suitable administration building. Plans are now advancing to rectify this through the development of a new landmark building. This will accommodate the University's Student Services functions, its Executive Office and a Visitor Centre on the site facing the Civic Centre, a dismal open car park since 1963. The new building will form a gateway to both the University and the city, and complete new foundations for the new century. It will be followed by the development of Science Central and a new Business School.

John Lambert

165

NEWCASTLE REVIVED

In 1933, in his book *English Journey*, J.B. Priestley saw Tyneside for the first time, in its all Depression misery. He saw the rusting shipyards, the broken-down cottages and the forlorn allotments, the consequences of the severe surgical operations in Britain's post-war economy. He noted grimly that society bore no gratitude, nor even a balancing mention of what the region had contributed. And for decades it only got worse.

In their heyday, the Tyne shipyards employed 80,000 men, and built the greatest ships of their day – the *Turbinia*, *Carpathia*, *Mauretania* and the first supertanker *Esso Northumbria* – until cheap Asian labour and chronic underfunding killed them off. The Great North Coalfield employed 250,000 men in 400 pits, and they too either slowly expired through natural means, or by political dictat. But the oral traditions of poetry, song and storytelling lived on in the songs of Shildon's pitman poet Tommy Armstrong, the novels of Ferryhill's Sid Chaplin and the paintings of Ashington's Norman Cornish.

But what links those ships and crafts and skills, those workers, to the Millennium Bridge, The Sage and the Angel of the North? What links them are those very same skills, translated into a different form for a new century. The arcing bows of the Bridge, the riveted torso of the Angel, the swooping roofs of The Sage – all the old skills employed by new masters, re-engaging people with the collective self-esteem that creativity engenders.

Newcastle was not 'run down' when I came to the University in 1973, not really. The best days of the river had gone, true, but they'd been gone since the railways arrived and moved the lucrative trade up the hill towards the new station and Grainger's new town. It was an aggressive, filthy and vigorous place, a small city that felt like a pit village, from the tough Quayside pubs to the working men's clubs still dominating entertainment.

And the Georgian elegance of a 19th-century city had been challenged by the biggest man on the river, T. Dan Smith, the Tammany Hall man par excellence, who took them all on and eventually lost in a tale of hubris to quiet us all. But Dan had left his mark in the passionate brutalism of the new Central Library, Dobson Street and Pilgrim Street. And it was he who said, in 1965, that having led the world in the Industrial Revolution, Newcastle would lead the world in the Leisure Revolution.

Top left: The Angel of the North by Antony Gormley

Above: The Sage Gateshead, music and arts centre on the River Tyne

For three years I soaked up Newcastle, and when I left they were digging the holes for the Metro. Less than a decade later, in 1985, I returned to work for the BBC.

But if time ever took a cigarette and put it in your mouth, it was then. Thatcher's assault on Britain's industrial base hit the North East harder than anywhere. It had always defined itself by its work. It had produced great artists and writers – but they all mirrored industry, came from it, reflected it. Newcastle felt physically ravaged, like Carthage after the salt was sown. Dan Smith's buildings were derelict and unloved, and looked it. The glories of John Dobson's buildings were hidden under decades of filth and industrial pollution, the city centre looking as black as post-war Vienna, in the least-green town in Britain.

Amidst the carnage there remained a few souls dedicated to the traditions of representing the region's traditional culture – modern poetry fiercely championed by Tom Pickard and Jon Silkin; the Amber collective's film-makers showing northern working life, warts and all; Live Theatre from its Quayside outpost, Bruvvers (another theatre group) eternally out on the road, reflecting through local writers and actors the folk

JOSEPHINE SCRIVEN

SPEECH THERAPY / 1976–80

I have many recollections but most notably: the coastline just a train ride away (no cars for students then!); the Gilbert and Sullivan Society, which ignited an interest I still pursue today; the green hoardings that hid the Metro excavations; the friends I made and continue to keep in touch with; and, of course, the bridges and the view as you cross the river into the city and know you're home.

memory of work. But overall, Tyneside exported its talent, the young and ambitious seeing little here to detain them.

So what was the bridge between the desolation of the 1980s and the hope of a few years later? The major breakthrough came when the Year of Visual Arts in 1996 was won by the North East and Cumbria region. Every one of the 32 local authorities in the North East and Cumbria got a designated week when it was the centre of attention, and the projects lived up to any expectations. The smallest authorities were stimulated to heights they'd never imagined, working with the best artists in the world – sculptors Andy Goldsworthy (sheepfolds in Cumbria) and David Mach (*Brick Train* at Darlington), Bill Viola (*The Messenger*, a video installation in Durham Cathedral) – and then there was Antony Gormley. The year opened with his *Field for the British Isles* in railway sheds in Gateshead, but his major new commission that year was to become *The Angel of the North* in 1998. The greatest artists in the world now come to the city to create special works for it, and not just at the BALTIC Centre for Contemporary Art. Thomas Heatherwick's *Blue Carpet* outside the Laing Gallery created a rare piece of beautiful street furniture in Newcastle, to be joined by inspired seats on Grey Street. The Wilson Sisters came home with new films and 1,700 went naked on the Bridge for Spencer Tunick.

And it was the Angel that did it. No doubt about it. For months Gateshead's councillors had been bombarded by the most vituperative local newspaper campaign. Councillors George Gill and Sid Henderson, in particular, the champions of Gateshead's remarkable public art policy, stuck by their guns that the old pit site needed a great work and Gormley was the man to provide it. And as it was erected, as the bits forged in

Below: Performance by Live Theatre

Below right: The Blue Carpet by Thomas Heatherwick outside the Laing Gallery

Bottom: The Millennium Bridge by Wilkinson Eyre Architects and Gifford at Newcastle Quayside

Hartlepool yards fitted together so perfectly, and people saw the art and craft and skill, they melted to it as it slotted into the landscape. It touched the central nervous system of Tyneside, a system that had built the best ships and provided the best engineers. And now it's more, so much more, than merely the symbol of a new modern Tyneside. It's as recognizable an icon as the Eiffel Tower or the Statue of Liberty.

From this base, which confirmed what people thought was happening – that Tyneside was ready to fulfil a new role in Britain and Europe – came everything else, hot on innovation and design, connecting with the same joys of the built thing, from Dominic Williams's use of the old flour mills to create BALTIC, to Wilkinson Eyre's Millennium Bridge to Norman Foster's triple-shell design for The Sage, with the new Dance City (a specialist space for dance) and Seven Stories, the Centre for Children's Books, following.

In the midst of all that building and creation, the new identity of Tyneside was forged and Newcastle–Gateshead was born. Two small cities only united by the shared angst of supporting the same football team became one powerhouse. Gateshead's iconic buildings and vigorous will, Newcastle's regional capital status and massive arts funding. So together they bid for the title of European City of Culture for 2008. Of course they were favourites. Of course everyone neutral wanted them to win – by this time they'd become distinct, and distinctly fashionable. And of course Liverpool won, its massive whinge drowning out Newcastle's confident plea. Perhaps while they deserved it, Liverpool *needed* it. But the great thing was it changed nothing. Newcastle felt aggrieved and annoyed, but just got on with all their plans anyway.

But it's not just buildings, however iconic, that make a renaissance. It's the soul of the city – the souls of Stephenson and Scott connect to the Angel and the Bridge via the people who built them – the storytelling tradition continues through the generation of playwright Lee Hall, the late Julia Darling, and novelist Pat Barker. It's about a fiercely sceptical people who want to see the worth of something before believing it. But perhaps the most striking thing is the city's refusal to recognize it as total success.

Newcastle–Gateshead still has serious problems, not least low educational attainment and huge deprivation. Projects to tackle inner-city problems have led to the renovation of Graingertown, bringing people back to

DHRUV ADAM SOOKHOO

ARCHITECTURAL STUDIES / 2002–6
Northern Young Writer Award / 2004

Cities Slur
Day follows night the cities slur
As foist-leaflets find out every-corner.
The Tyne would offer no sympathy to drunks
And swallows culls easy-as yesterday's bigg-light.
This panics the sackless rowin' team
      -This dark Town.

Not us. Not now.
The night is on our hair
And we are quick-silver.
Some lasses kicked the street and sent more
Than bottles fleein'.
But cobbles yield to femmer-persuasions.
We are part of its fabric.
Sleekit sandstone.
      -This dark Town.

Sobered by our wishbone bridge
See you, losers! After Summer, after Easter,
After Christmas. Grit from black-diamonds tasted
Caviar for the new-connoisseur of style
Come back, return to
      -This, our dark Town.

live in the centre again, but the old industrial areas' problems will be harder to solve. The University is playing its part with the Partners programme with local schools, and is also a key player in the cultural regeneration via the Cultural Quarter and the Great North Museum projects.

Newcastle has come far in the past decade. Remember the opening sequence of *Get Carter*? The embodiment of 'it's grim up north' with blackened railway bridges and pit villages. Travel on the same route now and you're greeted by the Angel, The Sage, BALTIC, the Centre for Life, new Hilton, Holiday Inn and Vermont hotels. Perhaps the gratitude Priestley looked for from the nation has finally arrived, 70 years on, and with paint, not coal-dust, on its feet.

Mark Scrimshaw

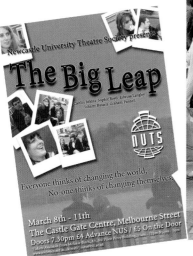

Above: A poster advertising The Big Leap, *a production by NUTS*

Below: The logo for Newcastle Student Radio

Bottom: Crowds of new students during Freshers' Week outside the Union Society building

STUDENT LIFE – OUTSIDE THE LECTURE ROOM

Expectations of student life at the University of Newcastle upon Tyne bring thousands of school leavers to the North East every year. Newcastle is a perfect town for students: small enough to find your feet and feel part of the city, yet big enough to have something for everyone, and the University has a history of providing an excellent base from which to establish yourself.

The starting point for the brave is undoubtedly Freshers' Week. Renowned as one of the best in the country, Newcastle University's Freshers' Week is a mini festival for university beginners, offering night-time events and parties, daytime activities from paintballing to beach trips – and even a free lift home!

Freshers' Week is arranged by students for students. This is a key aspect of student life in general in Newcastle: the majority of student activity is student-led. The University and Students' Union boast hundreds of societies and sports clubs, most of which were initiated and all now run by the student body, keeping them fresh and up to date when it comes to current trends.

A prime example of such a student-led society is the Newcastle University Theatre Society (NUTS), which has been an active part of University life for decades. NUTS is a breeding ground for talent and has seen many of its members follow successful theatrical careers through acting, directing, production, comedy and music. However, it has been, like so many student societies, a social group that has brought together hundreds of students with varying degrees of talent. The societies at Newcastle University are entirely non-discriminatory so, whether destined to play Hamlet or better suited to a pantomime cameo, everyone is encouraged to get involved. NUTS has covered everything from Shakespeare to musicals and student-written comedy, and few people at the University could have failed to notice something that the Society has staged, be it serious drama or a charity social event.

NUTS is just one of hundreds of societies, all of which have an active membership and arrange events that are designed to reach out to students across the campus. For example, the International Society puts on the International Grand Festival almost annually. This introduces the University population and the people of Newcastle to a little of the cultures of the many countries from which the University's students hail. The Debating Society takes teams around the world and has had members who have been international champions. The Newcastle University Jazz Orchestra gives musical students the opportunity to play at a professional level. The Short Film Society organizes a challenge every year where groups of students are given 48 hours to devise, write, shoot and edit a short film, which is later screened at Newcastle's favourite local cinema, the Tyneside.

Student media inform both students and staff of the latest news and events. *The Courier* has traditionally been the first port of call for student news, reviews and sports reports and has been running for over 50 years. It serves both the reader and the writer as it gives budding journalists invaluable experience. Newcastle Student Radio is also now a huge part of the student media network and broadcasts to students across Newcastle. Both *The Courier* and Newcastle Student Radio provide an opportunity not only to students wishing to follow a media career, but also to those who want to have their opinions heard.

For those whose life in Newcastle is more widely based, there have always been countless ways to become involved with the local community. Conventionally, the most common starting point has been Student Community Action Newcastle (SCAN). SCAN started as a settlement project in the late 1960s, becoming a registered charity in 1973. SCAN aims to serve the community, whilst also encouraging personal development in students, who can learn new skills and enjoy themselves through volunteering. Volunteering in the community is a good way to get to know Newcastle as a city and branch out a little from University activities. SCAN runs student-led projects throughout the North East, including environmental activities, helping refugees and asylum seekers, and assisting people with disabilities.

R.M. WHITELAW / ECONOMICS / 1963–6

I guess that every student believes that their university was the best place to be, but I know that Newcastle was the place to be in 1963–6. The 'swinging Sixties' found Newcastle at the heart of youth culture – the Animals were a 'fill-in' band at University dances in 1963, and the Rolling Stones would play at the Club-A-Gogo on Percy Street. My first digs were in Fenham, across from the park where Hank Marvin first used to practise his guitar.

I watched Newcastle United win promotion to the First Division, amongst crowds of 60,000, beating Sunderland and Jim Baxter along the way. Newcastle Brown was the coolest drink in the land – I introduced it to my local back in Exeter, and wished I'd agreed a commission! As well as the female population of the University, the Polytechnic, and all the teacher training colleges, we had all the wonderful nurses from the RVI. Saturday night dances were a sure fire certainty!

Lest it seem that life in Newcastle was purely hedonistic, I do have some memories of the academic side. I remember the Senior Lecturer, David Watkins, telling me in a tutorial to be bold and say what I really thought 'because this will be the last time you can be wrong and get away with it'. I remember the Sociology lecturer whose arguments were so convoluted we used to bet on the length of his sentences. But most vividly of all I remember a lecturer in Contract Law – a barrister whose lecture was always packed to the rafters. He would start to talk as he burst through the swing doors, continue citing case after case, without notes, for the full hour, and finish the last one as he made his way back to the swing doors. Carlyle v The Carbolic Smoke Ball Company lives with me till this day!

JANET JONES / MODERN LANGUAGES / 1966–70

I was a Modern Languages student and joined the SRC (Students Representative Council) in my first year. I volunteered to take on the organization of the Freshers' Conference in October 1968. I was the first woman to do so. There was no competition for the job – it took a year of hard work and planning and was generally considered to be an albatross!

It turned out to be a memorable year – my team worked incredibly hard, but also had great fun. We had offices on the top floor of the Union Building and secretarial help from the union secretary. We planned talks, entertainment, displays and met students and academics from across the University. To celebrate a successful conference, we went for a meal at the Gosforth Park Hotel, but the bill came to more than we could afford and I can remember the emptying of pockets and serious consideration about doing the washing up! A very kind gentleman on the next table made up the difference – he said the entertainment had been worth it!

NEIL MURRAY / ENGLISH AND PHILOSOPHY / 1967–72

I remember hearing that Paul McCartney and Wings had arrived and performed unannounced at the Castle Leazes Halls. My social circle even included Lindisfarne for a short time. An English Literature student called John Wilkinson (known as Wilko) reinvented himself as Wilko Johnson and turned up to play with his new band, Doctor Feelgood. A Scouse flatmate introduced a weekend visitor in the Men's Bar on one occasion and it was Alexi Sayle.

The political scene gripped me, and we produced a regular weekly paper called Pravda (this was supposed to be a humorous title but was probably taken at face value in some quarters! I still have all the editions). A delegation of Newcastle students went to Ashington to march in support of the 1972 miners' strike and were embarrassed to find themselves cheered along the streets.

PETER HARVEY / GEOGRAPHY / 1983–6

I was the Newcastle captain in the TV quiz University Challenge 1984–5. The team, selected by the Union in a lunchtime handwritten test, comprised three people from the North East – Dr Steve Martin from Redcar, a lad (whose name escapes me) from Durham and myself from Newcastle – as well as a chap called Bright from Coventry. The tale was written up at the time by myself and featured on the front page of the Student Union paper (with photograph in full colour).

As I recall we were drawn against Cardiff in the first round and did very well throughout the rehearsals (even our wild guesses were on target) – so much so that Bamber Gascoigne (original and best quizmaster) sought to console the opposition with 'Don't worry Cardiff, these things have a way of reversing themselves in the live programme'. And of course Bamber was always right.

It wasn't nerves or stage fright – he just stopped asking questions to which we knew the answers. And we should have known the fates had abandoned us when we were asked for the English version of the old Greek adage 'Owls to Athens', a dead cert for our team, we felt, as Bright buzzed in first and said 'Carrying coals to ... COVENTRY!?' Our humiliation was complete.

It was a long ride home for three of us to Newcastle with our supporters that night and a short sending to Coventry for the man we came to call 'notso' (Bright – get it?).

Student Community Action Newcastle

Top: Rag Float for SCAN, the University's community action group with their logo (above)

Many students also make their own contacts with the local community through other types of volunteering, working locally, and popularly arranging various social events in the city. A large number of graduates remain in the city after their degrees in order to pursue their careers, allowing even more involvement.

There has always been more to student life than officially organized events. The real buzz from living in Newcastle comes from the city life and the social occasions that students have either planned themselves or fallen upon at the last minute. Newcastle has a reputation for offering one of the best nights out in Europe – and with good reason. There are many clubs, bars and pubs, which are ideal as a distraction after a hard day's study. And, of course, dinner parties, coffee breaks and trips to the Tyneside Cinema for a slightly off-the-wall film are very popular as well.

Perhaps these unplanned social occasions are often the most memorable. Few recent students could honestly claim they have never been to 'The Boat' (or the *Tuxedo Princess* as it is officially known), the hideously designed nightclub on a liner that has been the venue for so many first-year socials. Few have never enjoyed a pint in the Union or on Osborne Road, and most have probably stopped to chat to someone outside the Library and ended up having a four-hour coffee break. Less recent students might remember the cinema next to the Union, gigs at the Polytechnic (as it was then called) and the Bigg Market before it was overrun with more modern bars.

From arrival in Newcastle as timid first years in halls to leaving a few years later as confident twenty-somethings with letters after their names, most University students will remember their student lives extremely fondly. Whether involved in sport, societies, student media or nothing in particular, the social aspects and extra-curricular activities often make up for the particularly hard times of study and allow all University graduates to leave with far more than just a degree.

Francesca Naish

THE COURIER

On Thursday, 18 November 1948, *The King's Courier* was born. Initially the newspaper for King's College, Newcastle, in the University of Durham, *The Courier* began as a four-page newsletter whose purpose, according to the President of the King's College Students' Representative Council, William Brough, was to 'clearly bind the separate parts of the college more closely together'. He described it as a 'painless way of keeping in touch' with student and University life, and *The Courier's* first editor, Stuart Shaw, added that 'perhaps the most important aim [was] the fostering of interest in all college activities'. In *The Courier's* 58 years, it seems that little has changed in this sense. It has always prided itself in being the voice of Newcastle students and remains the most accessible regular update of university goings-on.

The first ever article was written by the Rector, Lord Eustace Percy, whom Castle Leazes' residents will recognize as the namesake of one of their halls. Topics covered in the first issues included the future of King's College, student apathy, women at work, the International Union of Students, societies' news, arts reviews and sports' reports, covering rugger, soccer, fencing and rowing, to name but a few.

Top left: The first issue of The Courier *student magazine, 18 November 1948*

Above right: *Issue 1116 of* The Courier*, 31 October 2005*

The Courier's popularity saw it grow in size and circulation during its early years and, by the 1960s, it was an eight-page publication covering all the basics of student life. The 1960s *Courier* became more lighthearted, with pictures of students, pieces on travel and a more jovial attitude. Important issues included the establishing of the University of Newcastle upon Tyne, the problems of leaving university and getting a job and, perhaps most outrageously, the indignation caused when a group of women infiltrated the Men's Bar on a Friday night.

By the 1970s, *The Courier* had seen its first pornography: exotic dancers had entered the Union and a lot of women were disgusted. There was anger at rising tuition fees for international students and fear about accommodation. But perhaps most notably, *The Courier* had become yet more relaxed, with far more tales of boozy student shenanigans.

Arguably, *The Courier* is so invaluable because it is one of the truest reflections of popular student feeling of the moment. This could be seen in the early 1990s, when it became rather ruder, unafraid to print the odd impolite word and certainly willing to mock itself. The paper was crisper and a bit more colourful, and readers were not only treated to 12 pages of entertainment, but also a free burger on presentation of the infamous front-page Burger King voucher still seen today. Big stories included the City Council's proposal to fine students for putting up Union election posters and the 'agrics' being allowed back into the Union after bad behaviour (they have now long since been banned again). The everyday student was given more of a say, with more columnists and the still popular 'Vox Pop', allowing students to give their opinions on issues of the day.

The Courier of the new millennium seems to be a natural development from its early days. It is bigger, brighter, and the entertainments section – now referred to as Pulp – is far more comprehensive due to the current trend to socialize away from home as much as possible. There are more contributers and therefore more stories, but in many ways *The Courier* today, though developed and expanded, has much the same feeling as it always had. Although some of the issues have changed – women are most certainly permitted to drink in the Men's Bar, for example – the inherent feeling of 'studentness' still remains. *The Courier* continues to 'bind the separate parts of the college more closely together' because it is the simplest and most effective way of keeping up to date, keeping in touch and having a voice.

Francesca Naish

NEIL MURRAY

ENGLISH AND PHILOSOPHY / 1967–72
The Northerner and *The Courier*

I buckled down to work but also started contributing to *The Northerner* magazine and *The Courier*. It was around the summer of 1968 that the traditional *Northerner* title was renamed *Package*, having been taken over by new joint editors Mike Jones and Gordon Sharp, and became something very trendy, appearing literally as a 'package' on occasions. I don't think it lasted much longer after that.

In September 1968 came the phone call that changed things for me. The appointed editor of *The Courier* had failed his resits and would not be returning, so would I do it? Other *Courier* colleagues were the lovely Caroline Dees as features editor, Brian Cummins from whom I learnt page layout and Sam Swallow as sports editor, the stereotypical bluff Yorkshireman. The everlasting Monica Doughty was in harness as *The Courier* secretary (a staff post), forever doing battle with Students' Representative Council officials about overtime, which *The Courier* and its disorganized student staff usually required.

I remained involved with *The Courier* after giving up the editorship, and actually enjoyed it more now doing layout and occasional features. The work was mainly done on Sundays. Access was by the fire escape, though the Union was experimentally opened on Sundays a year or so later. Working through Sunday night was normal, and new editor Brian Horne or myself would catch the first train on Monday morning to South Shields and deposit the completed copy through the letterbox of the *Shields Gazette*. A few of us would return to the printers mid-week to supervise the final work on the linotype trays and see the printing done, bringing the bundled copies back to the Union by car on a Wednesday afternoon. Needless to say lectures were usually out of the question.

NEWCASTLE UNIVERSITY BOAT CLUB

The Newcastle University Boat Club (NUBC) evolved from its former guise as King's College Boat Club at the same time as the University itself was founded in 1963, but it shared the Newburn site with Durham University Boat Club right through until 1999. Insufficient space for racking the boats at the Newburn site, coupled with an almost unbearable competitive tension between the two clubs, prompted the move to the Club's present boathouse near Newburn Bridge. The first occasion in the history of Durham Regatta where Durham University did not win the top competition of men's elite VIIIs was in 1980. And who beat them but Newcastle University, much to the dismay of the home crowd!

Rowing equipment is expensive and difficult to maintain. A new VIII boat, for example, costs nearly £20,000 and a set of eight blades costs £1,600. These

SPORT

FRANCESCA NAISH / *THE COURIER* EDITOR / 2004–5

Sport at the University plays a major part in student life. Wednesday afternoons have long been given over to sporting activities in over 40 pursuits, ranging from football and netball to tae kwon do and Ultimate Frisbee. Sport is an unbeatable way of physically working hard, keeping fit and enjoying yourself – while representing your university. Newcastle University's teams have been successful in the British Universities Sports Association (BUSA) leagues and competitions, as well as in derbies against Durham, such as the annual boat race, and against Northumbria in the Stan Calvert Cup every December.

Since 1994, the Stan Calvert Cup has been perhaps the biggest event of the sporting calendar at both Newcastle and Northumbria Universities. It is held in memory of Stan Calvert, who was the first director of sport at Newcastle University in 1981. Usually on a cold and otherwise miserable day in December, thousands of students descend upon Gateshead Stadium, bringing with them an atmosphere to rival a football derby between Manchester United and Manchester City. The mascots come out and over 1,000 students compete in 20 sports. It is the climax to the year-round friendly rivalry between the two universities and always attracts students not normally involved in sport, who come to support their respective teams. Over the years, the battles have been close, but up to 2006, Newcastle have taken the cup a few more times than their neighbours.

To play sport at Newcastle University, you don't need to be a supreme athlete. The University's Intra Mural leagues allow groups of students to set up their own teams in order to compete against each other on a slightly less official level. Any students can put a team together with friends from halls of residence, course mates or people they meet in the pub, and matches are held each week in sports such as football, rugby, netball and hockey. The Intra Mural leagues are extremely friendly and allow students of all abilities to play games in a relaxed atmosphere.

One of the best aspects of sport at the University is its social side. There are few athletes who would deny that playing sport has brought them new friends. The sports teams arrange regular social events and, on a Wednesday night, the Union's Men's Bar is usually full of players either celebrating a win or commiserating over a loss. The highlight of the sporting social calendar is probably the annual Athletics Union Ball, which celebrates University sport each year through team awards, the presentation of University colours – and a very good party.

M.A. HIGGINS / GERMAN AND SWEDISH / 1963–6 / Rugby

I arrived in Newcastle on the Saturday before term started. I found out, when I went to Eustace Percy Hall, that the Rugby Club were holding trials that afternoon. I caught the number 19 bus to get to Cochrane Park, only to find that I was going the wrong way round on the circular journey. When I eventually arrived at Cochrane Park, I discovered that

Cecil Elliott (second from right, ringed), a history student during 1924–8, is shown here in the University's rugby team

because I had not been at Freshers' Week, I was not registered to play in the trial and so I only came on late in the second half as a substitute. I seemed to do quite well, however, and was picked to play for the 1st XV on the following Saturday against Percy Park. I played at centre and scored the University's first and second try in its history and was written up in *The Sunday Times* the following day.

KEITH POWELL / CHEMISTRY / 1965–71 / Rugby

I played for the University rugby 2nd team from about 1968 until 1970. During that time we had Brian Keen and Ken Goodall in the University 1st team. Brian played for England at prop and Ken played for Ireland at lock. Shortly after that we had Dick Cowman, who subsequently played fly half for England. I am not aware of having so many international players from Newcastle University since then.

Top right: The Stan Calvert Cup

Above: The Ultimate Frisbee team

Right: In April 1965, in only its second season, Newcastle University's 1st XV beat Rockcliffe 12–3 to win the Northumberland Rugby Senior Cup. John Tarbit was their captain

173

RAG WEEK

The Rag Revue Chorus in 1947

JEAN NICHOLSON / FINE ART / 1945-8

In my second year it was suggested that there should be a Rag Week, including a Rag Revue, the first since before the war. The producer was Maurice Brand and he was a dynamo – a fifth-year medical student. He asked me to design the costumes. I also danced and sang in the chorus, which involved a lot of tap dancing and high kicking, and took part in a couple of sketches. I remember that the producer of the Rag Revue traditionally failed his finals; I know that Maurice did and had to do another year and resit – and he passed well. The music (and the words) were composed by Peter Whittingam, also a medic – I think he passed first go. The music was lovely.

There was a male chorus – all large sporty types, mostly medics and agrics, but dressed very carefully and properly in women's clothes and wigs and highish heels (very hard to get because of five years of clothes rationing). They were wildly popular and got several encores and deafening cheers.

The finale consisted of several couples in laundry baskets wrapped in cotton wool (probably stolen from the Royal Victoria Infirmary) hoisted up and down over the stage and singing, 'Floating away in a cloud for two'.

PROFESSOR DEREK GELDART / MECHNICAL ENGINEERING / 1950–4

The Rag Day held every autumn term was a huge event, intended to raise funds for charities. The mechanical engineers constructed a full-size elephant out of plywood on a wooden frame. Its stomach was partly cut away to reveal a red light bulb

The first post-war Rag Procession in October 1946. The All But Beer Machine was the Engineering Department's float and the man clutching his hat in the centre was Sir Robert Malpas, a benefactor of the University

The astonishing full-size elephant constructed by the mechanical engineers for Rag Week 1951

flashing on and off during the parade up Northumberland Street, carried on the back of a flat-top lorry. 'Wor Elefunt' with its articulated legs was surmounted by a turbaned mahout, a charming, clever, hard-working student by the name of Muckerji, the only Indian in our year.

KEN PRINGLE / PHYSICS / 1949–52 / Rag Caterpillar

I was one of the middle legs of an extensive caterpillar that wound its way down Northumberland Street on Rag Day 1951. In those days the spectators appeared to thoroughly enjoy the proceedings and contributed generously to the collection boxes wielded by the most attractive girl students – the men were well camouflaged within the caterpillar 'skin' and similar artifices. I hope the relationship between town and gown is still as good as it was then.

SIR TERRY FARRELL / ARCHITECTURE / 1956–61

The agrics always had tremendous floats and one year the Architecture students stole their float, and drove it to Holy Island. The agrics caught the Architecture students, stole their trousers and left them stranded – they had to hitch back to Newcastle in their underpants. When they got back, they found that the vehicle that they had used to go to Holy Island had been carried up two flights of stairs and left on the landing of the agricultural building.

PETER VALE / MECHANICAL ENGINEERING / 1965–8

Freshers' Week was like being a child in a sweet shop. There must have been over 100 clubs vying for our patronage. The Ski Club? Never done that before, they have snow in the North East and it sounded fun. It raised a few eyebrows when I took a pair of skis on the 28 bus to Fawdon in the Friday rush hour, and returned from my digs with them on the Sunday! The day was simplicity itself. In his sloping snow-covered field, a farmer had set up a tractor-driven winch to haul skiers to the top. I had great fun launching myself down the slope, generally finishing up in a heap but never actually learning anything. Nonetheless, the university experience whetted my appetite.

SUSAN WHYTOCK / ZOOLOGY AND BOTANY / 1959–63

After 40 years, I still have vivid memories of Rag Week! A whole week was filled with fundraising events, culminating in a Grand Parade of decorated floats complete with Rag Queen and tiara! A political issue of the day was De Gaulle's reluctance to let the UK join the Common Market, and many of the floats were devoted to this theme. There were shows, balls, stunts in the street, and a Rag Band with majorettes marching round the town. A large amount of money was collected for charity; I recall one year it totalled £15,000!

Thomas Henry Brown in strappy flapper shoes and a hat rides on a float with other dental students in Rag week 1925

175

A float reflecting a political issue of the times *Students dressed to kill at the Arts Ball* *A duel in the streets of Newcastle, staged as a Rag stunt*

TONY DUHIG / GENERAL ARTS / 1961–4

I was Rag President in 1964. Through negotiations with University authorities, it was agreed that there would be no lectures, seminars or technical work from midday on the Wednesday to the following Monday. In return, Rag agreed that events would take place only in that time and not over an extended period as in the past.

The Rag magazine was put out to contract as far as the advertising was concerned. We signed a five-year contract that guaranteed an income of £500 in 1964 and rising each year thereafter. All we had to do was to produce the copy on time and the magazine was delivered fully printed and ready to distribute.

The Rag Ball had been a financial loss for many years. I made local enquiries as to who in Newcastle knew how to organize a successful charity ball, and the name that came to the fore was that of Mrs Bosanquet, wife of the Vice-Chancellor. After supper at their house (me in my shabby student clothes), she agreed to run the Ball Committee and become a member of the Rag Committee!

Mrs Bosanquet not only ran the Ball Committee, but also spent hours in the Rag Office with teams of students addressing hundreds of envelopes by hand from lists that she had acquired from many local sources. Donations poured in as the invitations went out, and our costs were more than covered before the Ball began. Another piece of history! Our total revenue was over £13,000 and we gave over £8,000 to charity – a much healthier proportion than the previous year!

PAUL F. MILLER / AGRICULTURE / 1983–6
The Great Stretcher Race

As stretcher races go, the ones organised by the Agric Society for Community Action Week in the 1980s took some beating. Teams of six entered in fancy dress. St Trinians were there, men in drag, country yokels, escaped convicts, and a full 'pas de six' in Day-Glo tutus.

All of the stretchers were lined up on the grass in front of the Students' Union with a team member sat on each waiting for the start. The rest of the team took up their positions at the other side of Kings Walk. It was a Monte Carlo start as each team raced across to their respective stretcher, picked up their charges and headed off into town to cajole as much money as possible from defenceless Geordie shoppers in Northumberland Street.

Meanwhile, an obstacle course had been set up along Kings Walk, up the steps and through the arches to the Quadrangle. The teams arrived back from town, handed over their collections and prepared for the hazards ahead. To add interest, two of the stretcher bearers in each team were tied together in three-legged fashion and the other three were tied together in five-legged style.

The agric night 'buzz' table was set up on beer barrels and this was the first feature to be climbed over without losing the patient off the stretcher. Next came the beer barrel slalom, which caused much confusion within the teams, no one quite knowing which tied leg was going where.

On completion of the tour around the Quad every team member was rewarded with a pint of cold custard, the refusal of which incurred instant disqualification or having it poured over your head. There were some sorry sights by the end.

CAROLINE AND DAVID GILL / CLASSICS / 1979–82
Rag Day Recitation

It was anything but a rosy-fingered dawn. There was, in fact, a distinct chill in the air at the start of a snowy Rag Day. Classics and Ancient History students huddled under the arches waiting for Dr Peter Jones to launch the departmental 'Homer-athon'. Dr Jones had decided to swell the Rag Day coffers by organizing a sponsored read of Homer's Odyssey in classical Greek. The bard, clad in sky-blue (in what uncannily resembled a dressing gown) leaned over his bema (reading desk) and began to boom out the tale of Odysseus's return from Troy. At the end of his oration, Dr Jones prepared to pass the baton to members of his Classical flock. Faces turned as white as the snow on the roof tops – was this a case of pre-performance nerves or acute frostbite? Some of us were wondering whether a public recitation of Homer was a bridge too far! It was all great fun – and many of us enjoyed our epic moment.

Above: Ed Coode with his Olympic Gold Medal

Bottom: Angelo Savarino, an Italian national rowing coach, came from Rome to become head coach at Newcastle University Boat Club

costs are currently met by the members through a combination of fees, sponsorship and other revenues. Since 1996, the University has wisely invested in the part-time employment of a boatman, Brad Jewell, for the upkeep of the fleet.

Brad received his degree in Naval Architecture from Newcastle University over 30 years ago. Although never an oarsman himself, Brad has said, 'I'm full of admiration for the rowers. Rowing is a most demanding sport and their commitment is tremendous. They train very hard – twice a day – in all weathers, and their team spirit is first class.' The rowers too are very fond of him, and he has become an integral part of the social scene.

The social scene is an important part of the Boat Club. Approximately 75 per cent of the Club is made up of people who never rowed before they came to university. Everyone has their own reason for being lured to the sport. But what makes them stay is the emotional extremes shared by a crew over a season, which can create a bond that lasts a lifetime.

A recent addition to the social calendar has been the inclusion of a dinner at the end of the first semester in memory of a former member of the Club, James (Jim) London. Jim graduated in 1996 with an Honours degree in Civil and Environmental Engineering. An active member of the Club as both a rower and a coach, he tragically died aged 23 in 1998. At the dinner, an award in his memory is given to those who share the passion and commitment that Jim held for NUBC. The current men's 1st VIII boat is also named after him.

The creation of the Northumbrian Water University Boat Race between Durham and Newcastle upon Tyne is the pinnacle of the Club's public calendar in the North East. The first of these races was held in 1997 and has grown in terms of success and stature year upon year.

The event feels almost gladiatorial due to the large crowds, often several thousand, looming over the two crews as they surge downstream side by side along the Quayside. Initially the event was only for three crews: Men's 1st VIII, Women's 1st VIII and Freshmen's VIII. The introduction of the Freshwomen's race in 2004 proved to be an immense success, as it brought about some very close and competitive racing.

In the nine years of the race to date, there has been a steady increase in the number of victories attained by NUBC. First blood was drawn in 1998, when the Freshmen crew coached by Jon McEvoy became the first NUBC crew to reign victorious over Durham. It was the Senior Women who struck next in 1999 and 2001. The 2001 winning crew was stroked by Ros Carslake, who later that same year won a gold medal at the U23 (under 23) World Championships in a coxless pair. Further victories did not occur until 2005, when for the first time since the event was created, NUBC drew the event with two wins for each university. The Men's 1st VIII, the flagship event, was won for the first time by NUBC by a narrow verdict of 6 inches. The photo finish confirmed the result that the home crowd were all desperate to hear. The event could so nearly have been a NUBC outright victory if the Freshmen hadn't been inched out again in a photo finish.

For many years NUBC was portrayed as Durham's poor relation, but in recent times it has evolved into a highly competitive rowing centre. In the last decade, the Club has enjoyed a good measure of success on the international scene, most notably with our 1997 Senior Men's captain, Ed Coode MBE. Ed graduated at the end of 1997 and went on to attend Oxford University to further his rowing credentials. Rob Latham was Ed's pairs partner back in 1996 and represented Great Britain at the U23 World Championships in the VIII.

While still at NUBC, Ed attended the U23 World Championships in a coxed IV, where he won a silver medal. He made such an impression that, in the same year, he was invited to attend the Senior World Championships, again in a coxed IV, where, incredibly, he won a bronze medal. The following years would see Ed in and out of the famous Sydney Olympic coxless IV, containing the formidable duo of Redgrave and Pinsent. When the final selection was made, Ed was selected to represent Great Britain rowing in the pair, where he narrowly missed out on a medal, finishing fourth. During the next Olympiad in Athens, Ed suffered a shoulder injury, but following an operation, he regained full fitness and secured a seat in the flagship boat, the coxless IV. The most exciting race in memory ensued, and the IV surged to victory in one of the tightest races imaginable, winning gold over Canada by 0.08 seconds.

More recently, the Club has enjoyed a succession of young talent promising to emulate the success of Ed. Henry Pelly competed in the U23 World Championships in a quadruple scull. He was the Club's President from 2004 to 2006, and has been very influential in leading NUBC to its recent Boat Race victories. In 2005, NUBC was represented by two oarsmen at the U23 World Championships, George Laughton in the VIII, and Stephen Feeney in the lightweight quadruple scull. Stephen won a silver medal at those championships, and who knows what further success the future may hold for these or any other of the NUBC athletes.

Joe Leiserach

THE GREAT NORTH MUSEUM

The Great North Museum is the focus of the new Cultural Quarter, part of Sir Terry Farrell's Masterplan for opening up the University to the city of Newcastle. Culture, in the form of art galleries, museums, public lectures, etc, is an excellent 'gateway project', helping to draw people onto the University campus. Central to the concept of the Cultural Quarter is the idea of bringing together the three campus museums: the Hancock Museum (Natural History), the Museum of Antiquities and the Shefton Museum (Ancient Greek collection) into one location, which would also be linked with the Hatton Gallery (Art) in terms of its organization and management.

An ambitious scheme for a combined museum was submitted to the Heritage Lottery Fund in June 2003. This bid was revised the following year and, in January 2005, the Trustees approved an allocation of £8.75m toward the total costs of around £26m.

The Great North Museum – a project title that has aroused strong views both for and against – is the product of a new partnership comprising: the University of Newcastle upon Tyne; the Natural History Society of Northumbria, owners of the Hancock Museum and its collections; the Society of Antiquaries of Newcastle upon Tyne, owners of much of the collection within the Museum of Antiquities; Newcastle City Council, contributors along with the University to both the capital and revenue costs of the new museum; and Tyne and Wear Museums, who will manage the Great North Museum.

The world-class design team comprises architects Terry Farrell and Partners and exhibitions designers Casson Mann. Sir Terry Farrell is a Newcastle alumnus; his firm's projects have included the Dean Gallery, Edinburgh, and The Deep, Hull. Casson Mann have won acclaim for their British Galleries at the Victoria and Albert Museum and the new Churchill Museum at the Cabinet War Rooms.

The Great North Museum will be located in an extended Hancock Museum building and a separate off-site store. The elegant Grade II*-listed building, dating back to 1884, has suffered from various accretions during the last 120 years and every square centimetre is packed with stored objects, many in far-from-ideal conditions. The project will transform the Hancock's interior to allow all three museum collections to be displayed within the one building, together with certain items from the Hatton Gallery such as the Uhlman Collection of African Art, which will be combined with other fine ethnographic

The new North Gallery where the dinosaurs lurk

Above: An artist's impression of the Great North Museum, showing the barrel-shaped addition to the Hancock Museum

Below: The Biodiversity Wall in the South Gallery giving a taste of the wide diversity of the natural world

material, including some items traceable back to the voyages of Captain Cook.

The design for the new Hancock building will open out what are currently three entirely separate spaces by creating a central route right through the building. The South Gallery, by the entrance, will house a stunning 'Biodiversity Wall', displaying from floor to ceiling the huge variety of the natural world. The Central Gallery will focus on the Roman collections from the World Heritage Site of Hadrian's Wall, with an interactive model of the Wall, presenting these unique objects from the viewpoints of various different historical characters who lived along the Wall and its hinterland. The rear North Gallery will contain some of the Hancock's wonderful geological specimens, complete with dinosaurs. The first-floor suite of galleries will explore the ancient civilisations of Egypt, Greece and Rome, as well as related modern world cultures, using a mix of displays and technology. One gallery will be devoted to the magnificent Shefton collection; currently hidden away in the Armstrong Building and seen by only a few thousand each year; as part of the Great North Museum it will be seen by over 300,000 real visitors, as well as by countless virtual visitors through the Museum's website.

A new barrel-vaulted extension at the rear of the building will provide: dedicated ground-floor education space to enhance school visits, complete with a study garden for activities such as pond-dipping; a first-floor high-specification temporary exhibition space to house national and international touring exhibitions; and a second-floor library containing the combined natural history and archaeology libraries of the two societies, making an important research resource available to the public for the first time. In addition to this truly Great North Museum, many objects not on public display will be accessible off site in the new purpose-built store. The Great North Museum is due to open its doors in January 2009.

Eric Cross

VISION OF THE FUTURE

Wise men do not predict the future. However, this book is an opportunity to reflect on the past and to try to use this as a guide to where this University might go in the years to come.

As the previous chapters have so clearly shown, the formation of the University of Newcastle upon Tyne in 1963 was a seminal event. In many ways it was as though the child had outgrown the parent, the federal University of Durham, and needed now to have the independence of a separate identity. Forty years later, in 2003, we had a joint dinner with the Council of Durham University and looked again at the issue of how we might best collaborate with Durham. The formation of the new University of Manchester, the largest in the UK, was a spur to this. We were prepared to consider all options, including the possibility of re-merger. Durham preferred to focus on individual areas in which we might collaborate to advantage. This led to a sensible rationalization of Linguistics and Religious Studies. Both were small but had high-quality research. Durham planned to close Linguistics. We agreed to take their Linguistics staff and to transfer our Religious Studies staff to Durham. In recent discussions I was delighted to hear how well both groups have fared in their new environments. We now have one of the largest and best Linguistics groups in the UK, and Durham a much more broadly based Religious Studies department.

What of the future? We have been awarded additional student numbers by the Higher Education Funding Council for England on condition that the Universities of Newcastle and Durham continue discussions on strategic collaboration.

The articulation arrangement with Durham for the teaching of Medicine has been a good example of the two universities working well together. Approximately 100 students per annum start with Durham on the Stockton Campus, then move to Newcastle after two years for their clinical training and graduate with a Newcastle degree. In this respect we have a regional Medical School and have students in nearly every major hospital in the North East. In addition to teaching, we are developing close links with Bioscience in Durham and have plans to form a joint Institute of Stem Cells and Regenerative Medicine. Bioinformatics is another important area of collaboration.

I strongly believe that, with time and with the appointment of two new Vice-Chancellors, there will be increasing pressure for these collaborations to grow. The

North East needs a very successful Higher Education sector if it is to compete in 'the knowledge economy'. In John Gibbins' article, 'Origins of Armstrong College', on the history of the College of Science, he refers to the decision by the Durham Senate, on 11 March 1871, to provide a grant of £1,000 so that a College could be established in Newcastle 'to provide advanced scientific education in the North region'. Now, 135 years later, we have an opportunity further to capitalize on this legacy with the development of Newcastle Science City. This University, together with the City Council and the Regional Development Agency, has bought a 14-acre, city-centre site (the old Newcastle Brewery) to act as Science City, and plan to use this to create a unique interface between academe and business/industry. The four areas that have been chosen reflect Newcastle's major strengths in Stem Cells, Molecular Engineering, Energy and the Environment, and Ageing (to be based at the Newcastle General site). We very much hope that, with our shared history, Durham University will play an active role in the Stem Cell Research and, possibly, in other areas such as Molecular Engineering. This is an ambitious project which will cost £450-600 million and which aims to make Newcastle a world-class environment for science and science-based businesses. Science City will need to be closely integrated with two other major initiatives, the Science programme of the Northern Way, which involves the eight research-intensive universities in the North, and the Regional Development Agency's Strategy for Success. All three have common scientific themes.

The Mission Statement of the University is 'to be a world-class research-intensive university, to deliver teaching of the highest quality, and to play a leading role in the economic, social and cultural development of the North East of England.' Our approach has been summed up by 'excellence with a purpose'. This application of knowledge for economic/social benefit should become an increasingly important part of our strategy. We have been judged to be one of the top four universities in the UK for technology transfer and Science City should further enhance this reputation. We propose to build a new Business School and to have technology transfer as its major focus.

The Sunday Times stated that it would be 'difficult to imagine a better place to be a student' than Newcastle. The continuing improvement of the quality of our teaching and that of the total student experience must continue to be a major aim of the University. We need to attract the best

students and to widen participation. Only 23% of our students come from the North East and the region has the lowest uptake of Higher Education in the UK. We must play a leading role in changing this. Our PARTNERS programme has been very successful in building partnerships with over 90 schools and colleges in the North and in identifying those with the potential to benefit from coming here. This is based around an assessed summer school. It needs to grow in the years ahead.

The University has pursued an aggressive international policy over the last few years and I see this expanding. We have more than doubled our international student numbers and plan to increase them further. We will only be able to do this if we offer excellent teaching and support services. In Malaysia, we are exploring a joint venture for us to deliver the Newcastle MBBS degree on a new campus. In Singapore, we have set up a company, NUIdeasBank, which is a shop window for our intellectual property. This is proving to be a very effective way for companies which have recently been spun off by the University to interface with new markets in the Far East. Other significant projects include stem cell links with Monash University, a major energy project in Shanghai and another in Singapore with Nanyang Technological University.

Interdisciplinary research will almost certainly continue to be a strength in the future of Newcastle University. We have set up ten Institutes designed to facilitate this. These include:

An aerial view of the University Campus in 2006

Informatics Research Institute (IRI)

Institute for Ageing and Health (IAH)

Institute for Cell and Molecular Biosciences

Institute for Nanoscale Science & Technology (INSAT)

Institute for Policy and Practice (IPP)

Institute for Research on Environment & Sustainability (IRES)

Institute of Human Genetics (IHG)

Institute of Neuroscience

Newcastle Institute for the Arts, Social Sciences and Humanities (NIASSH)

Northern Institute for Cancer Research (NICR)

Institute of Cellular Medicine

Institute of Health and Society

It is at the interface between subjects that research often has its greatest dividends. A good example here is the interface between cancer, medicine and chemistry. This has led to the development and clinical trials of a new group of drugs, the PARP-inhibitors. These inhibit DNA repair and the aim is to make current cancer therapies more effective. Serendipitously, these drugs have been found to have a specific ability to target and kill breast cancer cells from patients with the inherited form of the disease (about 5% of patients).

Three years ago I asked the following questions: 'What are the critical issues of today and the horizon issues of tomorrow that concern you most?' and, 'In which areas of society do you feel change is most needed to benefit current and future generations?' I suggested that these are the questions that really matter to all of us. I had recently explored these issues with Rick Smalley, the Nobel Prize-winning scientist – then at Rice University in Texas and now sadly deceased. Our starting point was Rick's list of the ten greatest threats to mankind. These related to: Energy, Water, Food, Environment, Poverty, Terrorism and War, Disease, Education, Democracy, and Population. Two things struck me when looking at them: the first is the requirement for interdisciplinary approaches to find solutions; the second is the extent to which internationally recognized activity led by colleagues at Newcastle University has a role to play.

Since then we have set up a Development Council to help us focus our fundraising activities and have identified five themes where we think that we are best placed to have a transformational effect on the big issues of the day. Transforming the Environment, Transforming Health, Transforming Culture, Transforming Business, and Transforming Lives: the aim overall is to transform horizons for our students, staff, the North East and the wider world. The challenges are immense, but I am proud of what we have achieved in a short time.

I hope that you have enjoyed reading this book. For some, it will be a trip down memory lane. For others, it will give a flavour of a rapidly evolving University with a proud history in one of the UK's most vibrant cities.

Eric Thomas, the Vice-Chancellor of Bristol University, has suggested that 'Human society requires universities – they are not an added extra, they are an essential part of the fabric of our civilization, our educational provision, our search for new knowledge and our civic life'. This need has never been more pressing. In a society in which governments spin an increasingly complex web of regulatory control, it has become even more important to have institutions in which freedom of speech and independence of mind is preserved. In the past, universities were elitist organizations and were often regarded as 'ivory towers' and described as 'seats of learning'. They admitted about 10% of the population. Modern universities are very different. The Government would like 50% of the 18–30-year-old population to have experience of higher education by 2010. It has also become increasingly aware of the importance of universities in economic regeneration. I have no doubt that in both these areas of international quality education and research, Newcastle University will continue to play a leading role.

Vice-Chancellor Christopher Edwards

Newcastle University Timeline

1832	Private lecture courses given by local medical practitioners at Bell's Court, Pilgrim Street		**1913**	Chair of Economics
			1914–18	The buildings of Armstrong College used for a military hospital
1834	Lectures at Barber-Surgeons' Company's Hall in the Manors: the true start of the Medical School		**1917**	Chair of Fine Art
			1918	The first public lecture was founded as the Earl Grey Lecture

1832 Private lecture courses given by local medical practitioners at Bell's Court, Pilgrim Street

1834 Lectures at Barber-Surgeons' Company's Hall in the Manors: the true start of the Medical School

1851 New Medical School building Victoria Street
Major personal quarrel; split between minority in new building and majority in improvised premises

1852 Majority establishes 'Newcastle upon Tyne College of Medicine in connection with the University of Durham'

1857 Reunification in new premises in Orchard Street

1870 The School renamed as 'University of Durham College of Medicine'

1871 The College of Physical Science established (with Chairs of Mathematics, Chemistry, Physics and Geology)

1874 Chair of Natural History

1875 Chair of Mining

1883 College of Medicine moved to Northumberland Road
College of Physical Science moved to Lax's Gardens (site of the present Armstrong Building) and was re-named 'Durham College of Science, Newcastle upon Tyne'

1888 NE Wing of Quadrangle opened

1890 College of Physical Science strengthens Arts: start of teacher training and appointment to Chair of Literature

1891 Chair of Agriculture and Forestry (Cockle Park); Chair of Engineering

1892 Chair of Botany

1893 Chair of Bacteriology

1894 SE and NW wings of Quadrangle opened

1895 Teaching of Dental Surgery by local practitioners starts
Chair of Education

1896 Formation of Medical Students Representative Council

1898 Chair of English Literature; Chair of Classics and Ancient History

1900 University *Medical Gazette* first published

1904 Durham College of Science re-named Armstrong College

1906 Official opening of Armstrong College and King's Hall by King Edward VII
Chair of Naval Architecture

1907 Chair of Electrical Engineering

1908 University of Durham Act: constitution of the federal University of Durham comprising the colleges at Durham and the College of Medicine and Armstrong College at Newcastle
Chair of Midwifery and Gynaecology

1909 Chair of Pathology

1911 Chair of History; Chair of Philosophy

1913 Chair of Economics

1914–18 The buildings of Armstrong College used for a military hospital

1917 Chair of Fine Art

1918 The first public lecture was founded as the Earl Grey Lecture

1920 Tutorial system for undergraduates introduced

1925 Joint Armstrong and Medical Students Union Building

1926 Armstrong College Library (also housing the Medical College library)

1927 Department of Geography established

1928 Faculty of Applied Science formed

1931 Dental School incorporated in the College of Medicine
Romano-British Archaeology introduced

1932 Opening of New Hall donated by George Henderson, a major University benefactor

1934 Royal Commission on the constitution of the University

1937 Re-constitution of the federal University of Durham merges Armstrong College and the College of Medicine to form King's College

1937 Lord Eustace Percy appointed Rector of King's College

1939 New Medical School building opened by King George VI

1939–45 Establishment of Chairs of Architecture, Geography, and Civil Engineering and Readerships in German, Metallurgy, Romano-British Archaeology, Engineering and Town Planning

1945–63 Substantial academic and physical growth including the establishment of many new chairs, the formation of many independent departments, the opening of new buildings for Chemistry, Engineering, Arts and Physics, and the continuing major reorganization of the estate.

1950 Ethel Williams Hall opened

1952 Mr Charles Bosanquet appointed Rector of King's College

195–56 Leazes Terrace acquired for student residences

1956 Building acquired for the original Eustace Percy Hall

1961 Close House and its grounds purchased for the provision of outdoor sports centre

1963 Dissolution of the federal University of Durham. King's College becomes the University of Newcastle upon Tyne with the Durham colleges constituting the University of Durham

1964 The Duke of Northumberland installed as the University's first Chancellor
University Refectory and Agriculture building opened

1965 University Library receives the Pybus Collection

1967 Dr Martin Luther King awarded honorary degree

1968 Dr Henry Miller appointed Vice-Chancellor
The Claremont complex opened

1969   Castle Leazes Halls of Residence opened
        Opening of University Theatre
1974   Richardson Road student flats opened
1976   Centre for Urban and Regional Development Studies (CURDS) formed
1977   University Development Trust established
1978   Professor Laurence Martin appointed Vice-Chancellor
1978   Opening of the new Dental School and Hospital
1981   Merger of the Union Society and the Students' Representative Council
1983   Graduates' Society launched
1984   New Medical School opened by Her Majesty Queen Elizabeth the Queen Mother
        Celebration of the 140th anniversary of medical teaching in Newcastle
        Opening of the new University Library named after Philip Robinson, a major benefactor of the library
        Opening of the Claremont Sports Hall
1987   Medical School's main laboratory building named after Dame Catherine Cookson, major University benefactor
1988   The School's clinical building named after Dr William Leech, also a major University benefactor
1989   Viscount Ridley installed as Chancellor in succession to the Duke of Northumberland
1992   Mr James Wright appointed Vice-Chancellor
1993   Alumni Association formed to succeed the Graduates' Society
        St Mary's student residence opened
1994   Modularization of all degree courses over two semesters
        Stan Calvert Cup launched
1995   University hosts the British Association's Festival of Science
        Northumbrian Universities Royal Naval Unit formed
        Robinson Library, the first university library to be awarded the Government's Charter Mark for Excellence
        Formation of the Knowledge House, providing access for business and industry to the expertise of the University and other universities in the North East
1997   Inauguration of the annual Durham and Newcastle Universities' Boat Race
        Opening of the Language Centre's Open Access Centre
1998   National funding changes: student tuition fees increased and maintenance grants replaced by income contingent loans
1999   The Right Honourable Christopher Patten installed as Chancellor in succession to Lord Ridley
        Launch of 'PARTNERS' programme complementing the

University's Students into Schools programme
Medical School Library named after Lord Walton, former Dean of Medicine
2000   Opening of International Centre for Life in Newcastle
        The University wins *The Sunday Times* 'University of the Year' award
2001   Professor Christopher Edwards appointed Vice-Chancellor
        Major endowment for the School of Management from the family of David Goldman, founder of the Sage Group
        Launch of major expansion in medical student numbers and of partnership with Durham University in development of medical degree programme
2002   Re-structuring of the University: merging of seven faculties into three and of 75 departments into 27 new schools, supported by ten large research institutes and a number of research groups
        National Research Assessment exercise confirms the excellence of the University's research
        New Medical Lecture Theatre opened by, and named after, Professor David Shaw, former Dean of Medicine
        New music studios and practice rooms opened by Mark Knopfler, rock musician and honorary graduate
2003   Formation of the Development Council comprising alumni and friends of the University
2004   Newcastle scientists awarded the first UK licence to create stem cells from unfertilized human eggs for pioneering research into a range of major diseases
        Enterprise Centre for students and graduates launched
        Opening of the Devonshire Building housing the Environment and Sustainability Research Institute, the North East Regional e-Science Centre and the Informatics Research Institute
        The Paul O'Gorman Building housing the Northern Institute for Cancer Research
        The 'Beehive' established in the Old Library Building for the discussion and cross-fertilization of research ideas
2005   University awarded Queen's Anniversary Prize
        Newcastle designated by the Chancellor of the Exchequer as one of six Science Cities
        The Institutional Audit by the Quality Assurance Agency confirms the high quality of the University's teaching and learning
        New indoor Sports Centre opened
2006   Grant of £9 million from the Heritage Lottery enables work to begin on the Great North Museum

Honorary Graduates

Honorary DCL

1974 Alexander, John Osmond MacDonald*
1993 Ariff, Mohamed Ishak Bin Haji Mohamed
1974 Attenborough, Lord Richard (Samuel)
1967 Baird, Sir Dugald
1998 Barbour, Margaret
1992 Beecham, Sir Jeremy
1998 Beith, The Right Honourable Alan James
1998 Belafonte, Harry
1970 Bessey, Gordon Scott
1977 Bettenson, Ernest Marsden*
1970 Booth, Norleigh*
1978 Bosworth, George Simms
1965 Bradlaw, Sir Robert Vivian*
1984 Brearley, John Michael
1990 Brittan, The Right Honourable Sir Leon
1972 Campbell, Mungo*
1966 Campbell-Robson, Lorne*
1989 Carr-Ellison, Sir Ralph
1998 Carrington, The Right Honourable Lord
     Peter Alexander Rupert
1984 Chao, Frank Sze-Bang*
1971 Christopherson, Sir Derman Guy*
1974 Cookson, Roland Antony*
1998 Davies, Cyril
1964 Daysh, George Henry John
1977 Dower, Pauline*
2001 Downer, The Right Honourable Alexander
1984 Her Majesty Queen Elizabeth The Queen
     Mother*
2001 Edwards, Jonathan
1993 Erskine, Ralph
2000 Farrell, Sir Terry
1995 Fasella, Paolo Maria
1998 Faulkner-Brown, Harry
1964 Festing, Field Marshal Sir Francis
     Wogan*
1976 Finniston, Sir Harold Montague*
1976 Galleymore, Harry Reginald*
1981 Gibson, Joseph
1998 Glenamara, The Right Honourable Lord
1972 Godber, Sir George (Edward)
1989 Grant, David James*
1988 Hall, Sir John
1979 Hamilton, Sir Denis*
1995 His Majesty King Harald V of Norway
1991 Harbottle, Stephen
1980 Harness, Edward G*
1964 Hogg, Quintin McGarel (Baron Hailsham
     of St Marylebone)*
1966 Holm-Olsen, Ludvig

1968 Howick of Glendale, Lord*
1995 Inge, Field Marshal The Lord Peter
2992 Irvine, Sir Donald
1973 Jacobson, Lionel*
1992 Jenkins, Jennifer
1988 Jones, Sir John Harvey
1992 Jopling, Michael
1967 King, Martin Luther*
1983 Kummerman, Henri*
1975 Leech, Sir William Charles*
1996 Lim, Boon Heng
1990 Mackay, The Right Honourable Lord
1983 Mann, Reginald William*
1977 Mawby, Russell George
1973 Martin, Sir David (Christie)*
1991 Martin, Sir Laurence Woodward
1985 Moffitt, John Edward
1998 Mowlam, The Right Honourable Marjorie
1980 Murray, Margaret Stevens
1974 Nattrass, Frederick John*
1968 His Majesty King Olav V of Norway*
1999 Patten CH, The Right Honourable
     Christopher
2000 Pettifor, Ann
1966 Pybus, Frederick Charles*
1980 Richardson, Lord
1989 Ridley, The Right Honourable Viscount
1964 Robens, Lord
2003 Robson, Sir Bobby
1964 Robson, Robert Errington*
1966 Russell, Theresa Science
1999 Seitz, The Right Honourable Raymond
     George Hardenbergh
2002 Sherlock, Nigel
1966 Smith, Thomas Daniel
1991 Spoor, Roger
1987 Straker, Sir Michael*
1969 Taylor, Sir James*
1996 Tu, The Honourable Mrs Elsie
1988 Walton, Sir John
1969 Wilson, John Pearce*
1971 Woodeson, James Brewis*
2001 Wright, James

Honorary DSc

1984 Acheson, Ernest Donald
1974 Adams, Raymond D
1965 Alfvén, Hannes*
1975 Anderson, Ephraim Saul
1975 Artobolevskii, Ivan Ivanovitch*
1965 Babcock, Horace Welcome
1980 Bacon, Francis Thomas*
1981 Bartlett, Neil

1974 Beevers, Harry
1969 Beloussov, Vladimir Vladimirovich*
1995 Bell Burnell, S Jocelyn
1984 Black, Sir James Whyte
1984 Blaxter, Kenneth*
1966 Burns, Wilfred*
1988 Carter, William C
1965 Chandrasekhar, Subrahmanyan*
1965 Chapman, Sydney
2002 Colwell, Rita
1967 Cottrell, Sir Alan Howard
1964 Cox, Sir Gordon*
1994 Day, Peter
1975 Den Hartog, Jacob*
1972 Dickens, Frank
1969 Doll, Sir Richard
1988 Elsasser, Walter M
1977 Flowers, Thomas Harold*
1970 Goodeve, Sir Charles Frederick*
1987 Hawking, Stephen William
1979 Hirsch, Sir Peter
1965 Hodgkin, Sir Alan Lloyd*
1970 Hooker, Stanley George
1976 Hoyle, Sir Fred
1968 Hunter, Sir John*
1978 Johnson, Alan Woodworth*
1997 Jones, David Edward Hugh
1965 Libby, Willard Frank*
2003 Loebl, Herbert
2000 Lucas, Adetokunbo Oluwole
1977 M'Ewen, Ewen*
1966 McKissock, Wylie*
1993 McLaren, Dame Anne Laura
1965 McMichael, Sir John
1997 Metakides, George
1969 Miles, Sir Ashley
1971 Mosby, Hakon*
1968 Nagata, Takesi*
1965 Néel, Louis Eugene Felix
1964 Nicol, Davidson Sylvester Hector
     Willoughby*
1992 Payan, Jean-Jacques
1968 Penrose, Lionel Sharples*
1985 Pittendrigh, Colin Stephenson*
1980 Press, Frank
1966 Prigogine, Ilya
1995 Rees, Sir Martin
1973 Rochester, George Dixon
1964 Rothschild, Lord*
1965 Sabin, Albert Bruce
2003 Schneider, Frederick
1965 Severny, Andrey Borisovich
1971 Stephenson, Henry Shepherd

1998 Sujin Jinahyon
1995 Sykes, Sir Richard
1968 Thellier, Emile*
1970 Thompson, Sir Harold (Warris)*
1974 Venus, James*
1979 Warner, Sir Frederick
1983 Wheeler, John Archibald
1967 Wigglesworth, Sir Vincent
1972 Wilkes, Sir Maurice Vincent
1994 Wolfendale, Sir Arnold W

Honorary MD
1995 Calman, Sir Kenneth
1991 Foulkes, Ernest
1980 Grey-Turner, Elston*
1990 Mahler, Halfdan
1996 Ogilvie, Bridget
1994 Sjöqvist, Folke
1993 Tomlinson, Sir Bernard Evans

Honorary DCh
1980 Peel, Sir John (Harold)
1978 Watt, Sir James

Honorary DLitt
1996 Astley, Neil
1994 Barrow, Geoffrey W S
1988 Baxter, Biddy
1983 Bell, Quentin Claudian Stephen*
1969 Bruford, Walter Horace
1971 Bunting, Basil*
1976 Crowe, Dame Sylvia
1964 Darwin, Sir Robin*
1964 DeLoach, Daniel Barton*
1987 Drew, Dame Jane Beverley*
1981 Elton, Sir Geoffrey Rudolf*
1995 Hall, Peter Geoffrey
1970 Hay, Denys*
1966 Humphreys, Robert Arthur*
1991 Kennedy, Paul
1993 Kermode, Sir John Frank
1996 Kunzmann, Klaus R
1970 Lancaster, Sir Osbert*
1972 Lough, John*
1999 MacFarquhar, Roderick Lemonde
1969 Mahon, Sir Denis
1985 Muir, Jean Elizabeth*
1976 Needham, Joseph*
1966 Page, Denys Lionel*
1967 Pasmore, Victor*
1979 Pincher, Chapman
1985 Quirk, Sir Charles Randolph
1999 Rawson, Jessica Mary

2003 Reynolds, Fiona
1984 Reynolds, Joyce Maire
1965 Richmond, Sir Ian Archibald*
1998 Rothschild, Lord Nathanial Charles Jacob
1977 Southern, Sir Richard William*
1973 Summerson, Sir John (Newenham)*
1967 Toynbee, Jocelyn Mary Catherine*
1978 Trevor Roper, Hugh Redwald
1997 Whitaker, Sheila
2001 Woof, Robert

Honorary DDSc
1995 Andreasen, Jens
1978 Boyes, John*
1978 Chalmers, John*
1981 Cohen, Bertram
1981 Lawton, Sir Frank Ewart*
1995 Seward, Margaret

Honorary LLD
1975 Micklethwait, Robert*
1990 Taylor, Lord Justice*

Honorary DMus
1968 Boulanger, Nadia*
1996 Bowman, James Thomas
1990 Gibson, Sir Alexander*
1974 Goodall, Reginald*
1978 Josephs, Wilfred*
1993 Knopfler, Mark
1972 Schwarz, Rudolf

Honorary DD
1998 English, Donald*
1979 Hume, Cardinal Basil*
1981 Newbigin, James Edward Lesslie*

Honorary DEng
1991 Harrison, Sir Terence
2002 Hawley, Robert
1987 Hildrew, Bryan
1984 McDonald, Sir Duncan*
1991 Malpas, Sir Robert
2000 Parnaby, John
1997 Ridley, Tony Melville
1985 Russell, Sir George

Honorary MDS
1981 Armstrong, Francis

Honorary MA
1990 Adie, Kate
1984 Allen, Thomas

1979 Armstrong, Sheila Ann
1971 Atkinson, Frank
1980 Bennitt, Albert John*
1987 Bibby, (John) Roland*
1983 Bluett, Thompson Hall*
1969 Brannigan, Owen*
1973 Brymer, Jack
1978 Chaplin, Sidney
1983 Cookson, Dame Catherine*
1974 Cornish, Norman
1985 Denyer, James Henry*
1975 Gilroy, John Thomas Young*
1966 Hand, Winston*
1970 Humphreys, Sydney†
1997 Kay, Alison*
1970 Keenlyside, Raymond†
1970 Major, Margaret†
1976 Murray, Edith*
1981 Nunn, Sir Trevor Robert
1981 Philipson, John*
1987 Phillifent, Robert
1977 Robinson, Henry Russell*
1978 Robinson, Lionel*
1988 Robinson, Philip*
1965 Rolt, Lionel Thomas Caswall*
1972 Shott, Norman
1992 Shukla, Hariprasad Mohanilal
1970 Simpson, Derek†
1975 Swindale, Alfred*
1976 Towers, The Reverend Thomas*
1974 Wainwright, Alfred*
1966 Ward, Cyril Randolph*

Honorary MMus
1980 Orde, Valentine*

Honorary MSc
1994 Alder, James
1971 Brown, Geoffrey Francis*
1966 Cotton, William Henry Basil
1970 Floyd, Arthur*
1971 Horsley, William Douglass*
1968 Myers, Ernest Myers*
1993 Sinden, David
1970 Walker, Arthur*

Honorary MEd
1976 Foster, Brendan
1966 Neill, Alexander Sutherland*
1965 Stewart, Muriel Acadia
1992 Uttley, Roger

† *Aeolian String Quartet*

List of Subscribers

Alan Adamson	1953	James S. Carruthers	1959	Dr Mary Edminson	1955	Keith Gunning MB BS	1986
Rosemary Adamson (née Muras)	1951	Marie Cashman	1950	Christopher Edwards		Regina Haba	1982
Helen M. Akroyd	1972	Mr Ian Chadwick BDS	1957	**Current Vice Chancellor**		Dr D.W. O Hagan (née Pledge) MBBS	1941
Prof. Grace Alderson	1982	A.C.F. Chan-Dominy	1991	John Edwards OBE BA MRTPI	1965	Christopher J. Hall	1982
Dr Brian Angus	**Retired Staff**	Ng Chee Leong	2001	John H. Edwards	1958	John Hall	1944
Paul and Sarah Arden	1984	Chai Foh Chin	1982	F.J. Elliott DIP Arch. (Dunelm) ARIBA	1963	Martin Hallam	1976
Keith Armstrong	1953	Renos J. Christodoulou	1960	Anita Elliott	2004	Gordon James Hammond	1947
J.G. Arumathurai	1994	Chris Claridge	1967	Dr Faraj El-Mabruk	1998	J.M. Hardcastle	1964
Nicholas Athanassoglou	1968	Mr D. Clarke MB BS	1966	N.A. Elvin	1954	Philip Hardy BDS	1973
Michael Aubrey	1987	Chris (Harry) Clayton	1989	Alan English	1976	R.B. Harper	1965
Stuart Bailey	1985	Peter G. Coates	1970	Dr Eric Evans	1969	S.J. Harris	1970
P. Balasubramaniam	1991	Fenwick Limited		Mr David Evans MBBS	1978	Guy C. Harris	1960
Elaine Bartlett (née King) BSc	1966	Peter Cobbett	1949	Dr J. Eve	**Retired Staff**	Jeremy K. Harris	1989
Alison R. Broadbent	1992	Rupert J.H. Cole	1991	Anthony D. Everitt		Neville V. Harrison	1954
Henry Beckwith	2000	Dr Bryan Coleby BSc	1950	Faculty of Medical Sciences		Andrew S. Harton	1973
Bryan Bell	1967	PhD	1954	Dr David Fairbairn	1987	Peter Collier Harvey	1986
Irvine H. Bell	1966	Mike Collier		P. Fairfax	1967	Roger S. Harvey	1972
Prabhjot S. Bhatia	1991	Diane M. Collings	1970	J.A. Fallows	1980	Keith A. Haynes	1973
David Bibby	1996	Susan Connors	1970	P.S. Fairfax	1967	Martin Hayton	1976
Nigel Bidwell		Nick Cook	1975	Kathleen Fardey	1936	K.L. Hayton	1958
A. Stuart Binks	1965	Sheila Cookson BA Hons	1971	Kirstin A. Farquhar BDS	1992	Pamela Hebblewaite (née Kilner)	1969
Frank Binns	1953	Graham Cooper	1969	Peter Farrar	1968	Santiago Henao-Perez	1987
David Bispham	1961	Peter Cove	1961	J.G.W. Feggetter MBBS	1966	Richard P. Hennessy	1975
Fawaz K. Bitar	1988	Mark Crowther	1981	Miss Roshni Fernando	2003	Robin Herzberg	1979
Dr Brian A. Black	1956	Moira Crowther (née Hill)	1982	Peter Ferrow	1970	Christopher Hewitt	1969
Roger W. Blake	1971	Paul R. Coxon	2005	Dr Nicholas Fisher	1971	John Ashley Hey	1991
Richard Boak	1980	Sir Alan Craft	1969	David Fitz-Patrick MB MS	1974	Cedric Hinchliffe	1961
Regis Boisbluche	1996	Sam Creed	1995	Alan J. Flintham	1974	Mrs E.M. Hirst	
Philip Bolam	1943	Stafford Critchlow	1988	Neil Forker	1976	Dr David Hodgson	1955
Mick Bond	**Former Staff**	Margaret Cummins Walloe	1967	Dr K.B. Forster	1955	Denise Hogg	1993
Alastair Boobyer	1971	M.T. Cunningham	1948	Air Core I.H. Forster OBE	1955	Donald L. Holmes	1965
Dr F.W. Boon	1935	Mr G. Dane	Staff	Mr Fountain	1965	N.M. McQ. Holmes	1973
Wendy Boothroyd	1967	Andre Danjoux BDS	1959	James Fox	1965	Stuart Holmes	2003
Sally Ann Boucher	2004	Dr Noel Davies		Mr Nick Francis	2004	David Holmes	1984
Graham Bowes	1990	R.M. Davis Dip Arch	1958	Dr Jane E. Frew	1978	Stephen Holt	1964
Gerald Bowlt	1988	Terry F. Davies	1971	Josephine Fuhse	1970	Sheila Hood	1971
Professor Clive Bradbeer	1954	J.M. Davison	1966	Maria Filomena G.F. Crujo Camoes	1973	Lynne Howlett (née Taylor)	1983
Richard J. Bradburn	1974	John D. Davison	**Retired Staff**	Peter A. Gee	1967	David Hudson	1970
John and Caroline Bradley		Mrs Anne Dawes (née Pickering)	1969	Professor Derek Geldart	1986	Dr Brian Hughes BSc	1972
(née Baker)	1981	Andrew Dawson	1984	Robin T. Gibson	1955	Katherine Hunter	1998
Stanley Bradley	1966	Joanne De Lange	1969	Peter W. Gibson (Dunelm) DDPH RCS	1952	J.K. Hutchinson	1960
Professor Paul Brenikov	**Retired Staff**	Jeff De Lange	1966	Dr Bob Giddings	1978	Professor Ken Jack OBE FRS	1939
Paul Brenikov	**Retired Staff**	Colin A. Dearlove	1973	Dr David Gill and Caroline Gill		Professor Peter Jacob	1963
John B. Brennand		K. Deary BA	1974	(née Dudley-Smith)	1982; 1982	Ole J. Jacobsen	1983
BSc CEng FIMechE	1944	Rex Dempsey	1953	Martin R. Gillespie	1986	Rakshit N. Jagdale	2002
E.A. Bristow	1951	Tom Dening MB BS	1980	Keith Gilroy	1973	Lisa James Todhunter	2004
David S. Brooks		Emily Dening (née Lan) BA	1978	Lesley D. Gilroy	1958	Alan M. Jarvis	1948
Hugh Brown	1949	Ann Dennis	1973	H.D. Glenwright	1957	Jack Jeffrey	1953
Dr Ian Brown OBE FRCP FFOM	1972	Hewan A. Dewar MB BS	1935	Mr Roger Gomersall MB BS	1966	Carole Jeffrey	1975
Mary Brown (née Miller) BSc	1965	John R. Dilks	1947	Paul Gosling	1993	Joy A. Johnson	1976
Nicholas Bryars	1991	Maria Dimitroulia	1996	Amy Gospel	2002	J. Andrew Johnson	
Michael Buckley	1963	Dr W.B. Dobie	1944	Dr Dipak Gosrani BDS DPDS	1980	Huw Jones	1983
Hilary Bugler	1983	Dr Simon Dobson	1989	Henry H. Gossman	1949	A.F. Kelley MSc	1939
Melissa Bunyard	2001	Major G.H. Donaldson	1956	Roger Graham	1963	Anthony Kershaw	1992
Prof. Russell W. Burns		Ann K. Donaldson (née Wilson)	1948	Carolyn Grant (née Wood)	1993	Dr Dermot Killingley	**Retired Staff**
Dr Susan Burrows	1981	John S. Dowden	1981	Fay Gray MA	1986	Ian Kitchen	2000
David Burton	1968	Marc O. Drobe PhD	2000	Dr Damian C. Green	1993	D. Kobasa	
Sandra Cadima		Dr Ian Dugdale	1956	George Greener BSc	1969	Leonidas Korbetis	1977
Richard Calasca	1972	Andy W. Duncan	1966	Dr Martyn W. Griffiths	1986	Jason Korbetis	2005
Dr George Yuille Caldwell	1951	Mrs P. Duncan		John E. Griffiths	1962	David S. Kurilla	1993
Hugh Carr	1983	Sarah Dungate	1989	Judith Griffiths (née Bolam)	1970	Kwasi Kwakwa	1995
Dr P. Carrington		Fiona Durham (née McArthur)	1979	Jennie Lynsey Gundill	2006	Harold Lake	1947

Name	Year	Name	Year	Name	Year	Name	Year
Dr A.G. Larson	1952	Dr Andrew I. Naylor MBBS	1985	James Sargeant	1966	Dina Tiniakos PhD	1998
Dr Gerry Lawson BDS	1956	Steve Newberry		Rosemary Saunders	1958	Nick Tinker	1991
John N.L. Latham	1971	Mr W. Newton		Colin G. Saysell	1992	Gillian Featherstone	1979
Dr T.J. Laundy	1969	B.M. Nicholson	1967	Dr David M. Saysell	1996	David Tonks	1964
James Law	2001	Nick Nicholson	1967	Helen Scanlon	1996	R.L. Townsin PhD DSc	Retired Staff
Dr Chris E. Lawrence	1979	James Nightingale	1997	Maurice Scanlon	1970	Elsie Tu (née Hume)	1937
Janet Laycock (née Whitwell)	1975	Frank Nolan	Retired Staff	Robert Schofield	1991	Dr Elsie Tu	1937
Alan Leading	1975	Bernard Nolan BA (Hons) MA	1996	Dr Shelagh J. Scott	1980	John Turner	1961
Mr Yuen-ho Lee and Mrs Lai-ping Lee	1983	Emeritus Professor Pavel Novak		Mark Scrimshaw	1976	Graham Peter Tye	1981
Drs D.N. and D.A. Leitch	2002		Retired Staff	Josephine Scriven (née Eccles)	1980	Roy R. Tyerman	1955
Kate Lemon	2005	Peter H. Nunn	1949	Deva Senanayake	1991	Edwin Underhill	1963
Audrey Leng	1994	Steven Oakes	1997	Mr J.I. Sharp	Retired Staff	Geoff Usher	1992
Dr Tony H.L. Leong	1983	John W. Osselton	1950	Mike Sharpe	1968	Peter D. Vale	1968
Professor Ruth Lesser	1971	H.R.C. Owen	1963	Kenneth Shenton Med	1977	Elise Vandervelde (née Ross)	1961
Dr D.C. Park Lincoln	1953	Susumu Ozeki	1996	Oli Shepheard	1987	Paul Velluet	1970
John L. Lloyd	1967	Debbie Palmer (née Powell)	1993	Suzanne Elizabeth Sheppard	1996	Barry Wade	1959
Brian Lloyd-Davies	1956	Dr T. Pankhurst	1995	Dr Robert S. Shiel	1969	Alice Wainwright	2006
Dave Lockwood	1978	Nikolas Andeas Papalos	1995	Dr David Shirt	Retired Staff	Dennis N. Walder	Retired Staff
Dr Herbert Loebl OBE	1949	Mr F.J. Parker	1970	Chris Shorrock	1982	Margaret Watson	1972
Miss Ruby Loh		Professor David G. Parker		Dr A.I. Short MEd PhD	1972	Alex Wallace	2001
John R. Long	1982	C.Chem FRSC	1971	Gibert Short	1968	Andrew Walster	1970
Michael Loomes	1969	Brian Parker	1971	Robert Skelton	1960	Lord Walton of Detchant	1945
Charmian Lovel		Stan Patchet	1970	Dr Andrew Skillen	Retired Staff	Yongmei Wang	2004
Paul Lowe BDS	1982	Lauren Patterson	2004	Geoff Skinner	1969	Frank Ward	1963
Bruce Lowe	1967	Mr Norman C. Paul BA (Hons)	1955	Richard Skinner	1965	Mrs M. Anne Ward	1976
Francis John Macadam	1978	Matthew Payne	2005	Jane Slater	1987	Jean Ward (née Graham)	1953
Alexander Main MBE	1936	Mary Pearce	1972	Ernie Smart	1950	R.J.M. Watkiins	2003
Yannis Makarounis	1979	Dorothy Pearl (née White)	1963	Harry Smart	1989	(Em. Prof.) J.A. Watt	Retired Staff
Gisli Mar Gislason	1978	Linda Pearson	1966	Peter T. Smedvig	1970	Dr David J.T. Webb OBE	1989
Lamin Jonsaba Marenah ORG PhD	1956	Dr Philip J. Pearson	1972	Ian J. Smith BSc MSc	1950	Colin Weedon	1970
Dr Geoffrey Marsh	1953	Meriol D. Penn (née Godfrey) BSc	1951	John C. Smith	1964	A.P. Weetman	1977
Harry Marsh	1973	Judith A. Penny (née Mellor)	1967	Dan Smith	2001	Douglas Weir	1981
Sarah Martin	1998	Professor Huw R. Phillips	1971	Martin Smith	1977	Dr Iain and Elizabeth Weir-Jones	
Malcolm Mencer Martin MBBS	1945	John A. Pickard	1987	Christine Smith	1970		1965 and 1966
Melissa Mathur (née Somerville)	1995	Anne L. Pickering	1976	John T. Spain	1954	Humphrey Welfare	1972
Chikako Matsuura	1998	George R. Pickles	1966	Marie Spencer (née Giliker)	1943	Betty Elise Welford (née Hjersing)	1939
Ian Maxwell	1967	Dominic Pinto	1978	(Gp Capt.) Roy Springett	1962	Joseph H. Whiffen	1975
R.I. McCallum	Retired Staff	Dr Gordon Pledger	1953	Dr Leonard James Srnka	1974	Michael Whitaker	
John J. McGrane BSc (Hons)	1984	Alexandros Poutachidis	2003	Anthony and Susan Stanforth		David Whitaker	1984
Des McHugh	1974	Dr Philip M. Preshaw	1992		1956 and 1966	David White BSc	1974
Dr N. McKay	1997	Caroline Pryer	2002	Martin Staniforth	1975	Alex White	1993
Dr Christine McLean (née Brown)	1971	Eric Norman Quenet	1952	Dr Cathy Stark	1988	Dr Rebecca White MBS	2001
E.W.G. McNaught	1982	Dr S.S. Randhawa FRCS	1979	Dr Frederick W. Stephenson	1961	Ian M. White	1970
Miss Demetra Mentou	1997	Dr Anthony L. Reading	1954	J.C.C. Stewart CBE	1937	Bob Whitelaw	1966
S.W. Stuart Menzies MBBS	1962	Irene M Redpath	1988	Dr Geoffrey W. Stitt	1965	Dr John Whittle	1974
Stephen Metcalfe	1998	Ian Reynolds	1961	Professor Roy Storer	1950	Miss Susan Whytock	1963
Austin Miller	1953	Vincent Rice	1971	David William Stoten	1985	Iain Weir-Jones PhD	1965
Paul S. Mitchell	Former Staff	Nick Richardson	1977	Paul Sturgess (Brown)	1945	Elizabeth Weir-Jones (née Ingram)	1966
Timothy Mooleedhar	1976	David A. Richmond	1984	Ruth Sunderland Neill	1983	Bethany Wilcock	2003
W.G. Derek Morgan	1961	Andrew F. Riddle	1976	Charlotte Sykes (née Prater)	1954	Tim Wilder	1976
Ruth E. Morgan	1960	Frank Ridley	1945	Alan Sykes	1955	Dr Nicholas Wilford	1990
Dave Morgan	1979	Viscount Ridley Hon Dcl	1989	John C.S. Talbot	1970	Peter S.D. Williams	2003
Chris Morgan	1971	Mrs Pauline Rimer	1962	Peter J. Tallentire	1960	Dr Peter Willis	1956
Mr P. Morris	1943	Kathleen M. Robertson (née Walker)	1959	Dr M. Ali Tanor	1980	Ivor Wilson MBBS	1951
Dr Andrew J. Mortimer	1970	Dr Frank Robinson		Jeremy Taylor	1982	Linda Wilson	1995
Dr B. Moss	Retired Staff	Derek Robinson	1989	Dr Norman Taylor MBE	1998	John Wilson	1953
Dr Jeffrey Moysey	1976	Dr J. Stuart Robson	1964	Emma Elizabeth Litt Taylor	2004	Dr Adrian Winbow	1969
Douglas Fenwick Mullen	1967	David Rock PPRIBA Hon FAIA	1952	Paula Thomas BA (hons)	1991	David Woodcock	1936
Trish Mullins (née Britten)	1981	Dr H.D. Rowbotham	1965	Simon A. Thompson		Andrew J. Wright	
David Mullins	1982	Dr Lorna M. Rozner	1947	Brian S. Thompson	1972	N. Brian Wright	1954
J.J. Muray	Staff	Pieter Rutgers	1973	Dr Ian M. Thompson	1998	James R.G. Wright	Retired Staff
Neil Murray	1972	Heather A. Rutherford (Tucker) MEng	1998	J.E. Thorpe	1983	Sri Wahyuni Mohamed Yahya	2002
Dr David Nassif	1977	P.S. Sahni	1956	H.K. Thurlbeck (née Shenton)	1980	Emeritus Professor P.J. Yarrow	
Mrs Silvana Nassif (née Karam)		Dr S. Sahnoune	1989	Mr J.A.G. Tindall	Retired Staff	Dr J.C. Yule	1970

187

Index of Names

Acknowledgements

From College of Physical Science to Armstrong College
by John Gibbins
I should like to acknowledge the following sources:
Calendar/Almanac of Armstrong College, 1883/4; 1893/5; 1902/3/1911/12;1921/2; 1932/3; 1952/3; 1959/60.
Bettenson, E.M. *The University of Newcastle upon Tyne: A Historical Introduction, 1834–1971*, University of Newcastle upon Tyne, 1974
Collins, R. *Sociology of Philosophies: A Global Theory of Intellectual Change*, Harvard University Press, 2000
Gibbins, J.R. '"Old Studies and New": The Organisation of Knowledge in University Curriculum' in *The Organisation of Knowledge*, edited by Martin Daunton for The British Academy, Oxford University Press, 2005
Halsey, A.H. and Trow, M. *The Academics*, Faber and Faber, 1971
Whiting, C.E. *The University of Durham*, 1832–1932, The Sheldon Press, 1932

Origins of the College of Medicine
by David Shaw
I should like to acknowledge the following sources:
Grey Turner, G. assisted by Arnison, W.D. *The Newcastle upon Tyne School of Medicine 1834-1934*, Andrew Reid and Company Limited, 1934
Embleton, D. *The History of the Medical School, Afterwards The Durham College of Medicine at Newcastle upon Tyne, For Forty Years, From 1832 to 1872*, Andrew Reid, Sons and Co., 1890

Medicine Between the Wars
by David Shaw
I should like to acknowledge the following sources:
Bettenson, E.M. 'History of the Medical School', in *Newcastle School of Medicine 1834–1984 Sesquicentennial Celebrations*, ed. Dale, G., Miller, F.J.W., Bramley, K., University of Newcastle upon Tyne, 1984
Bettenson, E.M. 'The Hutchens Affair', *Durham University Journal* 1982; N.S. 43: 159–98.

Education
by Anthony Edwards
Historical information on teacher education at Newcastle is provided by Colin Tyson and Professor John Tuck in a 1971 departmental publication, and in the essay collection edited by Gordon Hogg as part of the centenary celebrations. My own recollections of the years 1979–97 have been updated by Professor Bruce Carrington.

Law
by Ashley Wilton
This history draws substantially upon an unpublished history to 1963 written by D.W. Elliott on the creation of the University of Newcastle upon Tyne.

Modern Languages
by Phil Powrie
I would like to thank Colin Riordan, Elizabeth Andersen and Allan Callender for their contributions to the article.

Chemical Engineering
by John Backhurst
I would like to thank John Harker for his invaluable assistance.

Civil Engineering
by John Bull
I should like to acknowledge the following publications:
Isaac, P.C.G., *Civil Engineering Diversity: Meeting the Needs of Tomorrow*, Proceedings of a Colloquium Celebrating Fifty Years of Achievement at Newcastle, Wylam, Allenholme Press, 1995 and Isaac, P.C.G., *Civil Engineering: The University Contribution*, Newcastle, Oriel Press, 1970.

Computing
by John Lloyd
Some of this history is taken from Dr. Page's contribution to *A History of Computing at Newcastle*, prepared for 40th Anniversary celebrations.

Geology
by Duncan Murchison
I wish to acknowledge the information gleaned from Bettenson, E.M., *The University of Newcastle upon Tyne: A Historical Introduction, 1834–1971*, University of Newcastle upon Tyne, 1974.

Mathematics and Statistics
by Robin Johnson
I am very pleased to acknowledge the information and reminiscences provided by Robin Plackett, John Ringrose, Neil Freeman and current colleagues, and the archive researches undertaken by Fred Bosanquet.

Mechanical Engineering
by Leonard Maunder
I wish to acknowledge that some of the information for this article was provided by Bettenson, E.M. *The University of Newcastle upon Tyne: A Historical Introduction, 1834–1971*, University of Newcastle upon Tyne, 1974 and *Engineering* Nov 30 1951, pp. 681–3

The publishers wish to acknowledge the invaluable help given by all the contributors who so kindly gave of their time and expertise. This book is not a straightforward history shaped by one point of view, but a compendium of voices, and their help in making it such is much appreciated. It was much appreciated. In addition the publishers would like to thank the following people:

Ally Robson (Union Communications Officer), Anne Murphy, Fred Bosanquet, Gerry Dane, Derek Hawes in Library Print Services, The Development and Alumni Relations Office, Marion Wilson and the Publications team, Melanie Reed and the Press Office team, Melanie Wood and the Special Collections team, Stephen Teal, Stu Vose (*The Courier* Editor)

Picture Acknowledgements

(Key T-Top, B-Bottom, L-Left, R-Right, C-Centre)

Harper Collins Publishers	64TR
Journal and Chronicle Newspapers	33TL, 146C
Literary & Philosophical Society	18R, 58B
National Portrait Gallery, London	143
Newcastle City Library	34BL
Peacock, Graeme (graeme-peacock.com)	8T, 13, 23T, 56
Print Services at the Robinson Library Newcastle University	
20, 21(all images), 22, 41, 69TR, 98TL, 98TR, 98C, 104TL, 104TR, 108TL, 115	
Punch	57
Royal Geographic Society	136R
Seven Stories: The Centre for Children's Books	70R
Society of Antiquaries	12
The Centre for Life	99
The National Museum of Science and Industry	31
University Photolibrary	
Colin Cuthbert:	45L, 87, 128BL
Keith Pattinson:	120
Graeme Peacock:	105, 120T, L166
Print Services at the Robinson Library:	68, 75L, 75R, 81R, 102B, 128TR, 161, 166R
Wood, Jonathan	46BR

PART OF NEWCASTLE UPON TYNE FROM T. OLIVER'S PLAN OF 1830

ORCHARD ST.
STREET
LIT. &
PHIL.
LIBRARY
COLLINGWOOD STREET
GROAT MARKET
CLOTH MARKET
WHEAT MARKET
POTTERY
GATE
BACK ROW
CLAVERING PLACE
BAILIFF GATE
CASTLE STREET
CASTLE
COUNTY COURTS
DEAN
THE SIDE
THE CLOSE
SAND HILL

THE EARLY HOMES OF THE COLLEGE OF MEDICINE.

A—Bell's Court.   C—The Cottage in the Physic Garden.
B—The Surgeon's Hall.   D—Orchard Street.

By courtesy of the Estate and Property Office of Newcastle upon Tyne